Ford in the Service
of America

Ford in the Service of America

Mass Production for the Military During the World Wars

TIMOTHY J. O'CALLAGHAN

McFarland & Company, Inc., Publishers
Jefferson, North Carolina, and London

LIBRARY OF CONGRESS CATALOGUING-IN-PUBLICATION DATA

O'Callaghan, Timothy J., 1930–
Ford in the service of America : mass production for the
military during the world wars / Timothy J. O'Callaghan.
p.   cm.
Includes bibliographical references and index.

ISBN 978-0-7864-4485-4
softcover : 50# alkaline paper ∞

1. Ford Motor Company — History — 20th century.
2. Manufacturing industries — Military aspects — United States — History — 20th century.
3. Manufacturing industries — Technological innovations — United States — History — 20th century.
4. Automobile industry and trade — Military aspects — United States — History — 20th century.
5. Industrial mobilization — United States — History — 20th century.
6. Technological innovations — United States — History — 20th century.
7. World War, 1939–1945 — Economic aspects — United States.
8. World War, 1939–1945 — Equipment and supplies.
9. World War, 1939–1945 — Technology.   I. Title.

HD9710.U54F67 2009   338.7'629222097309041 — dc22   2009027032

British Library cataloguing data are available

On the cover: Riveters working on the wing section of a bomber.
More than 300,000 rivets of more than 500 sizes were used in each bomber
(from the collection of The Henry Ford); employee pin, designed at the
direction of Henry Ford, for employees of the Aircraft Engine Division

Manufactured in the United States of America

McFarland & Company, Inc., Publishers
Box 611, Jefferson, North Carolina 28640
www.mcfarlandpub.com

In memory of my brother
OWEN THOMAS O'CALLAGHAN
7th Marines, 1st Marine Division.
Died Okinawa, June 6, 1945.

Table of Contents

Preface

When Henry Ford's Americana showplace, Greenfield Village in Dearborn, Michigan, was closed by the war in early 1942, Charles LaCroix, Assistant Director of the village, was given the assignment by Henry Ford to write Ford Motor Company's history of the war. Henry Ford's charge to LaCroix was, "Write me something I'll enjoy reading, not just a lot of statistics."[1] In completing his assignment, LaCroix produced 8 volumes summarizing the documents in 42 archive boxes of records as well as thousands of photographs covering the many facets of Ford's war production efforts. Unfortunately Henry Ford passed away in April of 1947 with the project unpublished.

These records have been available to researchers for the past 60 years and, while some have written about some portion of it in conjunction with a story of Henry Ford or Ford Motor Company, no one has ever published a book dedicated to this significant area of Ford's history. Ford R. Bryan, a distant relative of Henry Ford and author of numerous books and articles on Henry Ford and the Ford Motor Company, attempted in vain to persuade the Ford Motor Company or The Henry Ford[2] to have the LaCroix files edited and published. Bryan had indicated to friends that this would be his next project just before he died at age 92.

Having been a longtime employee of Ford Motor Company, I became interested in its aviation history in 1980. Not long after I retired in 1990 I became a volunteer in the Benson Ford Research Center of The Henry Ford, where I was asked to bring some order to its collection of aviation photographs. With this access and the leisure of time, I was able to search through all the Ford aviation related files and photographs — something few, if any others, have done — resulting in two Ford aviation books and a DVD.[3] Included in my research was the aviation history of Ford in World Wars I and II. I was fascinated with the information found in the LaCroix files documenting Ford Motor Company's other efforts in World War II, as well as other archive documents relating to Ford's other World War I efforts. With the urging of friends of Ford Bryan and myself, I decided to write the fascinating story of Ford Motor Company's service to America in both world wars. Once again, with access and the leisure of time, I was able to sort through every war-related Ford file in the archives that I could find.

The vast majority of Ford's World War II experience, detailed here, was drawn from LaCroix's extensive documentation (accession 435) which is well indexed. As a result the only footnoted statements in the present work are those *not* from this collection. One

1

surprise that surfaced in this research is the difference in production quantities stated by Ford in three different war-end reports. They run from identical, as in the case of Pratt & Whitney aircraft engines, Jettison Fuel Tanks and Universal Carriers, to a number of minor differences in other categories and to the loss of 4,458 Ford designed jeeps. The numbers used throughout this book are from the only audited record found that summarized production for *every item by month and cumulative* from January 1941 through August 1945.[4]

As an aid to researchers, the location of pertinent records of each war-time product within LaCroix's 8 volumes and 42 boxes are indicated in the notes for each chapter.

The LaCroix records are divided into four categories:

Boxes 1 and 2 contain the final draft (Volumes 1 through 8).
Boxes 3 through 22 contain back up information for the final draft.
Boxes 23 through 37 and 40 through 42 contain subject files containing rough drafts and additional miscellaneous details.
Boxes 38 and 39 contain a formal report to the War Department Price Adjustment Board for war-contracts terminated in 1945.

In 1947 LaCroix prepared a report for 1945 for submission to the War Department Price Adjustment Board. This report, consisting of three volumes, covers in great detail *only* the Ford war contracts that were *terminated* in 1945. Additional details are buried in the other boxes. Box 38 contains Volume 1 and 2 of this report and Box 39 contains Volume 3. Contracts for war products terminated prior to the beginning of 1945 are not covered in these three volumes. As a result the 1945 report contains no information on the following war products: Gun Director, Rate-of-Climb Indicator, Tank and Tank Destroyer, Amphibious Jeep and the Magnesium Smelter and Foundry. They are, however, covered in detail in LaCroix's final draft.

The Oral Reminiscences were another valuable and unusual resource. Following the deaths of Henry and Clara Ford a project was initiated by Ford Motor Company in the 1950s to capture the experiences of many of the former Ford managers and workers. These were taped interviews, later transcribed and now available in the Oral Reminiscences collection in the archives of the Benson Ford Research Center; 250 of these are contained in hardbound copies of the transcribed interviews with many more in unbound files. The histories run from as few as a couple of pages to as many as 1,536 pages. Some provide invaluable insights into many aspects of the activities of Henry Ford and the Ford Motor Company in both wars.

As a bonus to the researcher, in 1914 Henry Ford had established the Ford Photographic Department, one of the largest in the United States, providing a treasure trove of thousands of photographs, as well as 1.5 million feet of motion picture footage which documents much of Ford Motor Company's efforts in both wars.

One other source of great help was the history of Ford Motor Company, published in three volumes, by Dr. Allan Nevins, professor of American history, Columbia University, with collaboration from Frank Hill:

> 1954 *Ford: The Times, the Man, the Company*
> 1957 *Ford: Expansion and Challenge 1915–1933*
> 1962 *Ford: Decline and Rebirth 1933–1962.*

These books resulted from a grant to Columbia University from the Ford Motor Company on the occasion of Ford's 50th anniversary. The grant carried no restrictions or requirement of prior approval of the content.

Finally, an extremely detailed study of the Willow Run plant was published in August 1946 by the Air Materiel Command of the Army Air Force. It was one of a series of studies of aircraft plants built during World War II in order to provide guidance to the government in the case of future emergencies. This study was started in June 1945 right after production of the Liberator bomber ended at Willow Run. Entitled *B-24, Construction and Production Analysis*, this 105-page report is a critical study of Willow Run with all its warts and replete with many statistical graphs. It recognizes the uniqueness and enormity of the undertaking of mass producing the B-24 bomber and micro-analyzes the launch and operation of the Willow Run production system. While the overall conclusion is favorable, there are many detailed criticisms, which are to be expected in a project this unique. It was reviewed with Ford officials at the time and, while they concurred in the study, they felt it was prejudiced in favor of the Army and failed to appreciate the scope of the problems posed, especially by the lack of engineering data available from the Consolidated Aircraft Company, designer of the B-24 Liberator bomber.

Ford's overseas operations have no archives or research centers containing their contributions to winning World War II. Fortunately a small booklet, *Ford at War,* was published in Great Britain in 1946 by Hilary St. George Saunders. Illustrated with photographs and original colored artwork, it covers in detail the war production efforts of Ford of Britain along with commentary on the lives and activities of its employees. Without it there would be little information relating to Ford's contributions outside of the United States.

In all cases Ford, in this book, refers to Ford Motor Company. Henry and Edsel Ford are identified as such. All photographs and illustrations not otherwise identified are from the authors collection.

I am indebted to the staff of the Benson Ford Research Center for their assistance in this endeavor as well as their help in the past when researching the history of Ford aviation. In addition, I am grateful to Ford Bryan, mentioned above, and Dr. David Lewis, retired professor of business at the University of Michigan and the outstanding expert on the Ford family and company, for their use as resources and their friendship and encouragement over the years. Also, to Michael Skinner, past president of the Henry Ford Heritage Association, for his encouragement, critical review and valuable suggestions in furthering this project.

1

World War I

Introduction to War

World War I was triggered in June 1914 by the assassination of Archduke Franz Ferdinand, heir to the throne of Austria-Hungary, while visiting Serbia. The following month Austria-Hungary declared war on Serbia and by 1915 nation after nation in Europe, answering the calls of various defense pacts with each other, had joined the list of belligerent countries resulting in hundreds of thousands of soldiers becoming casualties in the conflict. Many in the United States felt we should prepare for the probability that this country would be drawn into the conflict. Many others, safely on this side of the Atlantic Ocean, saw no reason to become involved. In any event the United States was not militarily prepared for war and, although re-arming was being actively discussed, no serious action had been taken to develop our armed forces or build inventories of war materials.

Henry Ford, an outspoken so-called pacifist, was against preparedness, proclaiming that war only profited the politicians and greedy businessmen. The first public hint of Henry Ford's attitude was in 1915 when the Germans advertised in American newspapers that so-called neutral ships were in fact carrying munitions for Britain and subject to attack. So, when the *Lusitania* was torpedoed shortly thereafter by a German submarine, Henry Ford declared that the 1,153 people lost "were fools to go on that boat." He not only expressed his views verbally, but also, starting in 1916, heavily advertised them by placing news releases in 12,000 small daily and weekly newspapers. Later, starting with full page ads in 40 metropolitan newspapers, insertions escalated to include more than 250 of the nation's largest newspapers.[1] These public anti-preparedness expressions of Henry Ford led to the resignation of James Couzens who was as important to the early success of Ford Motor Company as Henry Ford himself. Couzens, Canadian born and probably biased in favor of preparedness, felt Henry Ford's public views were harming the Ford Motor Company. Many agreed with Henry Ford as pacifism was not an uncommon position for many in middle America who still had vivid memories of the Civil War.

Late in 1915 Henry Ford had been approached by a pacifist group which embraced him as one of their own and was persuaded that, with his help, they had the power to bring peace to Europe by making a direct personal appeal to the leaders of the warring nations. They planned to be mediators by soliciting the positions of each side and then presenting them to the other side. They felt they could then mediate a common understanding leading to peace. Henry Ford, feeling he might indeed be able to influence these leaders, chartered the Scandinavian-American ocean liner *Oscar II* and on December 4, 1915, set sail from Hoboken, New Jersey for Norway with a great deal of fanfare and a boat load of supporters and newsmen. For months they had been proclaiming their mission was world peace and that they would "get the boys out of the trenches by Christmas." While Henry Ford returned home in early January 1916 he continued funding his peace commission until January 1917.

While it was undoubtedly an earnest effort on Henry Ford's part to bring peace, it was doomed to failure and was subjected, from the beginning, to unrelenting ridicule by the world's press, politicians and business leaders. Even vaudeville comedian Will Rogers, starring in one of Ziegfeld's Broadway productions at the time, quipped, "The Ford peace ship has kept me alive for a month." But, while the press scorned his efforts and others claimed it was nothing but an effort for free publicity, it generated an enormous amount of goodwill for Henry Ford by the common folk. At least he had tried and as one song published about his trip proclaimed, "Mr. Ford, You've Got The Right Idea!"

While Henry Ford was undoubtedly the most prominent industrialist with this anti-war attitude and reluctance to produce war materials, he wasn't alone. Henry Leland, General Manager of the Cadillac Division of General Motors, wanted to convert a General Motors property into an aircraft engine production facility. Billy Durant, who controlled General Motors, refused to allow production for the war effort stating, "This is not our war and I will not permit any General Motors unit to do work for the Government."[2]

Henry Ford continued his anti-war campaign until February 1917 when President Wilson severed diplomatic relations with Germany at which time Henry Ford was quoted as saying, "Well, we must stand behind the President." Henry Ford went on: "In the event of war I will place our factory at the disposal of the United States government and will operate without one cent of profit,"[3] a statement that would come back to haunt him long after the war was over. When the United States declared war on Germany on April 6, 1917, he said, "I am a pacifist, but perhaps militarism can be crushed only with militarism. In that case I am in on it to the finish." The Ford Motor Company would be turned into an arsenal of democracy and Henry Ford was now winning praise from both sides — he had at least tried to end the war with his peace mission and now he was a realist supporting the war. Some now called him "the fighting pacifist."

Henry Ford announced that his factories could build 1,000 small submarines, 3,000 motors and 1,000 tanks each day leading the public to believe, as they would also later believe at the start of World War II, that Ford and American industry could mass produce our war needs with little delay. His submarine, he explained, would carry only one man who would guide the small vessel to the side of an enemy ship and then with a pole attach a pillbomb to the ship's hull. The Navy dismissed the idea and Franklin Roosevelt, then Secretary of the Navy, was quoted as saying "until he [Ford] saw a chance for publicity free of charge, he thought a submarine was something to eat." While the pill-on-a-pole generated a great deal of ridicule his 1,000 tanks a day boast was not too far fetched as he was already making 3,500 cars a day. After all a tank only had a metal shell, a Ford tractor engine and tracks instead of wheels.

While government bureaucracies were trying to sort out just what war materials the United States should produce, Henry Ford was trying to obtain a captured German airplane with a six cylinder Mercedes engine. On August 31, 1917, Ford wired Percival Perry, manager of the Ford works in Britain, exhorting him to obtain from the British government one of the captured German planes. Ford's intent was to examine it and then design and build a superior airplane and engine for the United States. He advised Perry, "Expect to build one hundred fifty thousand complete aeroplanes for use in France." Perry replied that "the number of machines mentioned deemed incredulous and unattainable." Perry went on to comment that the number of airplanes he expected to build was obviously an error — that doubtless some lesser quantity was meant. He assumed that Ford intended to independently manufacture a large quantity of complete aircraft. "If you undertook such work, and delivered the goods, the reclame and public recognition would be enormous." Ford's quest ended when Perry finally advised him that, while such a plane and engine was available, the British government would not act without a request from the United States government.[4]

A master of publicity, Henry Ford's exaggerations were probably purposeful — who would pay any attention to a claim of building only 100 submarines, or tanks or airplanes!

In considering the accomplishments of the Ford Motor Company, and all other companies producing war materials during World War I, it must be kept in mind that in March of 1918 the influenza pandemic, called the Spanish Flu, attacked the world, killing an estimated 675,000 Americans alone. While it was deadly to the young and old, it also caused severe illness in many of those in a workforce striving to meet the government's war-time needs. Trying to maintain a full workforce, over 46,000 workers at Ford Motor Company alone, was an enormous task by itself and was greatly compounded by this pandemic.

Also to be considered is the fact that most of the various war-time items produced by Ford, excluding cars and trucks, required massive expenditures for tools, fixtures and jigs. And, in the case of the Eagle boat, a huge new facility was needed. In virtually all cases it required hiring and training of thousands of new employees, most of whom had little manufacturing training or experience. By August 1918 Ford, for the first time, began hiring women for war work. While there were only 500 employed it was a significant departure from tradition.

Tractors for Britain

Ford's first war-related action was a humanitarian effort to aid Great Britain in its dire need for food production. Britain was a manufacturing nation dependent on importing two-thirds of her foodstuffs as well as much of the raw material for manufacturing. German submarines, however, were taking a terrible toll on the ships carrying the desperately needed food, resulting in the British embarking on a major program to expand their own food production, which was sorely lacking in tractors. With the outbreak of World War I, but prior to America's entry, an emergency plea came from Great Britain for 7,000 of a new tractor Ford was developing. Two prototypes of these tractors had been sent to England in January 1917 with the result that British authorities considered them superior to any other tractor they had tested. Henry Ford was reluctant to accept the British order as he felt his prototype tractor needed further development. The British responded that they had to beat the Germans with what they had — they needed an imperfect machine now rather than a perfect machine later.

In May Charles Sorensen was sent to England to establish a tractor operation in facilities selected by the British. German air raids in June, however, shifted much British industry to aircraft engine production and the potential tractor plant was canceled. Henry Ford was asked, and he agreed, to produce 7,000 tractors at his cost of $750, in his Dearborn, Michigan, plant. The first tractor was completed in October 1917 with 254 tractors completed by the end of year. By March 1918 the *London Daily Mail* reported, "There are hundreds [of Ford tractors] now at work and soon there should be thousands" and by April 1918 7,000 tractors had been delivered to Great Britain. H.C.B Underdown of Britain's Munitions Department thanked Ford for its efforts in providing the tractors, stating that without them "the food crisis would in all probability not have been surmounted." Henry Ford and Son built more than 27,000 additional tractors during World War I for distribution to farmers in the United States and Canada.[5]

Vehicles

When war was declared, Ford Motor Company was producing 3,500 cars on a daily basis. Once fully engaged in war production, car production rapidly decreased to about

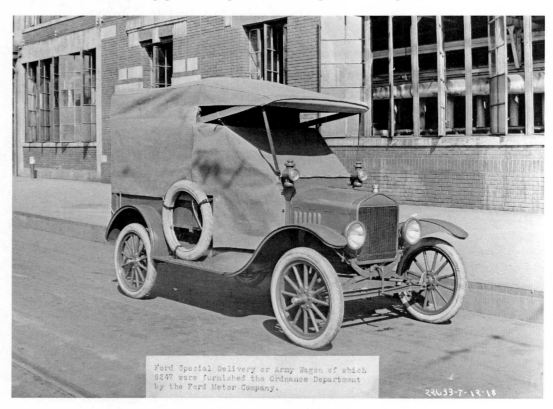

Ford service truck. More Ford vehicles were used by the U.S. Army in France than all other makes combined as it was known for its ease of operation and durability (from the collection of The Henry Ford).

100 cars per day, enough to fill estimated military requirements. Many United States government sources, aware of Ford's peacetime production records but not considering many of their facilities were now producing other war related items, expected Ford to deliver their orders for numerous motor vehicles on a moments notice. That said, Ford produced over 30,000 motor vehicles for war-time needs.

One of the major types of vehicles produced was a special ambulance designed by Ford after much collaboration with personnel from the United States Surgeon General's Office as well as with actual ambulance drivers from the battlefields in France. Early in the war Ford made a $500,000 donation to the Red Cross that was used to purchase 107 Ford built ambulances and 836 other vehicles. The Red Cross ultimately purchased a total of 2,397 vehicles.

There were a total of 30,734 U.S. built Ford vehicles delivered for military use at home and overseas: 16,899 passenger cars, 7,490 trucks, 600 chassis and 5,745 ambulances. (Records suggest Red Cross purchases were in addition.)

A special conveyor line was built for crating the vehicles destined for overseas shipment using a process Ford had developed before the war. The crates were lined with a special tar paper known as Slater's felt and all parts subject to rust were coated with Cedaroleum. It was so effective that other firms were requested to use the same method.[6]

Based on deliveries, there were more Ford vehicles used by the American Expeditionary Force in France than all other makes combined: Ford 20,652, all others 18,039.

Ford ambulance designed with input from soldiers in France and U.S. Surgeon General's Office (from the collection of The Henry Ford).

(This only includes vehicles shipped to France from the United States.) Not included are 8,500 regular Ford chassis delivered to the French government by September 1918. With the end of the war 13,160 pending orders for Fords were canceled by the government. At the end of the war, American dealers were concerned that the cars used in France would be returned to the United States, depressing the used car market, while in France they were desperate for these American cars as their total production had been for military use. In any event those cars still crated were returned to the United States while the remainder were used by the Army of Occupation and few if any were returned to the United States.

Several reasons stand out for Ford's dominance: the Ford was less expensive than the other makes; it was viewed as an easier car to drive, meaning the average soldier would know how, or could quickly learn, to drive it without special training; and it had a legendary durability and ability to navigate uneven ground.[7]

One comment about the versatility of Ford vehicles was received from a soldier at the front: "I have seen Fords used as tanks, armored moving forts, electric light plants, water pumps, ambulances, supply cars and many other things and they were always ready for anything at any time."

Liberty Aircraft Engines

The French and English had sent delegations to the United States in 1917 to sort out what the United States could do to aid the war effort in aviation. It was concluded that the Americans should concentrate on manufacturing training planes while the allies continued their efforts on building combat planes. The American made Curtiss Jenny was selected as the training plane to be produced and, as it was impractical to design, test and build a new combat aircraft in a timely manner, the United States copied the British de Havilland biplane to build for combat. It was further concluded that the "United States could rush quantity production of aircraft engines, which had always been a choke point in English and French aircraft production."[8] Unlike the decision to copy and build the uncomplicated stick and fabric British airplane, there were 60 different European aircraft engines. Most of these engines, handmade with parts that were seldom interchangeable, were all based on the metric system. Earlier experience with European engines had shown that copying them for mass production by American manufacturing methods was a trying process at best and not practical considering the urgency of the need for these engines. As a result the United States, with encouragement from the Allies, decided to build a new aircraft engine designed to give the Allies superiority in the air.

The government assembled a group of automotive engineers which included Elbert Hall of the Hall-Scott Motor Car Company, a well-known manufacturer of aircraft engines, and Jesse Vincent of the Packard Motor Car Company, who also had extensive aircraft engine experience. Packard had already developed an engine that met many of the government's requirements. The engine started life in 1916 as a 12 cylinder or Twin Six 905 cubic inch engine which was adapted for racing and had set a number of records. It was modified in 1917, and in early 1918 Hall and Vincent, with various staff, further modified this engine to meet government requirements, including those suggested by reports from the war front.[9] Originally classified as the U.S.A. Standard Aircraft Engine it was soon nicknamed the Liberty, a name that stuck and was ultimately registered as a trademark by the United States government. The design allowed for production as an 8 cylinder 225HP engine or 12 cylinder 400HP engine. It was felt that the 8 cylinder version of the engine would provide the power necessary for aerial warfare in 1918 with the 12 cylinder version scheduled for production in 1919. Aerial warfare was developing so fast, however, that only 90 days later the need for more powerful engines was recognized and all efforts were diverted to producing only the 12 cylinder version of the engine. The first engine was test flown in August 1917 and 52 engines were actually produced that month.

Ford received a contract for the eight cylinder version in October 1917 and C. Harold Wills, a Ford engineer who had been one of the chief designers of the Ford Model T and had assisted in the modification of the Packard engine, was placed in charge. Reconfiguration of the Highland Park plant was started immediately as well as actions to make or otherwise acquire jigs, fixtures and machinery and hire and train over 13,000 employees. Noted in a Summary of War Activities of Ford Motor Company dated September 27, 1918:

> The Liberty motor is an entirely new mechanism which naturally demanded changes as it progressed toward completion.... In all there were over 1,200 changes made from inception of the engine to production. These changes enforced delays in production as the fundamental changes entailed an almost complete revision of the motor in all its parts.[10]

The complete revision referred to above was the fact that Ford had started developing tools and fixtures and changing their facilities for production of the 8 cylinder engine when the government decided to produce only 12 cylinder engines. In addition, there were problems with the Packard engine that needed fixing. Ford had corrected a most serious problem in the Liberty engine by developing a more durable bronze back babbitt lined bearing for use in the crankcase and connecting rods that was causing repeated engine failures. Ford also devised an inexpensive method for cylinder construction. The cylinders were originally bored out of solid steel forgings, a laborious and expensive operation. Ford engineers produced a cylinder from steel tubing that saved labor and materials reducing the cost from $19.75 each to $8.25 each. Benedict Crowell, Assistant Secretary of War and Director of Munitions, commented,

> The final forgings were so near the shape desired that millions of pounds of scrap were saved over other methods, to say nothing of an enormous amount of labor thus done away with.... The most conspicuous success in the science of quantity production in the world was the Ford Motor Company, which devoted its organization to the task of speeding up the output of Liberty engines. In addition to the unique and wonderfully efficient method of making rough engine cylinders out of steel tubing, they also perfected for the Liberty a new method of producing more durable and satisfactory bearings.[11]

Over 118,000 man hours were expended by Ford in designing and drafting the necessary machines, jigs and fixtures. As a result the first Ford engine wasn't delivered until May 1918. Even with the late start Ford, building to a peak of 75 motors a day, built more engines in the last three months of the war than any other manufacturer. Overall Ford produced 3,950 of the total 20,478 engines built.

Ford's production of the new cylinder grew to 4,000 in sixteen hours which was way in excess of demand. Accordingly production was reduced to 1,600 cylinders a day. Both the bearings and cylinders were supplied to all other manufacturers. Because of Ford's production records, on October 18 Ford was directed "to proceed with all possible dispatch with the manufacturer of 12,000 additional Liberty engines," a contract canceled by the Armistice. Ford's cost to produce these engines was $5,000 versus a contract price of $5625. Both figures include a mandated profit of $625 and the Ford figures included nearly $3,000,000 in buildings, fixtures and machinery,[12] which meant the additional 12,000 engines would have been a great deal cheaper to produce. This ability to reduce costs through manufacturing innovations would be Ford's hallmark for nearly all war production in World War I as well as later in World War II.

The January 1918 edition of the *World's Work* magazine carried an extensive article about Ford's war efforts. Frank Stockbridge, the author, after spending a week with Henry Ford and other manufacturers, asked one of the other Liberty engine manufacturers, "Is there any difference between the Liberty motors you are turning out and those Henry Ford is making? No, he replied, except that Mr. Ford's are perhaps a little better quality." In a 1941 letter to Fred Black of Ford Motor Company, Erik Nelson, one of the pilots and the Project Engineer of the U.S. Army's Round-the-World flight in 1924, stated, "Having had a lot of experience with Liberty engines, the Ford-made engines were the

Soldier inspecting a Liberty engine at the Ford Highland Park plant. Ford engineers solved major production problem with the engine (from the collection of The Henry Ford).

'pick' and so specified [for this flight] — there was never a question among ourselves who built the best ones."[13]

Kettering Bug

Another World War I aviation project aided by Ford was the development of an engine for the Kettering Bug, a secret program that became known only years later. Captain Hap Arnold (Commanding General of the Army Air Forces in World War II,) directed a program to develop a low cost, long range, self-guided, self-propelled torpedo called a robot bomb, later known as the Kettering Bug. The missile was to be accurate up to 200 miles, carry a 200 pound warhead and cost no more than $200. Charles Kettering, the renowned General Motors inventor, was in charge of the project and would design the airplane while Ford's C. Harold Wills was given the task of developing a two cylinder engine which was desired due to simplicity and cost considerations. The Wills engine was a horizontal, two cylinder, air-cooled, 40HP, engine weighing 151 pounds that could be mass produced for $40. In testing, however, serious vibrations developed, forcing the development of an alternative engine.[14]

The first alternative was a three cylinder air cooled engine, reasonably free of vibrations but much too complicated for volume production. With these two engines eliminated, Wills, in collaboration with Jack Beebe of the DePalma Manufacturing Co., Detroit, Michigan,[15] developed a four cylinder "V" engine weighing 120 pounds, delivering 38HP at an estimated cost of $100. It was mounted on a 12 foot biplane with a 14 foot wing span and designed to fly 4 or 5 hours — just long enough to reach its objective. Flight direction was determined by gyroscopic controls and distance was controlled by a cam, set for a predetermined number of engine revolutions needed to reach the target. When the engine had turned the prescribed number of revolutions, the engine would cut out and the plane would dive into the target. Final testing didn't take place until October 1919, nearly a year after the armistice and the project was not considered further until the beginning of World War II. At that time it was decided that major targets in Germany were too far from British bases for a Bug type bomb to be effective[16] but the German V-1 missiles that showered London a few years later would use the same principle.

Eagle Boats

The largest of Ford's war production undertakings was in building the all-steel submarine chaser or Eagle Boat for the Navy. While it generated an enormous amount of publicity for Ford it had no impact on the war.

When the United States entered World War I, the United States Shipping Board was established to contract for the building of hundreds of new troop and cargo ships to supply the British Isles with food and desperately needed munitions to all our allies in Europe. In addition we needed to replace the extreme number of ships being sunk by German submarines. The original plan of the board called for 21 different types and sizes of ships. Henry Ford, appointed to the board by President Wilson due to his knowledge of mass production techniques, suggested the answer to the shortage of ships lay in the production of a large quantity of a standardized ship — the hull to be copied from some type of ship that had proved successful in ocean trade with the power plant and equipment selected from standard units currently available on the market — almost exactly how Henry Kaiser built the famous Liberty ships 25 years later.

In addition to merchant vessels to carry the goods there was great public demand, fanned by the daily press, for finding a means to deal with the submarine menace. New type ships were needed to find and destroy the German submarines that were taking such a toll on merchant ships in the Atlantic Ocean. A December 17, 1918, editorial in the *Washington Post* by Ira Bennett called for "an eagle to scour the seas and pounce upon and destroy every German submarine." The name stuck and the new ship became the Eagle.

Late in 1917 the Navy decided it needed steel ships, smaller than a destroyer, with about a 3,500 mile range, which was greater than that of the 110 foot wooden, gasoline powered submarine chaser previously developed for coastal protection. The problem with these 110 foot boats was their limited range of 900 miles and their large consumption of gasoline, which was not only difficult to obtain in a war zone but was an ever-existing potential fire hazard. These boats were adequate for patrolling in coastal waters but not capable of providing long range escort service. This led to the Eagle Boat,[17] designed to have a range of 3,500 miles with a cruising speed of 20 knots and suitable for escort duty as well as submarine chasing.[18] They would also be equipped with a submarine listening device devised by Thomas Edison. With all marine construction facilities swamped with war work, Ford was asked if it could and would undertake the task of building these boats without cannibalizing men or materials from other ship building facilities.

On January 14, 1918, Ford advised it was willing to accept a contract for the construction of from 100 to 500 Eagle Boats. They estimated the boats could be built at the rate of 25 a month once volume production was under way. Henry Ford had little part in design of the boats, except for plans that could affect the ability to manufacture them in volume and he warned, "We are builders and will not assume responsibility for performance." He suggested that hull plates be flat so they could be produced and installed in quantity and persuaded the Navy to accept steam turbine engines instead of reciprocating steam engines as they were more efficient, lighter and had a higher power-to-weight ratio. Henry Ford advised Secretary of the Navy Josephus Daniels that, rather than delay the project by waiting for a formal contract, he would proceed immediately based only on a request by the Secretary. In spite of Congressional opposition to appropriations for building the plant at government expense, Secretary Daniels wired Ford on January 17: "Proceed with one hundred submarine patrol vessels. Details of contract to be arranged as soon as practicable." In July an additional 12 boat were ordered for the Italian government.

Prior to the war Henry Ford had been planning a major expansion of his car manufacturing business and by 1915 had acquired over 1000 acres of land along a small river called the Rouge, located in what is present-day Dearborn. Henry Ford had suspended dividend payments by Ford Motor Company in order to fund his new Rouge project, an action contested by the Dodge Brothers, who were large Ford stockholders. Henry Ford was ultimately forced to pay dividends but pending the court's decision his commercial development of the Rouge site was suspended. However, the suit did not affect the plans for the new Eagle Boat factory. With the government paying for the development, five acres of Rouge land was chosen as a site for the factory. Designed by noted architect Albert

Kahn the building was 1,700 feet long, 350 feet wide and 100 feet high. The new building accommodated three assembly lines of seven hulls each allowing 21 boats to be worked on simultaneously. With the go-ahead wire from Secretary Daniels Ford started erecting a temporary building — the "B" building — under the direction of William B. Mayo, Ford's Chief Engineer. Production responsibility for the Eagle Boats would rest with William Knudsen, Ford's production manager, who was already in charge of most of Ford's war production activities.[19] Concurrently the government began widening and deepening the Rouge River, part of a previously planned harbor improvement program for the Port of Detroit, which allowed the Eagle Boats access to the Detroit River.

In addition to the construction of the new building, over 7,000 employees not working for other boat builders had to be hired almost immediately and trained. Almost as daunting was finding transportation for these new workers to a site that was formerly marshland, with no access to public transportation. It was months before trolley service was available and as an interim solution, Model T trucks with trailers were used to transport men from as far away as Highland Park.

Just as Ford had revolutionized automobile production with the introduction of the moving assembly line, he would be the first to apply many of these techniques to boat building. These boats were 200 feet long, weighing 615 tons, and the principle of Ford's moving assembly line process was modified to produce the boats in stages. In addition, due to the fact that all other normal sources were already dedicated to war production, Ford had to manufacture the steam turbines and boilers at his Highland Park plant and find sources for many other components from companies not producing war materials.

The Eagle was a single-screw vessel, driven by a high-speed Pool turbine designed for a speed of 18 knots with the engine developing about 2,000 shaft horsepower based on a 500 ton displacement and it had a cruising radius of 3,500 miles. They were armed with two 4 inch guns and one 3 inch anti-aircraft gun and a "Y" gun for firing depth charges. They were manned by 4 officers and 54 enlisted men to be trained with, and on, the ships as they were built. A cantonment containing a school and barracks for up to 1,200 sailors was built on site.

In late September 1918 it was determined that an additional facility on the East Coast would be needed to build the Eagles faster. Accordingly a contract was signed October 4 for Ford to build a second boat-building facility on land he owned on the Hudson River in Kearny, New Jersey.[20]

While the Rouge plant was being built, the hull for the first Eagle Boat was bolted together at Ford's massive Highland Park plant as a pattern vessel for perfecting the working plans and for making forms and templates which were used to duplicate parts for the other ships. When completed the boat was moved in sections on railroad flatcars to the new Rouge plant.

Groundbreaking for the Eagle Boat factory was in early January 1918 and by taking machine tools, presses and cranes from the Highland Park plant and other Ford branches, enough of the factory was completed to allow work to begin on Eagle No. 1 in May. There were three main tracks laid out to support the railway trucks on which the hulls were built. Each of the main tracks could support seven hulls allowing for twenty-one hulls to be under construction at one time. Along each track were piles of precisely cut and drilled steel plates for quick assembly. Over each track were traveling cranes for hoisting sub-assemblies into place on the hulls. Connected to the main assembly building was the

THE FORD MAN

Volume 2   Ford Factory, Highland Park, October 3, 1918   Number 19

Fourth Liberty Loan Now Due

Ford Men Should Buy Liberally, Sacrificing If Necessary, and Look Pleasant While Doing It

There is more reason than ever why we should subscribe liberally to the Fourth Liberty Loan in October. We know that sugar is doled out in little bits of 2 pounds per person per month; that some householders with hot air furnaces will have to burn soft coal, and that the coal will come high; that the newspapers prophesy that butter will go to $1 a pound and eggs to $1 a dozen by January 1st; and that $1 melts away in a grocery store like a flake of snow in a summer sun. These are all reasons why we should support the boys at the front with our money.

These are conditions brought about by the war, and of course we don't like them. Maybe we get fighting mad about some of the conditions, and that is the very reason we are fighting. We don't propose that these conditions shall continue any longer than possible nor there shall ever be another war. And if the present war is ended right, there never will be another. If it is ended wrong, there will be another. So while we are engaged in this one, let's go to it and end it right. We can't save a lot of money while we are doing it, but what good will money do us if we have to pay for another war a little later?

We have sacrificed a few things in the past, but the things that we have sacrificed is as nothing when compared with the sacrifices of the boys over there. Small indeed is he who would complain about the comparatively little sacrifice asked of us over here. One who is not willing to bear the little asked of us is not a very good American. Pay the dollar a pound for butter and do it cheerfully, if the price is approved by the food administration, or go without butter and do that cheerfully. In some training camps they go for days without butter and without sugar.

And let us not forget that the boys over there need munitions of war, clothing, transportation facilities, housing, and lots of other things. Then they need their wages, which do not compare with the wages of civilians. And all these needs are legitimate and must be met. Our dollars must meet them.

Congress has just passed a tax bill which will raise, it is estimated, about one-third of the requirements for the coming year. They are taxing incomes, war profits, gasoline, drugs, letter postage, and a hundred and one other things. When you pay a tax, you have no way of getting it back. But when you buy a bond, you will get all your money back, with interest.

There is every reason, moral, financial and patriotic, why you should go "over the top" in the matter of subscribing for the next issue of liberty bonds, and make even greater sacrifices to do so.—RIPPEY.

WORK WELL BOYS! IT'S FOR HIM!

OVER THERE

BUY BONDS

Originated and drawn by B. Caspar, an enthusiastic and 100 per cent loyal Ford worker. Thanks, Caspar, you've the right idea.

Uncle Sam to the Rulers of Germany

We tried to be neutral,
But you would not have it so.
You ravished your neighbors.
You outraged humanity.
And, failing to dominate us,
You reviled us.
You ordered us from the free seas.
You ambushed us on their highways.
You waylaid us in the night.
You killed our helpless people.
You drowned our women and children.
You destroyed our property.
You violated our rights.
You insulted our sovereignty.
You dishonored our flag.
You sneered at our protests.
You scorned our good will.
You flouted our friendship.
You mocked us as "money changers."
You derided our courage.
You jeered at our Army.
You scoffed at our means of defense.
You defied our offensive power.
You goaded us into war—and NOW,
You shall answer to 23 million men,
Placed at my command by Congress,
To make the world safe for Americans,
And other peace-loving people.
Civilization will subdue and disarm you.
Your vast machinery for torturing humanity,
Through your lust for pillage and conquest,
Shall be dismantled. You shall be made
Safe to live among law-abiding nations.
Take Notice!

UNCLE SAM.

Found

There have been turned in to THE FORD MAN 17 film negatives 2½" x 4", and 4 photographic prints. These were found on Manchester Avenue at noon Friday, September 20th. We hope this will meet the eye of the one who lost them and that he will call at office and secure them.

Direct from the Front

Here is a letter direct from the front and from an American soldier and former Ford worker to another Ford worker, who likewise has joined the defense for humanity and is now on his way to the front. The letter was dated August 11th and reads:

"Dear old Pal: Received your letter several days ago, but was too busy chasing the Hun to write you. So you are in the army too. Well, what do you think of army life? It's a great life if you don't weaken. I have the good fortune of being able to say that promotion has come to me, and I am now Battalion Sergeant-Major. Was acting Sergeant-Major for over two weeks and feel quite confident that I can make good.

"Our division played a very prominent role in the last American offensive and sure gave the Huns hell. From the number of German dead on the field they certainly lost heavily. In one little field and corner of the woods there were over 150 dead Germans. They seem mortally afraid of the Americans and will never put up half a fight. You no doubt have read about the Germans being chained to machine guns and doubted it; well it sure is the truth. Our troops drove them out of a town and the condition the Germans left the inhabitants was really a shame. They made them dig up their potatoes, gather up all the vegetables and then took everything away from them, and when we came they were almost starved to death. They robbed them of all their household furniture and destroyed everything they could lay hands on.

"The big guns seem to get on a man's nerves and after a steady all night bombardment, such as we were subjected to on several occasions, it makes one rather shaky in the morning. But, nevertheless it is a great game and lots of excitement. I will have a service stripe in another week, provided I don't have the ill luck of getting it in the neck before then. Will close with best wishes to wife and self and a safe journey over. I remain, Your friend and pal, Sgt.-Major Bob Cook."

In this letter you can see the spirit that makes the victorious soldier, the cheerful, optimistic, confident, sure to win spirit.

He Tumbled

A witness in a railroad case at Fort Worth, asked to tell in his own way how the accident happened, said:

"Well, Ole and I was walking down the track, and I heard a whistle, and I got off the track and the train went by, and I got back on the track, and I didn't see Ole; but I walked along, and pretty soon I see Ole's hat, and walked on, and seen one of Ole's legs, and then I seen one of Ole's arms and then another leg, and then over on one side Ole's head, and I says, My God! Something muster happen to Ole!"

Hold Steady, Men

Evidence has been brought to light which indicates that a well organized campaign is being carried on in the Ford organization to get our men to seek jobs elsewhere with the prospect of much higher wages. Needless to say, this work is being done by unfriendly interests bent only upon slowing up our war work.

Several instances have occurred where men have been lured away from the Liberty motor division with the promise of extremely high wages, only to find that the pay offered them was less than they received here.

Such experiences should teach the rest of us a valuable lesson. We are engaged in essential war work in the Ford Plant. Every man is doing as much good right where he is as he could do elsewhere. If for no other reasons than this, we should all "stick" to our jobs for the rest of the war period.

But here is still another point to remember. For seven years the Ford Motor Company has been paying uniformly higher wages than any other concern in the world. In times when work was slack and thousands have been thrown out of work by other firms, the Ford employes have worked right on, every day at the same big wage.

They have been given ideal working conditions and many other advantages not offered in other places. Yet a few of our employes, looking ever at "the green pastures just beyond their reach" have been unwise enough and disloyal enough to go to some other place where they may, perhaps, receive a few cents per hour more than they are given here. When the war is over and premium wages are no longer paid, these men will be coming back and begging for their old jobs.

How many of the great army of loyal Ford workers would vote to reinstate these traitors to their country and the firm that has done so much for them?

Let's stick tight, men, knowing that in so doing we are helping most of all to win the war and to show our employer in a practical way that we appreciate what has been done for us. And let us also nail the insidious lies of these German sympathizers, who would like nothing better than to see our work here crippled by thousands of our men quitting and searching for better jobs and better pay, which they will never find.

The Soldier's Chances

Great as the danger and large as the losses in the aggregate, the individual soldier has plenty of chances of coming out of the war unscathed, or at least not badly injured.

Based on the mortality statistics of the Allied armies, a soldier's chances are as follows:

Twenty-nine chances of coming home to one chance of being killed.

Forty-nine chances of recovering from wounds to one chance of dying from them.

One chance in 500 of losing a limb.

Will live five years longer because of physical training, is freer from disease in the army than in civil life, and has better medical care at the front than at home.

In other wars from ten to fifteen men died from disease to one from bullets; in this war one man dies from disease to every ten from bullets.

For those of our fighting men who do not escape scatheless, the Government, under the soldier and sailor insurance law, gives protection to the wounded and their dependents, and to the families and dependents of those who make the supreme sacrifice for their country.

Cartoon from *The Ford Man*, the Ford employee newspaper, urging employees to support the troops in France (from the collection of The Henry Ford).

Metal employee badge and security picture identification card issued to all employees working on the Eagle Boat. This type of ID was required for all employees producing war materials (author's collection).

"A" building or fabricating shop (150 × 450 feet) where plates, frames, shapes, etc., were manufactured and some assembled into sub-assemblies.

The boats were erected on timber cradles supported by twelve four-wheel railway trucks or 48 wheels to support an ultimate load of 200 tons. This allowed for progressive assembly by moving the cradle through seven stations. Based on the target of one boat a day, each station gang had three days to erect its share of the structure.

The first boat was finished and came off the line within five months, right on schedule. But production was not without serious problems. This was a brand new building to build a brand new boat to be built by a brand new process. A production system had to be devised, machinery that didn't exist had to be designed and built, over 7,000 inexperienced people had to be hired and trained by supervisors with no boat building experience and with all this the Navy kept making changes. Early on, Navy inspectors noted poor bulkhead work and defects in erecting, bolting, riveting, welding, patching, poor paperwork and poor inspection by company personnel. One problem was caused by the Navy trying to cram too much equipment in the narrowest size vessel. A wider vessel, favored by Ford, would have allowed for a much easier installation process. As an example, provisions had to made for using either fresh or salt water, which meant a duplication of the pipe systems. This meant 37 distinct pipe systems had to be crowded in, difficult to do in a large ship and doubly so in the limited space in the Eagle.

Among the many novel approaches to boat building was one for launching the vessel. A slip or channel one half mile long, 300 feet wide and 28 feet deep had been dug from the end of the "B" building, in which the ship was assembled, to the Rouge River. When completed, the hull of the vessel exited the end of the building on a cradle and instead of being launched from the ways stern first as all other large ships were, the cradle was lowered into the water by four hydraulic lifts until the boat floated off the cradle. At this point the ship was broadside in the canal and floated that way as it was towed down the canal several hundred feet to the channel to the Rouge River. It was then docked alongside the fit-out shops located along side the channel. At this time motor parts, boilers and armaments were installed at the fit-out shop (100 × 1,500 feet) which could work on up to eight ships at a time. The total time to launch a hull, starting from the last stage in the assembly building, was about 40 minutes.

Eagle Boat under construction with flat slab steel side recommended by Henry Ford to simplify and speed construction. Assembly line construction of oceangiong ships was revolutionary and similar to the way Henry Kaiser built Liberty cargo ships in World War II (from the collection of The Henry Ford).

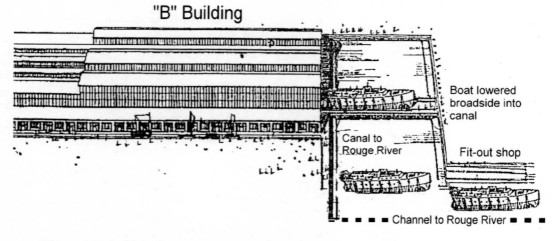

Illustration showing the unique manner in which Eagle Boats were launched broadside and then floated down the canal to the Rouge River (author's collection).

With Henry Ford's reputation for mass production, his decision to build Eagle Boats generated many comments, such as this cartoon of Ford's sub chaser chasing a German sub (***Bristol Herald Courier***, Bristol, Virginia, February 2, 1918).

A September 4, 1918, letter promised an aggressive production schedule.

| | Schedule | | Total | |
	Dearborn	Kearny	Launched	Commissioned
July/November 1918			12	3
December 1918	10	5	0	0
January 1919	15	10	5	0
February 1919	15	10	8	0
March 1919	15	10	14	0
April 1919	6	5	3	0

By Armistice Day, November 11, 1918, Eagle Boats Nos. 1 and 2 had been accepted by the Navy with No. 3 being accepted on November 14. No further boats were commissioned due to icing in the Great Lakes and St. Lawrence Seaway until April 1919, but boats were being built and launched each month — May, 6; June, 3; July, 5; August, 3; October, 1. With the end of the war the contract was reduced to 60 boats and plans for the Kearny plant canceled. Boat No. 59 was built in a record 10 days and Boat No. 60 was launched in October 1919.

Eagle Boat being tested on the Rouge River prior to delivery to the U.S. Navy. Only two boats were delivered by war's end. By the end of the contract Ford was building 14 boats a month (from the collection of The Henry Ford).

While no Eagles were launched in time to participate in the war a news report of August 4, 1919, reported all three of the first Eagle Boats were stationed at Archangel in support of U.S. troops serving in northern Russia.

Based on the initial order of 100 boats Ford estimated a per unit cost of $225,000. Considering all the expenses involved in startup up being spread over only 60 boats the actual per unit cost was about $750,000.

The Eagle Boat plant cost the government $3,500,000 and the contract gave Ford the right to prior sale at a valuation made by the government, and if Ford failed to exercise its right the plant would be dismantled and removed by the government. The "B" building where the ships were built was sold to Ford in December 1919 with all the other buildings being dismantled and removed by the government. Ford paid $663,500 less $180,000 for "outlays by contractor (Ford) for improvements that were of no value to the contractor." The contract was signed by Franklin D. Roosevelt, Secretary of the Navy.[21]

With all the publicity of Ford's submarine chaser, in 1918 Harry Coleman of Geary, Oklahoma, wrote the song *Ford's One Man Chaser* that started:

> *Henry Ford got a notion and he got it in his bean*
> *   that he could lick the Kaiser and all his submarines.*
> *So he made a "one man chaser" just as swift as it could be*
> *   and they took the foreign waters like a swarm of bumble bees.*

In January 1919, Senator Henry Cabot Lodge called for an investigation of adverse comments by the *Daily Iron Trade and Metal Market Report*. At the hearing, naval officers defended the boats as a necessary experiment, and as well made, and Ford profits were modest. A Navy Department letter dated April 2, 1924, commented on the performance of the Eagle boats:

The usefulness of the Eagles in the purpose for which they were designed was never demonstrated because the war was finished before any of the Eagles were in service. The circumstances that existed in early 1918 justified the Eagles, and if the war had continued a few months longer, these test would undoubtedly have been effective.... I may sum up by stating that the Eagles would have been of value if the war had continued through 1919, and their construction was justified.

Following the war some boats saw miscellaneous assignments with the Navy, others were used for training in the Naval Reserve and five were transferred to the Coast Guard. By 1941 all but 8 were sold, lost, or used as target ships. The remaining eight Eagles saw service in anti-submarine duty on both coasts during World War II. The story of the World War II activities of Eagle No, 56 in anti-submarine warfare off the New Jersey–Delaware coast in 1942 is related in the June 1973 issue of *Naval Institute Proceedings*. The article includes details of her being torpedoed off the Maine coast in April 1945.[22] Eagle No. 57, the last boat on the rolls, was sold in 1947.

Over the years, there has been much criticism of Ford's performance in building the boats, and many have made disparaging remarks of their performance based on naval design as well as Ford's construction. Three comments are in order:

First— A contemporary report: *Industrial Management, The Engineer Magazine*, January 1919, reported in a series on the Eagle Boat factory: "The result is one of the great industrial achievements of the war. [I]t staggers the imagination to realize that the feat was substantially accomplished, although the sudden cessation of the war somewhat dimmed the brilliancy of the performance."

Second— A personal report: The most telling comment of all is in a letter dated May 1919 to Ford from Lieutenant F. C. Forster, Engineering Officer on Eagle No. 2, covering his trip from Detroit to Russia. After discussing the typical shakedown problems encountered he wrote, "These boats for their size are very seaworthy little crafts and have stood up well under their hard strain of almost a seven thousand mile trip which is sometimes trying to larger and more sturdier craft. I think they have done excellently and no mistake."[23]

Third— Owen Gault's very extensive article "Ford's Proud Folly" in *Sea Classics*, October 1995, examined in detail the development of the Eagle Boat and all the charges against it. He summed up: "Their inherent flaws earned them the unenviable reputation of being 'Ford's Folly'; however, their shortcomings were better blamed on naval designers than on Ford's production criteria." Henry Ford's only design input was the use of flat hull plates to aid construction.

Ironically, the "B" building that assembled the Eagles would house a disassembly operation when, following the war, Ford would purchase 199 of the wartime merchant ships to be scrapped.[24] The Eagle Boats were the first product of Ford's Rouge Plant, which would eventually be the largest manufacturing complex in the world and be the home of the Fordson Tractor, the Ford Model "A" automobile, 1949 Ford, 1955 Thunderbird and the 1965 Mustang among others. The temporary "B" building remained in use until 2004.

Henry's Other Boat

In 1916 Henry Ford planned a trip to Cuba to explore the potential for obtaining iron ore and coal for the new Rouge plant he was planning to build. Ever mindful of the impact the Ford name had on real estate prices, he purchased the yacht *Sialia* for the trip to avoid the press and the potential publicity that would have inflated prices if he traveled on a commercial liner. Built in 1913 it was a 202½ foot, 552 ton steel schooner powered by oil-fired turbines with a range of 6,000 miles and cost Ford $250,000. In May 1917, having made just the one trip to Cuba, the schooner was sold to the U.S. Navy for wartime needs. It was commissioned as the USS *Sialia* and spent most of World War I at pier-side in Philadelphia, Pennsylvania, and Newport News, Virginia. Following the war Ford repurchased the *Sialia* from the Navy and retained it until 1929.[25]

Caissons

In November 1917 Ford was given contracts for 4.7 inch and 155mm gun caissons — two wheeled carts designed to haul large artillery shells of a specific caliber. Shortly after

Ford was the sole source for this 155mm artillery caisson (from the collection of The Henry Ford).

production started Ford was directed to concentrate on the larger 155mm gun caisson. Ford was the only producer of this larger caisson and reached a production of 150 per day. Ford developed a new axle for the 155mm caisson and in addition to being stronger, along with other manufacturing improvements, costs were reduced from the contract price of $1,250 to $700 each. Nine hundred of the 4.7 inch caissons were produced before all efforts were switched to building 8,937 of the larger caissons.[26] In addition Ford developed an overseas caisson crate containing 127 cubic feet less wood than the government design.

Tanks and Armor Plate

The massive use of the machine gun in World War I led directly to the development of the tank. In the trench warfare of that period, the machine gun was ravaging the allied infantry attacking across open fields. Some way had to be found to tear through the barb-wire entanglements and silence the murderous fire from the German machine gun nests. Developed by the British, the first tanks were monstrous 14 ton vehicles that proved effective against the German machine guns, however the need for smaller tanks was soon apparent. The French successfully developed a small six ton Renault tank manned by two

Front view of the first Ford-built 2½ ton tank. Several of the 15 tanks built were sent to France for testing and resulted in a request for a larger vehicle (from the collection of The Henry Ford).

Rear view of the first tank. The only two surviving tanks are at the Army's Aberdeen Proving Grounds, Maryland, and the George Patton Museum, Fort Knox, Kentucky (from the collection of The Henry Ford).

men and carrying a 37mm gun and a 8mm machine gun that was also used by the American Expeditionary Forces.

French factories, however, were not able to adequately supply their own troops, much less ours, resulting in a request to Ford in early March 1918 to design and build a small two man tank. Specifications called for a tank weighing two tons, mounting a 30 caliber machine gun with a speed of 8 mph and costing about $4,000. Within two days engineers drew up plans and within three weeks a two man, two and a half ton working model was built. Ford engineers determined that this tank could be produced as desired from 100 to 1,000 per day as Henry Ford had previously boasted. An initial order was placed for 15 of these two man tanks and a new building, 222 × 530 feet, was erected in 30 days. The tank was powered by two Model T engines, locked together and synchronized so that if one engine failed the other could still run both tracks. In effect they had an "H" type 8 cylinder engine that could produce about 35HP. The hand crank for the engines was replaced by an electric starter for obvious reasons. They were 14 feet long by 5 feet high, carried a 15 gallon gas tank and could travel 10 to 12 miles per hour. Space for the driver and gunner was extremely limited. The fifteen tanks were built by the end of the war with several being sent to France for evaluation. These tanks cost $7,273 each, a cost that would have been drastically reduced had volume production occurred.

Larger 3 ton type tank built by Ford. The Army ordered 10,000 but the war ended with only two being built. None survives.

Based on experience in France, the Army ordered 1,000 of this much larger 6 ton tank. Only one was built and this picture is the only known image (both images from the collection of The Henry Ford).

Based on the performance of the two and a half ton tank a contract for 15,000 three ton tanks was given to be built at the rate of 100 a day. Two were actually built before war's end. In addition a contract was awarded Henry Ford and Son in October for 1,000 six ton, three-man tanks, developed by Ford and powered with a Ford tractor engine and armed with a 37mm gun and a machine gun; $16,459 was expended on development of the six ton tank, only one of which was built.[27]

Two of the two and a half ton tanks survive. One, authentically restored, is on display in the Ordnance Museum, Aberdeen Proving Grounds, Maryland. It was sent there in November 1918 for testing and sat deteriorating until discovered and restored to running condition in 1964. The other, also restored, except for a modern Jeep engine, is located at the General George Patton Museum, Fort Knox, Kentucky.

Ford was also requested to develop and manufacture armor plate for the tanks that was strong enough to withstand the most modern armor piercing machine gun ammunition. In the development process a certain unknown element was found. Further investigation found that a German scientist had taken out a patent on this element, called zirconium, in 1910, with wording so vague that no one associated it with steel making. While unknown in the United States, the Germans had been using zirconium in steel making since 1913. This development led Ford to use the element allowing for the reduction in the thickness of the old armor plate by half while withstanding the same amount of fire and shock; $272,717 was expended in the development and production of this armor.[28]

In a publication by Ford on its war activities, submitted for clearance to the War Department, the government advised Ford "Delete the entire chapter headed "Armor Plate ... as such information inspires the production by the enemy of higher velocity ammunition."

Helmets and Body Armor

The modern military helmet, introduced by the French army early in the first World War, was an adaptation of a French fireman's helmet. Recognizing the value the British quickly introduced their own version. The United States Army, realizing the American soldier would be entering combat, reacted by directing research into a helmet for the American soldier.

Two of the early American designs were the Dean helmet, which required 10 operations, and a visored helmet requiring 15 operations. Ford was given samples of the two helmets to experiment with in manufacturing. In February 1918 Ford was given a contract for 11,200 of the Dean helmets, which was later reduced, and only 2,169 of these helmets were made by Ford in Detroit. Ten thousand Visor helmets were also ordered but there is no record of any being produced. The Dean helmet was probably the model 2 helmet (helmet on left) in the illustration that was discontinued as it looked too much like the German helmet.

After numerous attempts, a Model No. 5 helmet, substantially like that used by the British forces, was adopted. It differed from the British helmet only in the lining and the surface covering. The web lining in the American helmet fit tightly over the wearer's head, keeping the two pound helmet a uniform distance from the head which evenly distrib-

The Army ordered these helmets from Ford. The one in the middle was too complicated and the left one looked too similar to the German helmet. The English type helmet shown on the right in this Marine Corps recruiting poster was finally adopted (Americn Munitions).

Spray painting helmets at Ford's Philadelphia plant. Over 2,700,000 helmets were processed at the Philadelphia Ford plant (from the collection of The Henry Ford).

uted the weight on the wearer as well as the force of any blow to the helmet. The bare steel helmet, webbing and shipping boxes were provided by outside vendors and sent to Ford for finishing, assembly and crating. The original chin straps provided were cheap and tended to crack and Ford managers refused to accept them even though they had been passed by the government inspectors. The helmet was painted olive-drab and then sprayed with fine sawdust to eliminate glare and then painted again. (The British threw sand against the wet paint by hand which resulted in random small knobs that would break off revealing the shiny metal of the helmet.) The original contract called for production of 7,200 helmets a day, but by war's end 40,000 helmets a day had been reached and facilities were in place to deliver 75,000 a day.[29] A total of 2,731,573 helmets were actually processed. On an early contract for 725,256 helmets, Ford was allowed 31 cents per unit but the actual cost was 10.36 cents resulting in a $130,235.40 savings and a refund to the government.[30] This style helmet would be used by United States troops into the early days of World War II. Total cost for all experimental helmets manufactured by Ford and the standard helmets processed by Ford amounted to just 10.9 cents per helmet. All standard helmets and body armor were assembled or produced at Ford's Philadelphia Branch plant.

The references to Ford produced body armor are limited. Known facts include 6,454 sets (front and back) were manufactured by September 1918 along with 35,622 eye guards (no description available), at a total cost of $247,002.

Other War Products

The existence of some of these other war products is known primarily from their inclusion in a letter from Ford to the United States House of Representatives in March 1922.[31]

British naval officers brought an anti-submarine device to Ford where it was redesigned by Ford engineers under the officers' direction. No details exist about this device, only that it cost Britain $1,000,000.

Ford developed and produced a submarine listening device for installation on the Eagle Boats at a cost of $204,826.

Ford participated in the development of an experimental 75mm artillery shell at a cost of $2,457 and a sample tank ball-gun mount for a Browning machine gun for $463.

Ford also developed a non-porous aluminum casting, a vital factor in producing reliable gas masks. They also turned over their plant in Long Island City, New York, for the production of gas masks.

The entire facilities of the following Ford branches were leased to the government for war production purposes: Atlanta, Georgia; Cambridge, Massachusetts; Cleveland, Ohio; Louisville, Kentucky; Milwaukee, Wisconsin; Pittsburgh, Pennsylvania; St. Louis, Missouri; and Washington, D.C. In addition the following facilities were partially leased: Detroit, Michigan; Houston, Texas; Philadelphia, Pennsylvania; and Seattle, Washington.

In addition, the Ford Hospital, recently opened in Detroit, Michigan, was leased to the government for $1 a year, and renamed U.S. Army General Hospital Number 36. Between 1918 and 1919, 2,000 sick or wounded men from overseas were treated. Although the Army praised the hospital as one of the finest, records show it was left in deplorable condition when vacated in August 1919.[32]

Ford Overseas

Henry Ford's anti-war outpourings and the Peace Ship expedition did nothing to help the Ford image with his overseas subsidiaries, especially in Canada and Great Britain.

1. World War I 29

Although Henry Ford was looked on with great disfavor by those actually involved in the war, local Ford management was able to overcome this difficulty by keeping the image of the company separated from the man. Ford facilities in the British Empire, having been on war footing since 1914, were fully committed. The only definite information found concerning war production by Ford of Britain is that they built over 30,000 Model T troop carriers, water carriers, ambulances and munition carriers as well as an unknown amount of shell casings.[33] Ford of Canada built stacks and boiler castings for the Eagle Boat, some parts for the Ford tank and, along with Ford of France, supplied an unknown number of Model T cars and trucks.[34]

Home Front

Just as Henry Ford had used the media to push his pacifist views prior to the war, once he committed his plants to all-out wartime production, he unleashed a media blitz to support it. The Ford Photographic Department, established in 1914, had become one of the largest producers of motion picture films in the United States providing at little or no cost travel, nature and historical films for theater and dealership showings around the country. Ford used this in-house production company to further the United States war effort as well as tell the story of Ford's own war effort. Among such films, which were sent to 4,000 theaters throughout the United States, were: *How and Why Liberty Bonds Are Made* (used by the government), *The Truth About the Liberty Motor, The Story of the "Ford Eagle," Training Officers for Our National Army*, and *Heroes of the Coast Guard* as well as films for the Red Cross and Liberty Loan drives. Also, Ford made substantial contributions to the various Liberty Loan campaigns as well as to the Red Cross, YMCA and Knights of Columbus to aid them in serving the American soldiers in France.[35]

Wartime Profits

As mentioned earlier Henry Ford had been quoted as saying at the outbreak of the war: "Everything I've got is for the Government and not a cent of profit." Henry Ford directed that all war contracts be calculated without any profit but the War and Navy Departments insisted that contracts include profits for uniformity among manufacturers. Replying to a 1925 letter from Senator James Couzens, who had inquired as to whether Ford had refunded his wartime profits to the government, Ford's secretary Ernest Liebold replied in February 1925 that the "no profit" comment pertained only to Henry Ford's share of any profits. There were other Ford stockholders, including Couzens himself, who would have to give their consent to any such pledge. And in any event, calculations of profit or loss still could not be made as, five years after the end of the war, government accountants were still investigating Ford's wartime contracts.[36]

The final tally: Ford Motor Company earned $9,454,047 on total gross receipts of $108,851,320. Following the payment of federal taxes this was reduced to $4,357,485 of which Henry Ford's share as a 58.5 percent stockholder was $926,780 after taxes. There is no indication that any such sum was refunded to the U.S. government.[37]

Wartime Aggravations

To complicate Henry Ford's war production activities, he was persuaded by President Wilson to run for the Senate of the United States on the Democratic ticket in 1918. Wilson was having trouble getting his League of Nations proposal passed in the Senate. The proposal, a forerunner of today's United Nations, was encountering stiff opposition from the narrowly controlled Republican majority. The popular Henry Ford, known to favor Wilson's program, was a good bet to win the Michigan Senate seat for the Democrats and swing the balance of the Senate for the League of Nations proposal. Ford accepted the nomination but refused to campaign or spend a dime to promote his campaign, although others did, a position that cost him the election by only 2,201 votes. His opponent, Truman Newberry, spent lavishly and made many attacks on Ford's qualifications but two were directly associated with the war and eventually backfired on Newberry.

First was the fact that Henry Ford had obtained a draft deferment for his son, Edsel, as being necessary to the Ford Motor Company in producing materials for the war. This deferment request for Edsel had been rejected by the local draft board. In World War I (and again in World War II and today) a blue star flag was hung in people's window to indicate a family member was in the United States armed forces. (It was changed to a gold star for those killed in action.) The Newberry forces attacked Ford with a postcard size flier picturing the blue star flag with a caption "Henry Ford has nothing like this in his window." The reverse read: "His Country Needs Edsel Ford — Where is he?" Obviously, Edsel Ford was a great deal more useful as a senior executive in Ford Motor Company than as a soldier in any capacity in France.[38]

Second was the charge that appeared just before election day with a massive Newberry advertising campaign headlined "Henry Ford and His Huns," accusing Henry Ford of harboring German sympathizers on his payroll, a situation that could lead to sabotage. In particular a Carl Emde was named who worked on the Liberty aircraft engines. Emde, a Ford employee since 1908 and a loyal U.S. citizen, was in charge of designing tools, fixtures and jigs for the Liberty engine and one of a group that solved the serious problem in manufacturing the Liberty cylinders. The charge had no basis as Ford's Liberty engine work was considered by the Assistant Secretary of War "the most conspicuous success in quantity production in the world," and had saved the government thousands of dollars. Henry Ford was pressured to fire Emde but refused. Unfortunately, the Ford for Senator campaign made no immediately challenge to the ads and the accusation went unchallenged on election day.

Henry Ford was outraged by the vicious personal attacks, especially those regarding Edsel. An intensive investigation, funded by Henry Ford, was begun and ultimately charges were brought that Newberry had illegally and grossly exceeded spending limits on his primary campaign. He was convicted by a federal court but the conviction was overturned by the United States Supreme Court as no federal law was broken. In spite of the acquittal the Senate voted to censure Newberry for the exorbitant amount of funds spent which led to his resignation from the Senate. Ironically James Couzens, Ford's old partner who had left Ford after the bitter dispute over the war, was appointed to fill Newberry's unexpired term. Ford's refusal to campaign on his own behalf and the extravagant expenditures by Newberry's party coupled with the lack of response to the last minute Emde charges cost him the election. If Henry Ford had spent a small fraction of his Newberry investigation funds on running for the Senate he undoubtedly would have won.

Summary

Many United States companies were engaged in war production but Ford had more to contribute than any other automotive firm according to Allen Nevins.

Few organizations of any kind were potentially so important. Besides the many branch plants and the home center of Highland Park, there were two important sites for manufacturing, one for tractors in Dearborn and the other the Rouge. Even more important than factory potential were Ford's resources in manpower. He commanded a group of engineering and business executives with as much brains, resourcefulness and audacity as any other working force in the country ... all were trained to do the impossible. With them, no idea was too extraordinary to test, no problem too difficult to solve.[39]

Henry Ford and Ford Motor Company, which were one and the same to most of the public, received the lion's share of favorable publicity during the war. While most of Ford's public recognition was due to the uniqueness and enormity of the Eagle Boat program none of these boats saw action during the war. This was true of most war products made in the United States. Of greater importance were his efforts in solving problems with the Liberty engine which, although in small numbers, did reach the battlefront in France.

Ford's greatest contribution, however, was the thousands of motor vehicles they built in the United States and their foreign subsidiaries. Motor vehicles were common, every-

Postcard: France June 2, 1918, 23rd Engineers, AEF. "This little Ford has carried me thousands of miles thru mud, snow and shell holes. The large ambulances can't compare with it. This ambulance has been under fire many times and is still going strong" (author's collection).

day items and as such are seldom thought of as war production. However the role of the Ford Model T was regarded as a great asset by all of the allies. Poems such as *Hunka Tin* by an unknown Sammie[40] and *Elizabeth Ford*, about a Model T used by the Marines at Belleau Woods and throughout the war,[41] extolled the Model T. Lawrence of Arabia switched from camels to Model T's in the Middle Eastern Campaign and his boss, General Allenby, told radio commentator Lowell Thomas, "The Ford had decidedly helped to defeat the Turks. They were the only cars that would go across the desert. Any good car was usable on good roads. But the ungainly Fords were also reliable in rough terrain where there were no roads." According to Thomas, Allenby rode in a Rolls-Royce but always had a Ford on hand as a kind of insurance.[42] The *Hunka Tin*, a parody on Kipling's "Gunga Din," was used in Ford dealers' advertising all over the country and was cited by *Printer's Ink* as the most effective advertising to emerge from the war.

With the armistice eliminating most war production jobs Ford records indicate a major effort was made to retain unneeded workers on the payroll by finding work of some sort until the factories could be rearranged for normal car production. An example given was that of the 13,000 Liberty aircraft engine workers that were kept on the payroll until car production reached the pre-war level of 3,500 cars a day in May 1919.

2

World War II

Prelude to War

Following the inauguration of President Franklin Roosevelt in 1933 Henry Ford published a tribute to the President:

A great thing has occurred amongst us. We have made a complete turnaround, and at last America's face is toward the future.

Three years—1929 to 1932—we Americans looked backward. All our old financial and political machinery was geared to pull us out of the depression by the same door through which we entered. We thought it simply a case of going back the same way we came. It failed. We now realize that the way out is forward—through it.

Inauguration Day he turned the ship around. Having observed the failure of sincere efforts to haul us back the way we came, he designed a new method—new political and financial machinery—to pull us out the way we are going—forward. He is clearing international obstacles out of the way; he does not take advice from the "interests"; that he has courage and loyalty to work for one supreme interest only—the welfare of the American People.[1]

This optimism expressed by Henry Ford over President Roosevelt's inauguration quickly changed to disillusionment with the President's New Deal, exemplified by the National Recovery Act (NRA) that was signed into law in late 1933. The NRA program, which was one of the efforts by the President to end the Depression in the United States, imposed many regulations on business, including controls on employment which favored unionization. Henry Ford, along with a few other manufacturers, despised the terms of the NRA and, although he was not alone in refusing to sign, he was undoubtedly the most influential. He said the law didn't require him to sign it, just obey it, and he was already meeting or exceeding the requirements. This obviously infuriated President Roosevelt and in retaliation Ford was denied government contracts for motor vehicles until the NRA law was overturned by the United States Supreme Court in 1935. Still trying to get Henry Ford's cooperation in his recovery efforts, President Roosevelt unexpectedly invited Henry Ford to the White House in May 1938, and just as unexpectedly Henry Ford agreed. Commenting on his invitation, Henry Ford said, "I'm going to give the President a chance to look at somebody who doesn't want anything. I shall not give my advice." Although neither party made any comments after the meeting, this undoubtedly aggravated the already tense relationship, and what probably was mutual disdain, between Henry Ford and President Roosevelt as the war years approached.

Very much like World War I, the United States in the late 1930s was again not militarily ready to enter into a war. To put into perspective what the United States was up against just prior to the opening of hostilities in Europe, the U.S. Army General Staff noted in a 1936 report that, in the event of mobilization, the troops mustered during the first thirty days "can be supplied with all required equipment from storage or from procurement *except* for airplanes, tanks, combat cars, scout cars, anti aircraft guns and control equipment, searchlights and 50 caliber machine guns."[2] The situation did not improve. Major war games were held in the summer of 1941 to train and assess the Army's readiness for battle: tanks were trucks with *TANK* painted on both sides, antitank guns were lengths of drain pipes, obsolete World War I Springfield rifles had *.50 caliber* signs pasted on them for machine guns, and a wooden tripod was labeled *60mm mortar*.

As he was during World War I, Henry Ford was vocally against the President's efforts to involve America in another war. The relationship between Ford and Roosevelt was not helped, when, in 1938, both Henry Ford and his good friend Charles Lindbergh, both outspoken in their opposition to the United States being drawn into another European war, received high decorations from the German government.[3] Many severely criticized Ford for accepting the German decoration, but two conditions bear consideration. One was the fact that Ford Motor Company had a substantial operation in Germany valued at just over $8,000,000 (nearly $109,000,000 in 2006 dollars) which could very well have been jeopardized if the German award was rejected. In addition, Henry Ford certainly knew that President Roosevelt was not only displeased by his acceptance of the award but also his refusal to reject it. Henry Ford could be stubborn and probably all of the public antagonism expressed towards him for accepting the award just steeled his resolve to keep the German decoration. His only comment was that he was accepting the award as a gesture from the German people, not indicating that he, in any manner, approved of the Nazi regime.

Adding to the public perception of Henry Ford as a pacifist was his rejection of a government request, in June 1940, to build Rolls Royce aircraft engines for Great Britain. Henry Ford believed the contract, negotiated by his son, Edsel, and Charles Sorensen, with his approval, was between Ford and the United States government for domestic defense. He canceled it when he found the contract would be directly between Ford and Great Britain, one of the belligerents in the European war. Unfortunately, the perception left with the public was that Henry Ford's pacifist beliefs caused the cancellation of the contract.

Unlike 1917 however, the United States had at least started producing war materials for itself and, under the Lend-Lease Act enacted into law in March 1941, for our potential allies as well. By 1940 Henry Ford had finally acknowledged the threat of the war in Europe and was fully engaged in America's rearming for defense. Ford's principles in producing war materials for the government were the same policies governing the company since the introduction of the Model T in 1908: use mass-production techniques to build the best quality product for the lowest possible price. But, Henry Ford still harbored his distaste for war. In a September 1942 interview in *Liberty* magazine he was quoted as saying, "I hate war. I've always hated war ... you can't get me to say anything in favor of war." Actually, Henry Ford's actions in both wars demonstrated a deep conviction that America should avoid conflict except in defense of America itself.

Ford was, by Pearl Harbor day, actively producing or developing facilities to produce, airplanes, aircraft engines, jeeps and tanks — items that would be Ford's most high profile contributions to the war effort.

Beginning Dates of Pre-War Activities of the Ford Motor Company
September 17, 1940 — Ground broken for new airplane engine building in the Rouge.
November 9, 1940 — Ford submits bid for 500 jeeps.
December 12, 1940 — Ford investigates building parts for B-24 bomber.
September 17, 1941 — Government requests proposal to build 400 tanks a month.

In May 1940, President Roosevelt called for the production of 50,000 airplanes per year with 50,000 on hand by the end of 1942. In January 1942 he raised the ante to 60,000 by the end of 1942 and 125,000 more by the end of 1943. During this same period the public was complacent, in spite of President Roosevelt's demands, about the need for the production of weapons for defense. The public's assumption was the mighty production capacity of the United States could quickly produce any amount of needed weapons. This assumption was epitomized by the mighty manufacturing capacity demonstrated by the facilities of Ford, General Motors and Chrysler. The idea was further fueled by the rapidity with which Ford started producing jeeps in February 1941. Though it appeared to the public that the jeep could be produced on the same assembly line as the Ford car by just using different parts, there were numerous production changes required. That said, however, a jeep was widely publicized rolling off the line behind the last civilian car produced. But, while all existing facilities could, with some modification, turn rather quickly to producing jeeps and a number of other wheeled vehicles, they were not capable of being adapted to the task of building more complex products like aircraft engines or bombers. The production of these products was foreign to Ford's experience and required new skills, specialized machinery and dedicated buildings.

Ford brought to the war-production table a huge, efficient, integrated and mechanized manufacturing facility operated by highly skilled and experienced technical and assembly workers. The part the skilled worker played was paramount. Aptly put was the comment by *Time* magazine in 1942 about the men who were the foundation of America's war production effort:

The Industrys' front line is manned by a little battalion of unknown men in battered felt hats, sitting shirt sleeved in cubbyhole factory offices, and then darting out among the machines. These are Detroit's production men, fresh up from the ranks, a trace of grease still under their stubby fingernails. They know machines as only can men who have handled them. They are the men who plan by ear, with near-perfect pitch. With dog-eared notebooks, pencil stubs and know-how, they work out production problems that no textbook could solve. These production men have the same tactile sensitivity to machinery as a surgeon has for muscle and nerve: they can make the machinery and blue prints come alive as Toscanini brings notes off paper. They do not come ready made; they have to grow up with the machines."[4]

Ford's Rouge facility offered the other dimension. A *Life* magazine article in August 1940 best described the Rouge:

Ford Motor Company is important because it makes automobiles. To make them it has perfected a technique of mass production that long ago revolutionized the art of industry and is now revolutionizing the art of war. To make mass production more efficient, Ford built the largest integrated industrial unit the world has ever seen.... There are a hundred ways in which the self-contained might of River Rouge can — and certainly will — be turned to wartime use.... The first and most overpowering impact at the Rouge comes from the shear size of the place and the things it can do — the 17 acre foundry which can produce 1,000,000 castings a day, the mechanical shovels which can grab 15 tons of ore in a single fistful, the conveyor lines which have a total length of 125 miles.... Precision is at the root of all Rouge production. The plant has a special squad of gage inspectors who make daily tours, checking production gages against Johansson blocks [see Chapter 10]. These blocks, accepted world standards of production accuracy, are correct to the millionth of an inch.[5]

The Rouge, started with the temporary "B" building to build Eagle Boats in World War I, just kept growing after the war under Henry Ford's unrelenting drive to complete the vertical integration of his automobile — from obtaining iron ore from the Mesabi Range in Minnesota, transporting it on his Great Lakes ore freighter fleet, converting the ore into steel in his blast furnaces and then into parts to be assembled into a new Ford car on the assembly line in the "B" building. In addition was the array of other facilities like the great Highland Park and Lincoln plants and the many branch plants and village industry operations scattered around the United States.

One of the great bottlenecks for the United States in converting to a vastly expanded industrial production for war was the availability of machine tools and the capacity to manufacture them. Ford's entrance into war production made available to the government 29,332 machine tools as well as 10,190 presses, forging machines and so on as well as thousands of electrical motors, a critical item. Valued at nearly $275,000,000, the practical value was a great deal more than the cost when considering the time that would have been needed to duplicate them.

Some of the more important facilities available for defense production by 1939 and 1940, at the Rouge plant alone, included a power plant capable of producing enough power for a city of 250,000 people. It represented a $27,000,000 investment and produced one billion kilowatt-hours of electricity during the war, enough to supply 99 percent of the requirements of the Rouge operation. Equally as important was Ford's Tool and Die Department, a $14,000,000 investment expended to obtain the latest and best machinery available to make it the finest in existence. The ability of this department to make tools and machinery of original design for unique war contracts or replicate others that just were not available from a war-stressed tool industry was of incalculable benefit. During the war Ford expended 62,645,000 man-hours for tooling while contracting for another 30,500,000 man-hours from outside vendors. There was also the iron foundry, including its machine department, that produced and machined most castings. Another vital facility was the $43,000,000 steel making plant with its blast and open hearth furnaces, coke ovens and strip and rolling mills that supplied a large portion of the steel Ford needed for war production as well as providing steel to other contractors.

War Production

On February 10, 1942, production of all civilian cars and trucks ceased and the Ford manufacturing machine was now totally devoted to producing implements of war. Henry Ford and the Ford Motor Company were commingled in the public's mind and once again they forgave, or at least forgot as in World War I, Henry Ford's pacifist activities. Now,

Henry Ford was not only going to build the massive Consolidated designed Liberator bomber in the largest plant in the world, but also to build one of these huge planes each hour. It captivated the public's imagination as nothing else could. It also drew a great deal of ridicule and outright disbelief from the old-line aviation industry and assorted skeptics who forgot Henry Ford had successfully adapted the assembly line process to build Eagle Boats in World War I and the all-metal Tri-Motor airplane, used by over 100 airlines, in the 1920s and 1930s. In hindsight, the AMC (Air Materiel Command) report of 1946 perfectly summed up Henry Ford's philosophy. "Mass-production techniques developed in many years of automobile manufacture could be applied equally well to an airplane, a washing machine — or anything."[6]

Ironically Ford's two most serious war-production start-up problems involved the two most complicated products for the same reason: incomplete and in some cases non-existent plans. The designers and manufacturers of neither the Consolidated bomber nor the Pratt & Whitney aircraft engine were accustomed to production in the volumes needed by the government or envisioned by Ford. In both cases skilled workers literally hand-built the units, using their experience to make parts fit. In both cases Ford had to draw complete detailed plans, many virtually from scratch, to accomplish their mass-production goals.

Henry Ford, now in his 70s, had suffered strokes in 1938 and mid–1941 and was not always totally aware or in command of what was happening in his company. In fairness, though, he had established and developed the organization and manufacturing giant that was able to contribute so mightily to the nation's war production. He approved of the company's war efforts, participated in major policy decisions and spent a great deal of time at the Willow Run bomber plant. That said, however, there were still tremendous problems with the in-fighting between Harry Bennett, Ford's fixer, and Charles Sorensen, Ford's production manager, worsened by the death of Henry Ford's son Edsel in May 1943. Some government officials became so concerned about the ability of the Ford colossus, especially the Willow Run plant, to properly function under these conditions that there was talk of a government takeover. In the end young Navy lieutenant Henry Ford II was released from active duty in August 1943 with the hope that he might quickly assume a management role and bring some order to the feared chaos in Ford's war production machinery.

As you read through the following chapters of Ford engineers' designs, production techniques and innovations to simplify production, improve quality and in most cases reduce cost, keep in mind that only the major, and a few of the lesser important, production innovations are described. In each of Ford's contracts there are many more techniques and innovations found in the records but not covered here. In all cases the production innovations that are detailed here were selected because they were not only of major importance or unique, but also because they are ones I can comprehend and readily describe in understandable terms for the average reader.

War Production Facilities

In World War I Ford required only the "A" and "B" building for the Eagle Boat and the never used building for the tank to handle war contracts. The government paid for the ship-building facility and all equipment, giving Henry Ford the option, which he exercised, of purchasing it at the end of the war. Other Ford World War I production was accommodated in existing Ford facilities and leased to the government while several Ford plants were sold outright to the Government.

The same system held true in World War II. The government paid for the Willow Run plant, aircraft engine plant and several other buildings in the Rouge. As in World War I, several branch plants were sold outright to the government and other Ford facilities producing war materials were leased to the government with the government paying the cost of renovations needed to produce a given item. Lease rates were figured on the amount of space used in the plants for various contracts which changed over time as old contracts ended or were amended and new ones signed. In many cases Ford advanced the funds to start building and equipping a new plant with the most expensive example being the aircraft engine building. From 1941 to 1945, Ford had advanced $37,272,957 to build the aircraft engine building and start production with no reimbursement until 1944.

Unreimbursed funds expended by Ford Motor Company as of September 30, 1945:

Airplane Engine	$14,700,631
Defense Plant Corporation (facilities)	$3,967,250
Pulse Jet Engine	$769,336
Jettison Fuel Tanks	$3,465,756
Airplane storage and flyaway	$1,675,806
Universal Carrier (Bren gun)	$627,495
Other contracts	$746,435
Total	$25,952,893

The total government-owned plants and facilities in Ford's custody in January 1945 was:

Land and buildings with improvements and installations	$90,916,745
Machinery, tools, equipments, kilns, blast furnaces and steel-making equipment	$254,474,110
Total	$345,390,855

Employment Diversity

Henry Ford was probably the first major equal opportunity employer in the United States. As early as 1911 Henry Ford was paying attention to the handicapped and by 1916 Ford employed blacks, handicapped persons and ex-convicts as well as people of sixty-two different nationalities. They were all paid the same wage and some blacks had been promoted to white collar jobs and even foremen.

Following Ford's announcement of the $5 a day wage in 1914, "an order was issued to the employment office that no job-hunter should be rejected on account of his physical condition [excepting contagious disease] and no one should be discharged for physical disability." A card detailing the specification of every job in the company was kept by the employment office so every handicapped employee could be matched to a job he was capable of doing.

By the start of World War I there were 1,700 seriously disabled and over 4,000 other partially disabled Ford workers that would have found employment difficult. After the war Ford agreed to take 1,000 handicapped veterans as fast as they became available and by 1919 the company employed 9,563 persons with some kind of handicap. This included the blind, men with no legs, missing a leg or a hand or even both hands.

In the early 1920s plant managers were instructed to survey their communities to determine the makeup of disabled people and to make sure Ford plant's employment represented a cross section. If 1 out 1,000 persons were blind then 1 out of 1,000 Ford workers should be blind. If 2 out of 3,000 were deaf, then 2 of every 3,000 Ford workers should be deaf.

By World War II, Ford had perfected the matching of the disabled worker to an appropriate job, finding that the disabled worker's performance was equal to or better than the unimpaired worker and with fewer accidents. A 1943 Ford publicity release noted there were 11,652 men with various disabilities in Ford facilities receiving full pay.[7] In an employment report for July 1943 there were, at the Rouge alone, 1,200 blind workers or workers with seriously impaired vision. In addition there were 153 deaf workers, 15 in wheelchairs with missing legs, 1 missing both hands and 137 missing a hand or a whole arm.[8] In 1945 there were 4,976 workers in the Rouge with disabilities ranging from rheumatism to 32 totally blind workers and in no case were these jobs tailor-made to their handicaps. All received equal pay for equal job responsibilities.

Just before the start of World War II, nearly half of all black workers in the Detroit automobile industry worked at Ford. There were some race relation problems in Detroit, but Henry Ford's continuing efforts to provide opportunities to the black community and his attitude about the worth of every individual lessened or prevented some troubles at Ford that were experienced by other manufacturers.[9] Most black workers appreciated Henry Ford's effort on their behalf and were the last group at Ford to be unionized in 1941.[10, 11]

In the Willow Run plant there were about ten little people employed who were highly prized for their ability to work in tight spaces such as inside wings and fuel tanks and other places that others could not reach. Knowing they would not be accepted for military service, many saw this as their opportunity to contribute to the war effort. Then there were the women. With unemployment plunging from 14.9 percent at the end of 1941 to 4.7 percent by the end of 1942, staffing of Willow Run was a major challenge. Prior to World War II no women were employed on the final assembly line and Ford had not included them in plans when laying out the Willow Run plant in 1940. With the advent of Pearl Harbor and the decision for Ford to build the entire B-24 bomber the work force had to be expanded. With the added need for workers, and the draft cutting into the remaining work force, women were the answer, not only for office work, but also to keep the assembly lines moving. Building plans for Willow Run had to be redrawn to allow for the expansion, including women's restrooms.[12] At peak employment 15,412 women worked at the bomber factory — 39 percent of the total work force. As of August 1943 women comprised 22 percent of the company's employees, filling every type of job they were physically able to handle and at the same rate of pay as the men.[13]

Organized labor had decried the awarding of war contracts to Ford, which continued to reject unionization of its workers. The government refused to listen to the union demands, deciding that it was a matter for civil litigation and must not interfere with the national defense program. On the other hand, when the workers of the massive Rouge plant staged a spontaneous refusal to work in early April 1941, neither the federal nor state government would intervene. An appeal to the President that the walkout was affecting defense production, resulted in a comment that the President did not consider it a serious interference. (A cynical person might believe the President was getting even with Henry Ford.) The result was that Ford finally signed its first union contract on June 20, 1941, and both management and labor leaders, unsure of each others limits, fenced for power in the following months. In addition to the UAW and the Foreman's Association of America, Ford had to deal with ten other labor organizations. Following the war Ford claimed there had been 773 wildcat strikes or slowdowns in negotiations with the UAW since the first union agreement had been signed.[14] According to the AMC report, however, "Willow Run was completely free of serious labor troubles. Work stoppages occurred from time to time but were of brief duration, few lasting more than several hours."

Publicity

While Ford was not the largest producer of war materials during World War II, it got the lion's share of publicity. This was due to the sheer magnitude of the new bomber factory at Willow Run and the extraordinary, some said unbelievable, claim of building one of the large B-24 bombers every hour. Assembly of a giant airplane based on an automobile type assembly process had never been done before and the enormity of building these large airplanes, in the numbers forecast, grabbed the public's imagination.

Throughout the war a story on Willow Run was always good for newspaper articles and magazine features. Most of these were positive in the first year or so as government officials and Sorensen released statements implying great progress was being made towards producing bombers. When the truth became known about the lack of progress in actual bomber production at Willow Run the press quickly turned negative and it dominated Ford war production news. Largely ignored were positive stories about jeeps, aircraft engines and other war products.

Ford did very little advertising regarding his war production in the first months of the war, feeling that with all the press coverage he was receiving, people knew what Ford was doing. With the confusion about what was happening at Willow Run, advertising was not practical. It was not until February 1943, with no airplanes pouring out of Willow Run, that Ford finally ran his first ad on war products announcing, with car-like merchandising, "New Models for 1943." It covered all Ford war products and other ads, individually extolling the production of jeeps, tanks, aircraft engines and bombers, appeared in following months. Finally in 1944, with the production miracles at Willow Run, all press coverage turned favorable. It is not surprising, therefore, that a Roper survey in the spring of 1945 found that only Henry Kaiser and his Liberty Ship shipyards ranked higher than Henry Ford in people's opinion of which businessman did the most to aid the war effort.[15]

One of the first war-time ads illustrating Ford's major war products to counter adverse press about the perceived slow start in building B-24 bombers. *Detroit News*, February 28, 1943 (from the collection of The Henry Ford).

Key Participants

Obviously this list covers just the very senior Ford executives that managed the Ford wartime production miracles.

Edsel B. Ford (1893–1943). Edsel Ford became President of Ford Motor Company in 1918, but in reality Henry Ford remained in control of the company, making all major decisions and the person most always quoted by the newspapers. Edsel Ford was a quiet, unassuming individual who worked behind the scenes and was responsible for a great many things the public never heard about. He shunned the spotlight, seldom giving interviews and always deferring to his father and when pressed by others to confront his father he would demur, saying, "It's Father's company." Considering Henry Ford's age and physical condition, mentioned previously, Ford Motor Company, during World War II, was primarily directed by Edsel Ford and Charles Sorensen.

Charles E Sorensen (1881–1968). Born in Copenhagen, Denmark, Sorensen came to the United States in 1885 and attended school in Buffalo, New York. By 1904 he was working as a pattern maker for a Detroit foundry where he met Henry Ford. In 1905 he agreed to work for Henry Ford at his new Ford Motor Company. Because of his work on

One of the many prominent visitors to Willow Run. *Left to right:* Eddie Rickenbacker, World War I ace; Edsel Ford; Mead Bricker, general manager of the bomber plant; and Henry Ford, at Willow Run in January 1943 (from the collection of The Henry Ford).

the Model T he was made assistant superintendent of production. An aggressive, domineering and hard driving individual, he introduced innovative procedures in the foundry, including the casting of the one-piece Model T engine block and later the V8 cylinder block. From then on he was known as "Cast Iron Charlie." He was one of the influential people in establishing the moving assembly line at Highland Park and in charge of developing tractor production during World War I. Taking charge of the Rouge plant when it opened in 1919, he selected Mead Bricker as one of his chief assistants. A manufacturing genius and Vice President of Ford by World War II, Sorensen was involved in negotiating war contracts with the government. He became the chief of war production for Ford, ramrodding the construction of the Pratt & Whitney aircraft engine plant and the Willow Run bomber plant. He left Ford Motor Company in March 1944, joining a long list of able executives who were forced out by Henry Ford. Leaving Ford he became President of Willys-Overland, Inc., Toledo, Ohio, and was responsible for the production of the first civilian Jeep only 10 days after the end of World War II.

Mead L. Bricker (1885–1964). Bricker was born in Youngstown, Ohio. After becoming a machinist for a steam engine company in Ohio, he was hired by Henry Ford in August 1904 and left in late 1905. Returning in 1914 as superintendent of Fordson Tractor, by 1920 he was the General Production Superintendent of Ford Motor Co. Once Sorensen got the Pratt & Whitney aircraft engine plant started in World War II, Bricker took over, establishing procedures and policies resulting in record breaking production. By December 1941, Bricker was instrumental in setting up production of the high precision Gun Director and the Armored Car programs. In May 1943, with bomber production lagging, he was appointed General Manager of Willow Run and was instrumental in outsourcing jobs to Ford Branches, the Ford village industries and independent manufacturers. He was elected a director of the company in 1943 and a Vice President in charge of manufacturing in 1945. At his retirement from Ford Motor Company in 1950 Henry Ford II said, "Every major wartime production effort of Ford benefited from Mr. Bricker's great manufacturing knowledge and skill. In particular the output of 2,000HP aircraft engines and the unprecedented heavy bomber production at Willow Run were personal triumphs of his leadership."[16]

Logan Miller (1887–?). Born in Mattoon, Illinois, he began work as a machinist in railroad shops. Miller joined Ford in 1914 as a lathe hand at the Highland Park plant and by 1935 had advanced to Assistant Superintendent of the Rouge. In charge of the engineers, tool designers and production men sent to San Diego in 1940 to study Consolidated's assembly methods, Miller guided the development of production methods and tooling for Willow Run and became the Assistant General Manager in 1941. Known as one of the best sheet metal fabricating men in the country, he was largely responsible for the decision to use hard dies which greatly aided mass production by forming large quantities of parts with the same exact dimensions. He was also responsible for production shortcuts leading to B-24 bomber production records. Named a Vice President of Ford in 1950, he retired in 1953.

Harry Bennett (1892–1979). Born in Ann Arbor, Michigan, he sang in the choir and had an artistic bent. By 1909 he had become restless and joined the Navy, excelling in boxing which suited his style. About to reenlist in the Navy he had a chance encounter with Henry Ford in New York City who was impressed with his spirit and shortly thereafter hired him. Working directly for Henry Ford, he became the fixer whom nobody dared cross. He carried out Ford's suggestions to the letter and over the years rose to an unofficial position of tremendous power. Along the way he jousted with Sorensen for power within the company and by World War II he was in charge of personnel, labor relations, public relations and security. His conflicts with Sorensen continued until Sorensen was forced out by Henry Ford. Bennett was forced out a year later when Henry Ford II, released from the Navy to stabilize the company, finally became president and fired him in 1945.[17]

Charles Lindbergh (1902–1974). Lindbergh is included here, not only for the help he gave Ford during World War II, but also for his continuing relationship with Henry Ford in the 1930s. Lindbergh had first met Henry Ford in July 1927 following his world renowned flight from New York to Paris the previous May. A friendship developed over the years with Lindbergh staying with Henry and Clara Ford on occasions when he came to Detroit to visit his mother. Lindbergh had been active in the America First Committee to keep America out of the war and influenced Henry and Clara to join the organization. Lindbergh's effort in keeping the United States out of the war resulted in his being branded a copperhead, a Civil War term for traitor,[18] by Roosevelt, causing Lindbergh to resign his Army commission. When war broke out Lindbergh was refused reinstatement of his commission and defense manufacturers were reluctant to hire him out of concern for reprisals by the government.[19] He offered Henry Ford any aid or advice that might be useful in Ford's B-24 bomber project and Henry Ford, at odds with Roosevelt, hired Lindbergh in November 1941 as a test pilot and consultant for his Willow Run bomber plant. Ford employment records show he was employed from November 1941 to July 1942 at a monthly rate of $666.66.[20] While Ford was willing, and in fact offered a much larger salary, Lindbergh would only accept the pay he would have received if he had been reinstated as a Colonel in the Army Air Force.[21]

3

Consolidated Bomber

The story of the development of this airplane provides an interesting background to the B-24 Liberator story. Reuben Fleet organized the Consolidated Aircraft Corporation in 1923 and, in the late 1930s, hired an innovative aviation designer name Isaac M. Laddon. Laddon directed the development of the now famous PBY Catalina flying boat that was such a great search and rescue plane in the Pacific in World War II. In 1937 the U.S. Navy purchased 60 of these planes, one of the largest military airplane contracts since World War I. In the late 1930s the B-17 Flying Fortress was being built by Boeing Airplane and in 1939 the Army Air Corps asked Consolidated, with its proven aviation experience, to be a second manufacturer in order to increase production. After inspecting the Boeing plant, Fleet rejected the request on the grounds that it would be difficult to adapt Boeing's design to Consolidated's building methods. Instead, Fleet convinced General Hap Arnold, chief of the Army Air Corps, that they could design a new bomber, with a new wing design by David R. Davis, that would fly farther and faster with a larger bomb load than the B-17. Further, they would produce a prototype airplane in nine months, a nearly unheard-of feat. Under the direction of Laddon and Project Engineer Frank Fink, on December 29, 1939, one day shy of nine months, the prototype B-24 bomber made its initial flight from Lindbergh Field, San Diego, California.[1] The plane flew farther, faster and carried a larger bomb load than the B-17.

The plane as approved in 1939 weighed 37,000 pounds but by the time the first unit went into production it had been re-engineered up to 41,000 pounds. An order for 139 of these planes, designated LB-30s, had been originally ordered by France in 1940. On the fall of France to the Germans, they had been diverted to, and subsequently combat tested by, the British. They had been built to the British specifications and substantial changes and modifications had been required to meet the U.S. Army Air Corps requirements. Allowing for increased crews, self-sealing gas tanks, armament and increased bomb loads, the plane, as flown by the U.S. Army Air Force during the war, weighed in at about 56,000 pounds with one flight recorded at 72,000 pounds.

Relevant to the story of Ford's start-up experiences in producing the B-24 are these comments from the 1946 Air Materiel Command (AMC) study:

> The B-24 was a newly designed plane not thoroughly tested nor production engineered when Ford under-took its mass-production. In fact, only seven planes had been accepted

from Consolidated by the Army.... The flood of engineering changes resulted in serious delays during the early production period. Approximately 130 master changes were incorporated in Ford's first production B-24.... That any progress was achieved was due almost solely to Ford's complete mastery of mass-production, the organization's unqualified tooling facilities, its vast resources and purchasing power and its confidence in its ability to mass-produce pretty nearly anything.[2]

The Proposal: By the late 1930s the German Luftwaffe had demonstrated the importance of air power and the U.S. government, finally recognizing the urgent need to develop aircraft production and responding to Roosevelt's demand for 60,000 airplanes in 1942, had all aircraft manufacturers fully booked with contracts and were looking for much greater production capacity. Seeing the automotive industry as a solution, Ford was among the first to be approached. In December 1940 Ford was asked to use its mass-production know-how to help increase the nation's supply of warplanes by making parts and subassemblies such as wings and fuselages for the B-24 bombers. They would be assembled in new government plants to be built in Fort Worth, Texas, and Tulsa, Oklahoma. One of the reason for approaching Ford was that as a privately owned company, with enormous purchasing and production resources, it would be able to make decisions and take action almost immediately.

In early January 1941, Edsel Ford, Charles Sorensen, Logan Miller and other Ford production experts visited Consolidated's plant in San Diego to determine what would be required to accommodate the government's request. Sorensen's initial comment was that all existing aircraft manufacturers were building several types of planes for the Army or Navy as well as developing new models. As a result, these manufacturers, with their resources spread over several types of planes, could never produce aircraft in the volume the government needed. Sorensen, calculating the project as 25 percent manufacturing and 75 percent assembly, thought the plane was well designed and felt Ford could successfully produce the entire plane "if such a thing as freezing the design is possible." The only way to obtain volume, he insisted, was a plant dedicated to building one plane with minimal changes.[3]

Sorensen relates in his autobiography, *My Forty Years with Ford,* as he watched the piecemeal construction of the massive B-24 bomber at the Consolidated factory:

> What I saw reminded me of nearly thirty five years previously when we were making the Model N Fords at the Piquette Avenue plant.... The B-24's final assembly was made out of doors under the bright California sun and on a structural steel fixture. The heat and temperature changes so distorted this fixture that it was impossible to turn out two planes alike without adjustments.[4]

Sorensen was sure wing assemblies to be made by Ford would never fit the fuselages built by Consolidated. Their planes were literally hand built and it would be nearly impossible to mate them to the precision manufactured wings Ford would build.

That night in his hotel room Sorensen sketched out what he had in mind for a plant and wrote across the top "1 plane per hr, 400 per mo." Reuben Fleet's reaction was, "Why not make units for us, and we'll assembly them?" Sorensen replied "We are not interested in assemblies. We'll make the complete plane or nothing" and countered with a plan to build the entire bomber based on the precision manufacturing and assembly line methods that had been proven by Ford over the past 25 years. Sorensen's claim that Ford could built 400 bombers a month versus Consolidated's very ambitious goal of one a day or

365 a year, excited government authorities and caught them by surprise. As they were unable to immediately accept the challenge, Ford agreed to be a sub-contractor for Consolidated's bomber but, at the same time, fully expected to build the entire plane in the near future. (Even with hindsight the AMC report in 1946 ignored Sorensen's manufacturing expertise and downplayed his forecast of 400 units a month as a goal picked out of a hat.)

In February 1941 Ford accepted a $200,000,000 contract to build fuselage assemblies for 1,200 planes to be shipped to the new plants planned for Texas and Oklahoma. Building plans proceeded and by March over 200 Ford engineers were in San Diego to examine the mechanics of building aircraft wings, fuselages and other parts for the Consolidated plane.

The government let contracts in March 1941 for three new plants to build airplanes: Consolidated in Fort Worth, Texas, Douglas Aircraft Company in Tulsa, Oklahoma, and North American Aircraft Corporation in Dallas, Texas. By September the government, with these new plants under construction, reconsidered and gave Ford a contract to build 795 complete planes in addition to the 1,200 fuselage assemblies. In October a $420,000,000 contract was awarded Ford, divided between $48,000,000 for plant and equipment, $4,000,000 for an airport and $368,000,000 for complete planes and sub-assemblies. At the time of Ford's initial visit only the first six B-24s for the Army Air Corps were in production at Consolidated's plant. Now that Ford's proposal was accepted, its problem started.

Production Plans

Consolidated, while welcoming Ford's participation as a sub-contractor was wary, as were most other major airplane manufacturers, about Ford's entrance into the aviation field and its implication for postwar competition. They were not happy when the decision was made for Ford to build the whole plane but, in the spirit of cooperation, they took the attitude that they would teach Ford how to build airplanes. Ford men, on the other hand, having seen how Consolidated literally built planes by hand, took the attitude that they were going to show the aviation industry how to build planes better and faster. The aviation industry was miles apart from the mass production manufacturing concepts of the automotive industry, but by war's end they were all using portions of the Ford process.

The first task was in getting a set of plans from Consolidated. As the plane was already designed and in production, although just barely, Ford thought only a small engineering staff would be needed to refine the plans to fit Ford assembly methods. In reality, Ford engineers commented, it was like stepping into another world as up-to-date, detailed plans did not exist and those plans that did were for the most part out of date. In addition Consolidated had made running changes that were never recorded and they used fractional drawings while Ford was accustomed to using decimal drawings. Compounding the situation was the fact that Consolidated's skilled craftsmen were accustomed to hand fitting many parts. In March 1941, Ford sent Logan Miller, Roscoe Smith, Richard Pioch and a team of 200 engineers and production men to San Diego where they spent almost four months in studying a complex assembly process that was totally foreign to their experience. While the engineers gathered the information needed in making a complete, up-to-date set of plans others were developing layouts and production processes; the tool design team, unaccustomed to working with aluminum, studied the tools, fixtures and methods used to form the aluminum alloy that made up 85 percent of the airplane. Returning home, Ford's team of engineers, tool designers and others were housed in the old airplane factory at Ford Airport in Dearborn, Michigan, to complete their plans while the Willow Run plant was planned. Eventually the project was broken down into sixty-nine component parts for assembly purposes. Once the new plans were created Ford engineers then had to make an average of eleven drawings for each of the components to break down the assemblies into sufficiently smaller components to determine sub-assembly requirements. These drawings in turn had to be reduced to hundreds of additional drawings to develop each worker's individual assignment.

Site Location: While the engineers and production personnel were busy in San Diego, the hunt for a factory site began. Sites near Detroit, large enough to accommodate the original project of making only parts and assemblies, were limited and would have taken critical time to accumulate via condemnation proceedings for which there was, 10 months prior to Pearl Harbor, no legal basis.[5] With the decision to build the entire airplane, which now required an airport facility, land requirements escalated, virtually eliminating the Detroit area. The final selection of the site, located in both Wayne and Washtenaw Counties, Michigan, was chosen for several reasons. It was a desirable location and most of the necessary land was owned by Henry Ford and could be utilized immediately with options quickly obtained on any needed adjacent parcel. The land was part of the Ford Farms system used for soybean farming and was partially occupied by Camp Willow Run that provided farm work for sons of World War I veterans.[6] By early 1941 the camp had been closed and the small Willow Run Hydro Plant was opened providing 35 boys from the camp with the opportunity to work in industry and learn a trade.

Final planning located the plant site entirely in Ypsilanti Township, Washtenaw County, while the airport was entirely located in Van Buren Township, Wayne County (which includes the city of Detroit). Ford had the option to purchase the facility after the war and wanted to circumvent the postwar potential of higher Wayne County taxes on the building when converted to civilian ownership.

Construction: Expending its own funds, Ford started clearing the grounds in March 1941 even before a contract had been signed with the government. The Willow Run plant was designed by noted architect Albert Kahn who, starting with the mighty Highland Park plant in 1909, had designed most of Ford's buildings. (This was to be his largest single project and his last as he died in 1942.) Kahn proceeded immediately with the planning of a 1,176,900 square foot building to build knock-down components for other airplane plants. With the awarding of orders for a complete bomber, plans for Willow Run were dramatically enlarged to become the largest factory in the world with 4,734,617 square feet of floor space and a mile long assembly line. The project was too large to be let on a single competitive bid basis as there was no firm in the metropolitan Detroit area capable of handling it. As a result Ford selected five main contractors with whom they had had experience and were confident of their abilities. They negotiated terms with each and at a later date a prime contractor was appointed, at the request of Albert Kahn, to coordinate and oversee the activities of the five contractors. Portions of the plant started producing parts as early as September 1941. Thereafter, as sections of the plant were com-

Willow Run plant showing twin assembly lines ending in a 90 degree right turn. The plant was designed to keep all facilities out of Wayne County, Michigan, to avoid high taxes when converted to civilian production after the war (from the collection of The Henry Ford.)

pleted additional production facilities were added with plywood partitions being moved forward to block off that portion of the building still under construction. One year later, *Time* magazine (March 23, 1942) called it "the most enormous room in the history of man." It was finally surpassed in 1943 by the Chrysler aircraft engine plant in Chicago, but that plant never received the recognition that Willow Run did. By the end of 1944 working floor space, at all locations, dedicated to B-24 production would total 7,069,000 square feet.[7]

While Ford had started construction of Willow Run on its own initiative in mid–April 1941, ownership and responsibility was taken over by the government's Plancor (Defense Plant Corporation) in late June 1941. Actual responsibility for construction, however, remained with Ford under the direction of H.B. Hanson, who had been in charge of Ford power and construction for many years. The assembly line was 5,460 feet long, designed in an "L" shape to prevent the end of the final assembly line running across the Washtenaw County line into Wayne County. To compensate for the shortened assembly line caused by the "L" shape building, they made a dual assembly line that ended at the Wayne County line with the near-completed planes moving onto twin turntables at the end of the plant. This rotated the planes in a 45 degree angle to the right on the last leg of the assembly line for final detailing and towing to the Flight Department.

This twin assembly line ended up to Ford's advantage when production was cut back in 1944. The reduced production was accommodated by simply shutting down one assembly line and allowing the other line to operate at normal speed.

In all, there was almost five million square feet of building under roof erected on the 1,878 acres devoted to the entire project. While the plant was finished in November 1941, it took ten more months for the necessary tooling and various assembly lines to be set up and manned before the first B-24 was produced. In the interim, while crews were working in relays to complete the facility at Willow Run, jigs and dies were installed in the old airplane factory at Ford Airport in Dearborn providing the opportunity to not only train new employees in new ways of working but also to solve many assembly problems prior to full scale production at Willow Run.

While finishing the installation of the production system for building complete planes at Willow Run, Ford had not been idle. It was supplying fixtures, gages and tooling to the new Douglas and Consolidated plants as well as making parts and sub-assem-

Aerial view of the Willow Run plant and airfield, built on land formerly owned by Henry Ford. It was estimated that 100,000 employees would be needed (from the collection of The Henry Ford).

blies for Consolidated in California. It also supplied the two new plants with three complete sets of final assembly jigs and fixtures which prevented assembly difficulties when they later received Ford-built knock-down units.

Airport: The 1,484 acre site selected for the airport had poor drainage and preliminary work required moving 650,000 cubic yards of earth to install a 74 mile drainage system that took eleven teams working 107 days to complete. The runways were then constructed in 94 days using 84,600 tons of cement, enough to make a two lane highway 22 miles long. When finished there were six 160 foot wide runways with the longest being 7,365 feet. Three hangars were built, each with a 45 ton door that slid up and down with the touch of an electric button, with the two largest hangars capable of housing twenty B-24s at one time. In hangar Number 1 there was a center unit containing the control tower and five floors devoted to offices, hotel and a cafe. Willow Run Airport was officially opened on October 22, 1941, with Major Jimmy Doolittle, who would lead the raid on Tokyo just a few months later, making the first landing.

Some idea of the immensity of the Willow Run project can be gleaned from the size of the facilities and quantities of a few of the major materials used:

Plant and airport	1,878 acres
Total floor area including 3 hangars and 12 other smaller buildings	4,734,617 sq ft
Main plant length	3,200 ft
Main plant width	1,450 ft
Assembly line length	5460 ft
Concrete	1,575,356 sq yd
Steel	38,000 tons
Government Investment	
Land & Improvements	$5,075,500
Buildings	$58,762,800
Machinery & Equipment	$32,648,700
TOTAL	$96,487,000

Manufacturing and Assembly

In order for Sorensen to mass produce the B-24, and make one plane an hour, he divided the bomber into eleven major assemblies:

> One center wing section
> Two outer wing tips
> Two fuselage sections (fore and aft)
> Two sections for the nose and pilot's compartment
> Four sections for the empennage or tail assembly.

Logan Miller, in his oral reminiscences, related that on their trip to California they had visited Douglas Aircraft and saw how they manufactured their small airplanes. "They had the fuselage broken down so that each segment was an assembly in itself.... We conceived the idea of using the same procedure for the three large sections [of the Liberator]." These major assemblies were further divided into 69 sub-assemblies.

With the sub-assemblies decided the tools, gages, dies and fixtures could be determined and the machines and conveyors to be used could be designed. Then the sequence of forming each part and building each assembly had to be drawn up. Finally all of this had to be arranged within a huge new plant for building airplanes. It was so complicated that a 1/96th scale wooden model of the plant was made to plot the flow of the parts manufacturing into the assembly operation and onto the final assembly line. Black paper scale templates of the machines to be installed were set in the proper bays of the model against a white background and then photographed. These photographs were then given to the workmen to guide them in properly locating the machinery.

Willow Run was not only an assembly plant, it was also a major manufacturing operation which, by itself, required large numbers of workers. The plant was roughly divided into three main functions: parts manufacturing and component assembly accounted for about 20 percent each with the final assembly line accounting for about 50 percent and miscellaneous functions accounting for the remaining 10 percent. A spur from the Michigan Central Railroad Company provided rail shipments of vendor parts and raw materials to the plant, much of which was aluminum stock. These raw materials were manufactured into parts in four bays serviced by 15 ton cranes. The pressed or stamped parts were then moved by overhead conveyors to the small parts assembly departments. Each assembly bay was serviced by a five ton overhead monorail trolley, with crossovers, which permitted the load to be transferred to any bay. This system made it possible to transfer material from any point in the plant to any other point. The sub-assemblies produced in the plant merged with components produced by other Ford locations and outside vendors and then were channeled to build up the wings, fuselage and tail assemblies that fed the final assembly process. The final assembly process started with four primary assembly lines feeding the built up components into two final assembly lines, each of which was 1,500 feet long and 350 feet wide.

The backbone of the B-24 was the center wing section that was assembled in the Center Wing Vertical Fixture then moved on to be machined and bored by the Ingersoll machine and finally fitted with gas tanks, landing gear and all necessary wiring and controls. The center wing was then mated to the fore and aft sections of the fuselage. The fore section was mated first and, following the mating of the aft section, the landing gear was lowered and the assembly process moved forward on the plane's own wheels. At this

Model of the Willow Run factory at 1/98 actual size to facilitate layout of machinery and assembly operations. Black cut-outs of machines were placed in the small squares to guide placement of the actual machines (from the collection of The Henry Ford).

time the tail and nose sections were installed. These four assembly lines then converged into the two final assembly lines to add the wingtips, engines and all other items necessary to finish building a machine with 152,235 parts held together by 313,237 rivets of 520 different sizes plus government furnished instruments: engines, propellers, guns, radio equipment, etc. These two lines then merged into the final line for gassing, weighing and transfer to the Flight Department.

To build one B-24 a day, it was necessary to have 90 ships in some stage of construction[8] and was so involved that it was divided into 104 different departments. To maintain control over a workplace this dispersed, and insure workers were where they were assigned, identification badges were required to be worn at all times. These were two inch, round, stainless steel badges with the worker's picture in the center and came in three different designs which exposed 14 color combinations.

Production: The lead up to production was a confusing and frustrating period and the AMC report concluded, "The task of mass-producing airplanes proved more complex than Ford had ever imagined." Considering the nature of the project they were right, but then nobody, including the Army Air Corps, had any idea of the complexities to be faced. The Willow Run operation was without precedent with the result that Ford had to pioneer solutions practically every step along the way. Ford planned (unwisely in hindsight) to operate Willow Run as just one more of its off-site operations with nearly all operating departments and controls at the Rouge leaving only nominal authority vested in Willow Run management. This contributed to a bottleneck until the Spring of 1942 when the problem was somewhat eased as major departments and authority were transferred to Willow Run. Bickering among senior management at the Rouge and Willow Run, however, continued to aggravate already difficult operations until May 1943 when, under pressure from the government, Mead Bricker was named General Manger and

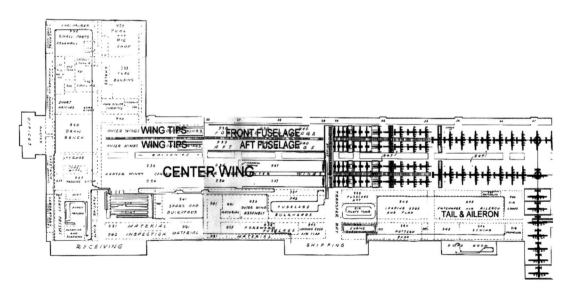

Illustration of Willow Run bomber plant showing progressive assembly of a bomber. To build one bomber an hour required 90 planes in various stages of production. Building bombers in the quantities envisioned by Henry Ford was scoffed at by experts (author's collection).

The bomber plant was so large that three types of factory badges with 14 different color combinations were issued to Willow Run employees so that security personnel could readily insure workers were where they should be (author's collection).

Logan Miller as Plant Superintendent with local management responsibility. The AMC report concluded, "This move for the first time removed Willow Run from the *small plant* class and gave it recognized local management. It did more than any other single thing to lift Willow Run out of the doldrums and send it on its way to real production."[9]

In addition to local Ford management problems, coordination of communications between Ford, the Army Air Force (the new designation of the former Army Air Corps, effective June 1941) and Consolidated also posed serious problems. Consolidated, the prime contractor, claimed it could handle matters with Ford directly, a major fault from the beginning when it was discovered there were no adequate plans available. In addition Ford had duplicated some 800 of Consolidated's templates in steel which were later found to be useless, requiring new templates and major re-working of the tools made from the old templates. Local Army representatives had trouble with the indirect management control from the Rouge which made getting decisions from local management difficult. Ford faced problems from the Army representatives as many were transferred to other plants just as they were becoming familiar with the problems faced at Willow Run while other Army personnel tried to dictate operating procedures to Ford. The first step towards satisfactory coordination between the three parties was the establishment of the B-24 Committee in May 1942. An engineering sub-committee was created and moved to San Diego to organize the flow of engineering data from Consolidated to Ford. It later moved to Willow Run to handle engineering matters there. The previously mentioned major changes and lack of adequate drawings from Consolidated resulted in 30,000 drawings being re-made for the first Ford-built B-24. From then on only another 10,000 drawings were required to cover changes for the next 490 bombers built to the introduction of the B-24H model and only 20,000 more drawings were required to the end of production.

Planned ten months before Pearl Harbor as an independent manufacturing and assembly plant it was estimated 85 percent of production would be retained at Willow Run with much of the workforce recruited from workers being laid off by the Detroit area automobile manufacturers. By early 1943, with only 344 planes delivered, and many delays caused by hiring problems described later, it became obvious that Willow Run could not maintain a workforce to handle 85 percent of the production process and outsourcing had to be implemented. Bricker, who was the driver behind outsourcing minor assemblies to other Ford facilities and sub-contractors at the Aircraft Engine Division, proceeded to institute the same practice at Willow Run. By January 1944, he had directed the outsourcing of 3,477 sub-assembly and assembly functions to other locations. While the smaller Ford plants and outside sub-contractors received some of the jobs, in an effort to control quality, most jobs went to Ford's main plants: 1,974 jobs were sent to the Rouge, 411 jobs to Highland Park and an additional 384 jobs went to the Lincoln plant. The largest was the transfer of the outer wing tips to the Lincoln plant as they had just been notified that the tank contract was coming to an end. It involved nearly 2,000 employees and 95,000 square feet of floor space.

Outsourcing was not just a simple transfer of job responsibilities. A thirty day float of spare parts had to first be created to cover downtime as in nearly every case the transfer of jobs included dies, jigs and presses that had to be removed, transported and installed in the receiving location. Workers then had to be trained in their new jobs and new equipment and all of this done in a manner so as to not interfere with the production of bombers at Willow Run. It greatly relieved the critical problem of not only expanding the worker base, but also of continually seeking and training replacement workers by moving jobs to plants that were already staffed with workers experienced in manufacturing. At peak production in March 1944 outsourcing accounted for one-third of total production at Willow Run.

Assembly: The final assembly process started with the center wing section, the backbone of the plane, being fabricated as described below. Four of these center wings would form the start of the four primary assembly lines. As they were built up they would merge into two final assembly lines, each of which was 1,500 feet long and 350 feet wide.

Several examples demonstrate how the assembly line worked and how the Ford system drastically reduced costs. Early on, Sorensen envisaged building the fuselage in two halves (fore and aft) so that all wiring could be easily installed before mating the two fuselage halves. The Consolidated method of assembling the whole fuselage and then dragging all the wiring in through the door for installation was "like a bird building his own nest while sitting on it," Sorensen commented. The most massive example of automation and cost savings, however, was the time to complete the assembly of the center wing section which was the backbone of the airplane. William Pioch, who had run Ford's tool design department for many years and had been put in charge of Engineering and Tool Design at Willow Run, commented that the major problem with Consolidated's assembly process was they never made two wings or fuselages the same. They had to use shims to make up the difference in the joints when they were assembled. He went on:

> I came to the conclusion that in order to make a good wing and make it accurate, make them identical and one right after the other, we would have to make it like we do an automobile part: that is, put it in the machine, machine it up, take it out, and put it on the assembly line.... I said we're going to design a machine that will machine all operations on the wing at one time. Of course, everybody thought I was nuts.[10]

The first step in assembly was starting the wing in the 27½ ton Center Wing Vertical Fixture. There were 35 of these units fixed on individual foundations embedded through the floor to a separate concrete base to prevent them from being affected by fluctuations

Rosie the riveters working on the wing section of a bomber. More than 300,000 rivets of more than 500 sizes were used in each bomber (from the collection of The Henry Ford).

of temperature in the plant floor. They were 60 feet long, 18 feet high and 13 feet wide and so complicated that no one but the Rouge Tool and Die Department would attempt to make them and it took them three months to build the first of the 35 fixtures. All parts of the main structure were made exceptionally heavy, in cast or welded steel construction. This insured that 0.002 inch limits were maintained throughout so that any center-wing assembly was fully interchangeable, regardless of which fixture it was made on. The assembly process was started by forming the outer skin of the wing. Ten sections of sheet aluminum for the top of the center wing and forty-four sections for the underside were cut to specifications at Willow Run, sent to the Rouge to be blanked and pierced by dies and returned to Willow Run. The upper skin pieces were riveted together as were the lower sections and with stringers set in place they were set up in the Center Wing Vertical Fixture to be attached to the spars and bulkheads by 78,606 rivets. There were also 6,439 other parts and bolts installed at this time.

When the riveting was finished and other parts installed, the clamp opened at the top and an overhead crane removed the finished center wing assembly from the Center Wing Vertical Fixture. Consolidated's method required days to erect a non-permanent jig to hold the wing in place during assembly and then hours to completely disassemble

Men inserting ribs and cross members in a bomber wing assembly (from the collection of The Henry Ford).

the jig to free the wing from the fixture. Ford's method took one man-hour versus Consolidated's, which took 250 man-hours. As well as saving time and money, these 35 fixtures guaranteed uniform precision of all center wing sections. End housings of the wing were machined within 0.0002 inches of one another.[11]

The completed center wing was carried to and then lowered into place on the Ingersoll machine, which was a machining and boring fixture built by the Ingersoll Milling Machine Co. The key to finishing the center wing was this machine, a most complex and innovative idea designed by Pioch's team. It was estimated this machine alone saved several million dollars for an investment of less than $250,000. The efficiency of this fixture was such that all center wing assemblies formed by the 35 Center Wing Vertical Fixtures were fed into and completely machined by this one Ingersoll machine.

It initially took 3¾ man-hours on this machine to perform 42 operations on the center wing, but with training and experience, by late 1943 the average time was dropped to 35 minutes. Following this operation the fore and aft fuselage sections, built as separate units as envisioned by Sorensen, were mated to the finished center wing section. As there was only one Ingersoll machine, and as a breakdown would have been disastrous, it was fenced off and under guard at all times.[12] Pioch comments in his oral reminiscence

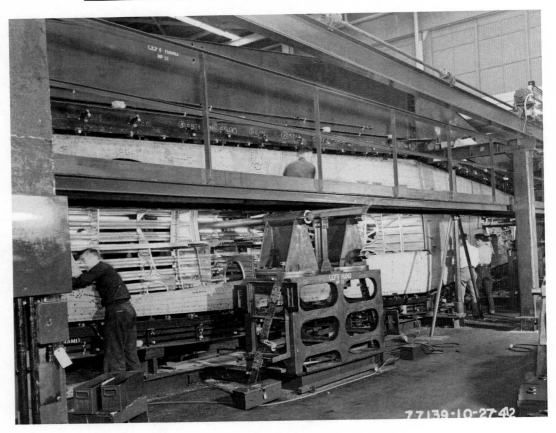

Precision manufacturing was essential for Ford to build one bomber an hour. This is one of 35 Center Wing Vertical fixtures that insured that each wing would be identical to every other wing produced (from the collection of The Henry Ford).

that when Senator Harry Truman and his group visited the plant they questioned the cost of this machine but after his explanation they left satisfied.

On August 7, 1943, the complete assembly of center wing number 600 took 800 man-hours to complete. With experience, by February 1945 the complete assembly had dropped to 385 man-hours.

Another of the complicated tasks unraveled by Ford engineers was the landing gear pivot. It was described as a half dozen pieces of steel, a couple of pieces of large tubes and some flat plates held together by 126 inches of welding, all of which had to be x-rayed. Ford's answer was three centrifugal castings. This was a process of spinning high quality molten steel to the outside of a mold which resulted in a uniform casting with fine grain structure. The Army Air Force, ever wary of Ford's innovations, in spite of its proven success, insisted that the landing gear withstand a load of 209,000 pounds. The Ford assembly withstood a test of 400,000 pounds, which was the limit of available testing equipment at Consolidated and was then sent for tests at a San Francisco laboratory with a bigger machine. At 412,000 pounds the shaft through the hinge snapped but the hinge held as it was run up to 480,000 pounds before it failed. But because of the crit-

Center wing being hoisted out of a Vertical Wing fixture. Ford's method took one man-hour compared to Consolidated's nearly 250 man-hours (from the collection of The Henry Ford).

ical nature of the landing gear each piece was still routinely x-rayed after rough machining. The new gear increased safety and reduced costs by 50 percent. Welding was another area that saw major improvement. To expedite riveting, engineers invented an automatic riveter which, using only three operators, drove 1,300 rivets in 37 minutes. Original plans were for a plane primarily designed for riveting with 13 rivets for every spot weld. However, through new machinery and procedures Ford changed the ratio to 5 rivets for every spot weld. For every 100 planes this meant 60,000 spot welds saving 125 man-hours over riveting, not to mention a reduction in weight and savings in material. Ten of the regular welding machines were allotted to one control man, each of whom had at least ten years spot welding experience. In addition there was one job foreman to each twenty-five operators. In this manner new men were quickly trained and schedules standardized without the usual confusion.

The Army Air Force instituted another cost savings in March 1944 when they stopped the camouflage painting of the airplanes, saving the cost of paint and the labor to apply it, as well as the elimination of the extensive paint department. Not only was it a cost savings but it also saved about 100 pounds reduction in weight that could either improve the performance of the plane or increase the bomb capacity. The biggest paint

The vital Ingersoll machine completed the center wing. This one machine was so efficient that it could handle all the wings prepared by the 35 Vertical Wing fixtures (from the collection of The Henry Ford).

job remaining, however, was sign painting. Each plane required 833 different markings on the inside of the ship and 400 markings on the exterior, all of which were applied by hand.

Parts Manufacturing: Ford had planned from the outset to manufacture parts for the B-24 with hard steel dies, a process it had perfected over the years that made possible volume production of automobiles. This was considered a radical decision and ridiculed by the old-line airplane manufacturers who used Kirksite dies. Kirksite, or soft dies as they were referred to, were dies with a rubber pad under the part being formed so that pressure on the aluminum parts was more evenly distributed, reducing the stress on some areas. The claim for the use of soft dies was that, with all the changes inherent in wartime production, they could be replaced quicker and at less expense versus the hard dies, which it was felt would also unduly stress the aluminum. This was a critical decision for Ford as the 85 percent of the B-24 was composed of aluminum structures and panels, a material Ford engineers were not accustomed to working with. Ford engineers ran extensive tests indicating that steel dies did not stress the aluminum sufficiently to seriously impair the strength of the part and with the equipment and experience of Ford's Tool and Die

Closeup view of the Ingersoll machine, which performed 42 operations in 35 minutes. Ford methods combined precision manufacturing with labor saving machines to save millions of dollars and thousands of man-hours (from the collection of The Henry Ford).

Department steel dies could be made as efficiently and almost as cheaply as the soft dies. Also the use of steel dies was a process that Ford was completely familiar with. Kirksite dies, moreover, wore out faster requiring constant maintenance and replacement. Also, the uniformity of parts stamped by the soft dies tended to degenerate progressively over time, slightly changing the dimensions of stamped parts as the dies wore out. In mass-production use this could mean parts, formed just before the die was changed, would have to be made to fit by the worker and could possibly fail in the aircraft at critical times. Steel dies, on the other hand, would provide uniformity of all parts stamped in high production runs, especially of larger pieces. The draw die for the pilot's enclosure, for example, weighed 15 tons and produced a stamping measuring 56" × 70" with a 10" depth. Using soft dies, the enclosure had to be composed of several parts, requiring welding, riveting and some degree of hand reworking.

The December 10, 1942, issue of *American Machinist* pretty well summed up the advantages of steel dies.

Ford-built cast-steel dies are high-production tools, an advantage in an expanding bomber program. The tools take in larger section of the work, minimizing press set-ups and reducing assembly labor. Stampings come out of dies to exact shape and contour. Methods in use by Ford will prove helpful to other mass-production aircraft enterprises. In addition, these practices should prove of benefit to plants outside of the aviation industry.

Steel dies' effectiveness was proved from an assembly standpoint by the complete interchangeability of all parts shipped as knock-down units to Douglas and Consolidated and by the volume of Ford production during the war. This use of steel dies was and has continued to this day to be a point of controversy. Senator Harry Truman, Chairman of the Truman Investigating Committee on war production, visited the plant in February 1943 and specifically questioned the wisdom of using steel dies. Edsel Ford asked Logan Miller to handle Truman's question.[13] Apparently satisfied with Miller's explanation, on leaving the plant Truman told reporters, "The Willow Run plant is incomparable. They are doing a marvelous job ... we were very pleased with what we saw."

The decision to use steel dies resulted in one of the biggest tooling programs of its kind, even in Detroit. More than 13,000 dies were needed immediately, a job too big even for Ford's massive Tool and Die Department. Excess needs were farmed out and every available shop in the Detroit area was pressed into service. It was likened to retooling for four new car model changes all at once. Fortunately Detroit Tool and Die shops had just finished the 1942 model die program for the automobile manufacturers and many were available to start immediately producing steel dies for the B-24.

Hand in hand with the use of steel dies were the blanking and piercing dies. To insure continuing uniformity of parts after forming, piercing dies were used to punch all the required number, size and location of rivet holes in a stacks of a single part at one time. This meant uniformity of all rivet holes in each of the pieces from top to bottom. The highest volume piercing operation punched 2,160 rivet holes at once. Another die had 721 individual punches at an accuracy of .002 inches. By contrast the airplane industry made rivet holes by separately stack drilling each hole in the part. It took much more time and the bottom of the stack of parts could be slightly out of alignment due to the fact that each hole was drilled separately. This could cause production bottlenecks due to out-of-line rivet holes. Aiding in the process was the Ford Press Room containing 60 heavy duty presses ranging in capacity from 150 tons to 1,000 tons.

By April 1, 1945, 30,739 dies had been made of which 15,659 were still in use — 8,357 at Willow Run and 7,302 at supplier plants. The balance were in storage or scrapped.

The AMC report of Ford's hard dies versus the aviation industry's soft dies is undoubtedly the most detailed study ever performed. Numerous operational drawbacks of using steel dies are listed but the most significant criticism was by using soft dies Ford could have produced airplanes sooner. The counter to that criticism was, that without the steel dies the volume of planes eventually produced by Ford would never have been reached. The major problem from Ford's standpoint was that many parts formed from the soft dies required "extensive hand hammering of individual parts to knock out flaws, to bring them within tolerance, or to make the part fit." The point is that the aviation industry had experienced workmen accustomed to reworking the parts. Ford had trouble finding workmen who had any industrial experience so any potential increased production by using the soft dies would have been reduced in trying to develop a qualified workforce and would have still cost greater production at a later date.[14] The report points out, however, that Ford was in a unique position to proceed with hard dies as it had enormous purchasing power and one of the largest toolmaking shops in the world and with this equipment and experienced workers, steel dies did not take that long to produce and were not that expensive. In some cases it was deemed cheaper to build additional dies rather than change some of the existing heavy dies. Some Ford personnel acknowledged that in the interest of flexibility and quick production there were some cases where soft dies should have been used, however, "The use of hard dies proved absolutely necessary in achieving mass-production of a large number of standard interchangeable sheet metal parts for the B-24."

The part made in the greatest volume and variety was the lowly rivet. Between 6,000,000 and 7,000,000 rivets were made daily in 519 different types and sizes.

Fifteen thousand gages were used and the inspection department had its own gage makers and inspectors routinely checking to insure continuing accuracy. All parts produced for the B-24 were 100 percent inspected and stamped by Ford.

Design Changes: Once production started, Ford made running *manufacturing changes* to constantly improve the process and save time and money. But, *design changes* of airplane parts and assemblies flooded in from the Army Air Force, proving frustrating to Ford in the early days. As Sorensen had originally stipulated, Ford needed frozen production runs to justify their hard steel dies and to mass produce planes in the quantity and quality they visualized; the Army Air Force wanted to make changes on every plane under construction every time a report came in from a war zone. Ford finally convinced

Evolution of the B-24E model on the left and center, with one to four manual machine guns in the nose, to the B-24H model on the right with the power turret featuring twin .50 caliber machine guns (from the collection of The Henry Ford).

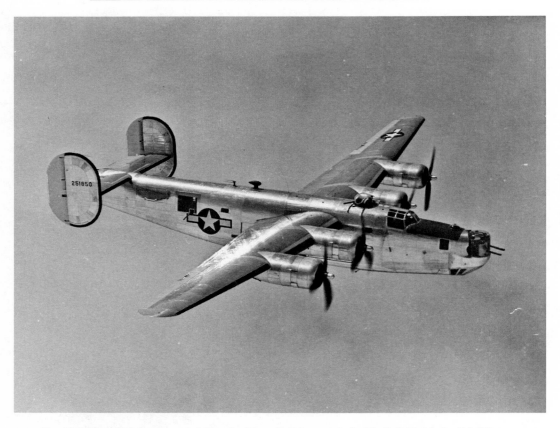

Ford build 8,686 flyaway and knock-down B-24s, nearly half of all B-24s build. Most were this B-24H model (from the collection of The Henry Ford).

the Army Air Force that making blocks of planes without significant changes and then retrofitting them at predetermined times was the most practical and expeditious method of production. By the end of the war most plane manufacturers were doing the same. But even this system of changes in blocks of planes resulted in huge engineering and retooling hours. The first changes applied to 20 blocks of 20 planes each or a total of 400 planes (B-24-E model) and resulted in 372 changes requiring over 48,000 engineering hours and over 290,000 retooling hours. Subsequent blocks were mostly for 400 planes each and changes ranged from 27 to 67 per block.

The redesign in March 1943 to accommodate the nose gun turret was the largest design change on a production plane. The first block of 400 of these new B-24-H models had 67 changes requiring 53,456 engineering hours and 208,271 retooling hours due mainly to changing to the new nose mounted gun turret.

The B-24-E nose gun had evolved from one machine gun in the nose to two, then three and finally four with all guns independently operated. As they could only be fired one at time they interfered with each other and the bombardier, making them vulnerable to frontal attacks, an opportunity quickly discovered by enemy fighters. A bomber unit in the South Pacific facing this dilemma took a tail turret off one of their B-24s and successfully installed it on the nose of another B-24, eliminating this fatal weakness. This

Single tail model YB42N. The plane had better flight characteristics than the twin tail model but was developed too late in the war to warrant a change in production. The modified model was produced by other manufacturers after the war for the U.S. Navy (from the collection of The Henry Ford).

was passed up the chain of command and finally approved. The nose on the B-24-E had to be redesigned to accommodate an Emerson Electric A-15 rotating turret containing twin machine guns, similar to the tail gunner's position, and a Briggs retractable ball turret had to be added underneath the fuselage. So extensive were the changes that it was designated the B-24-H model. The addition of the nose turret changed the center of gravity on the plane which actually improved the handling as the plane had been slightly tail heavy.

The Army Air Force wanted 50 of these modified B-24-H models for a scheduled attack on Berlin that July. Consolidated, as the lead contractor, was requested to make these changes, provide plans to Ford for subsequent planes, and deliver 50 modified planes by June 20. On March 10 Ford was asked to do the job, as Consolidated claimed it couldn't meet the time schedule. Ford was now expected to not only produce the plane, but to also do the developmental engineering as well. They replied, "Sure we'll try it, but probably can only get 25." An all out effort was made with half the Engineering Department involved. They designed a new nose that attached to the fuselage using the same holes as used by the old nose section. This meant the old B-24-E models with the Plexiglas nose could be easily upgraded by replacing it with the new nose and gun turret. While there were a number of other serious production problems and changes to resolve, by the middle of June, 15 planes had been modified and 42 were ready by June 30. Reports indicated that 16 of the new B-24-H models made the Berlin raid.

The largest of all changes was for the single tail YB-24-N model which had been under development since 1943. Ford had modified a Consolidated built B-24-D model by splicing the tail of a Douglas B-23 Dragon bomber to the rear of the fuselage of the B-24 and adding a forward nose turret resulting in the XB-24-K model. As suspected by the military this resulted in a more stable aircraft with better handling characteristics. This evolved into the fully redesigned YB-24-N delivered to the Army Air Force in November 1944. This was late in the war, however, and it was not practical to change the already reduced capacity of the production line for these limited benefits. Only seven planes were built by Ford. Substantially redesigned by the U.S. Navy, under the designation PB4Y-2, they were built by other contractors and served through the Korean Conflict. The change to the single tail and a number of other alterations on Ford's YB-24-N cost 135,120 engineering hours and 947,142 retooling hours. Both the engineering change on the new nose assembly and the redesign of the single tail assembly was under the direction of William F. Pioch's team.

There were a total of 1,079 changes from plane 1 to plane 8000!

Flight Operations

From the end of the final assembly line the plane was towed to the Flight Department where final checks and mechanical tuneups were made, the plane was weighed as a check for completeness, and fuel added. The next step was the Compass Rose located on the airfield west of hangar number 1. It was a 60 foot circular turntable, mounted at ground level, to check and correct bomber compasses and range finders. Rotating the turntable slightly aligned the bomber with a concrete gun butt for the ordnance check. Every other plane test fired its guns at the butt. Every 50th plane fired its guns over Lake Erie and every 300th ship expended a full armament load of machine gun ammunition and 50 concrete dummy bombs, flying at different altitudes and making bomb runs at extreme angles. Sixty-five thousand rounds of ammunition were expended in an average month.

The Flight Department consisted of thirty-four 4 man crews made up of a test pilot, co-pilot, flight engineer and radio technician. Following the Compass Rose orientation and ordnance check a flight crew took the plane aloft for the mandatory minimum 2½ hour test flight. Ford quality was such that the average flight time for complete acceptance of a Ford-built bomber by the Army was 2 hours and 43 minutes with a remarkable 39 percent of the ships accepted on the initial flight. Ford pilots conducted 21,109 test flights covering 5,241,013 miles.

A report made by a Curtiss-Wright Corporation representative in June 1944 is enlightening:

> Their record delivery day was a ship taking off every three minutes for a period of four hours and for a full day, they delivered 139 planes. The greatest single contributing factor is, all Ford pilots are authorized by the Army to accept ships for the Army. Ford is presenting to the Army good, clean airplanes showing high quality workmanship and performance.... For

the entire flight area operations there are only 30–40 crabs (problems) written on each ship. From our point of view, this was phenomenal.

By April 1945 the average *crabs* had dropped to less than 10 per plane.

Following acceptance by the Army Air Force all B-24s were flown to modification centers, set up around the country, to make necessary changes and to alter the planes for special needs according to the war theater for which they were destined. During the course of the war Ford was asked to assume responsibility for about 70 percent of these modifications. At that point in time about 15,000 workers were employed at the various modification centers. After a thorough analysis of the task Ford found that, instead of the expected huge increase of needed workers, they could incorporate most of these modifications in each plane at the time of assembly with no increase in the workforce.

In February 1944 the Material Command of the Army Air Force gave Willow Run their Quality "A" rating signifying that Ford pilots could put the final OK on the planes with only overall supervision by Army Air Force resident representatives. This "A" rating included B-24 parts and assemblies produced by the Highland Park, Lincoln and Rouge plants and selected village industry plants.

In *Willow Run: A Study of Industrialization and Cultural Inadequacy,* Carr & Stermer stated:

> In 1941 before Ford entered the bomber aircraft industry it required 201,826 man-hours to manufacture a single B-24 bomber. In March 1944, Sorensen's team of thinkers, hard-tooling procedure improvers of mass production, had reduced those man-hours to only 17,357.

Delays: Many reports of the start of parts production at Willow Run in February 1942 were interpreted as full production and about the same time a British production authority told the people of occupied Europe via radio that Ford was then producing a bomber an hour earmarked for the destruction of Hitler. This news of course filtered back to the United States and then, when the first Ford bomber was turned over to flight test, it was greeted with a great deal of public celebration — but it was a false start. Parts production had started but this first plane had been built up from parts for a complete bomber shipped from Consolidated to Ford, then dismantled and reassembled for training and educational purposes. Actually this training plane represented only the seventh bomber built by Consolidated for the Army Air Force, all of which were considered experimental at this early stage. In a June 1, 1942, issue of *Time* magazine, "Dutch" Kindelberger of North American Aviation commented on the automakers on fumbling their part of the plane program and was quoted "the biggest mistake they [the government] ever made was to break in high-production organizations to airplane-manufacturing method." Sorensen replied simply "that automen had always looked on the planemakers as little custom tailors." Apparently it got under Kindelberger's skin as he commented later in the article, "Talk about freezing the plane designs is as silly as freezing the design of a flint-lock rifle when the enemy is turning out a Garand." By late 1942 no bombers had been produced and the jubilant press of just a few months previous was now turning negative. The December 1942 issue of *Skyways* magazine berated Detroit manufacturers' production record while complimenting the old line aviation industry's record in a major article entitled "All-out Ballyhoo versus All-out Production." Taking particular aim at Ford it stated, "It was supposed to produce bombers at the unbelievable rate of one an hour ... where mass-production in world-record quantities is an every day affair, we find they have failed miserably." And, by January 1943, with only 56 planes built in all of 1942, the press was calling it "Will It Run?"

There were 130 major changes to the aircraft before actual production could start but, by late May, Ford had shipped the first sub-assemblies to Douglas in Tulsa, Oklahoma. However, all was not well. Early assemblies were returned to Ford for poor quality, due mostly to welding and inexperienced workers and supervisors. It was a short term problem and few subsequent shipments caused problems although it was claimed the first 100 Ford built fly-aways were not up to the increased demands of combat.[15] (This was a questionable statement at best, as no B-24s built during this time were combat ready leaving the assembly line. All had to be sent to modification centers for front-line use.) They were, however, classified as satisfactory for flying and were used for training.

Most people couldn't understand why it was taking so long for Ford to get going. They just could not comprehend the enormity of constructing a plant this size to build an item with 465,472 parts and rivets. The average person could not imagine the huge amount of scarce specialized machinery and fixtures that had to be designed and fabricated or otherwise acquired to build planes in a way they had never been built before; the need to hire and train over 40,000 unskilled workers and untrained supervisors; the enormous turnover of people due to the draft, going elsewhere to work and absenteeism as high as 14 percent in some months. In May 1943, a 56 percent labor turnover rate was reported for the prior eight months. The draft was another problem. Ford was spending thousands of hours training workers only to see large numbers, almost immediately, called up by the local draft board. The worst part was that the call-ups were indiscriminate; in some cases one department was crippled by excessive personnel being called up while few or any men were called up from another department. After numerous complaints, the draft board and Ford came to an agreement that allowed Ford to serve up lists of men, spread over many departments, so no one department would be crippled by excessive call-ups. Even after employees were recruited, hired and trained, absenteeism and resignations posed neverending problems. Between increasing production and labor turnover, at one point the unmet need was 400 new hires each day. Truly a difficult task with the remote location of the plant for people who drove or bussed and the wretched living conditions available for many out-of-towners. The difficulty in attracting potential workers was the major factor in the decision to outsource many jobs to other Ford facilities and outside vendors. Employment at Willow Run, initially estimated to reach 100,000, peaked at 43,369 in July 1943 and trailing off to an average of about 25,000 as many fabricating and assembly jobs were farmed out. But, the total employees in all plants working on B-24 related parts and assemblies peaked at 49,000 in June 1944.

Deliveries: Although the first complete plane accepted by the Army Air Force was not delivered until September 30, 1942, by the end of 1942, most problems had been or were in the process of being resolved. January 1943 production was 37 planes, February 70, March was 96 and April jumped to 146. Beginning with September 1943 Willow Run exceeded its schedule regularly, month after month. By November 3, 1943, substantial progress had been made and Ford had built its 1,000th plane. *Ford Times,* November 26, 1943, reported that bomber parts production had been farmed out to virtually every one of Ford's branch plants and village industries, and the War Production Board had announced the Willow Run plant was far above average for efficient utilization of manpower producing 80 pounds gross weight of aviation materials per man per month versus the 60 pounds per month average of other airplane manufacturers. The rate of efficiency had improved 40 times in the past year at Willow Run. By 1945 Ford was producing more pounds of aircraft material per man per month than any other manufacturer of Army Air Forces planes. Because airplanes differ so much in size, using pounds of weight of aviation material per man was a more meaningful comparison between builders than the number of planes produced.

With the arrival of the new year Ford began producing production miracles! In April 1944 Willow Run, working six days a week on two 9 hour shifts, produced 453 planes in 468 hours, one plane every 62 minutes.[16] Nearly 5,000 planes were built in 1944 alone! In August 1944, when Ford was gearing up to build 650 planes a month or a plane every 45 minutes, the Army Air Forces directed a production cut to 215 bombers for December, a number that would not be exceeded in following months. Production was severely curtailed in favor of the new long range B-29 bomber for missions over Japan. In spite of the cutbacks in production Ford was required to maintain all facilities and necessary personnel so that a 405-plane-per-month production level could be resumed at any time.

Human Resources

Medical Facilities — Plant: Included in the plant were provisions for a full size and fully staffed medical facility, common to all large Ford plants. It was headed by Dr. W.A. Dawson, who had many years experience in industrial medicine at the Rouge. The staff included eight doctors, forty nurses, a dentist and forty-two first aid men. Because of the size of the plant, there were seven first aid stations throughout the plant staffed with a first aid expert and a registered nurse. There were also 110 strategically located stretcher boxes containing two stretchers and four crash helmets plus cases containing supplies of first aid items. During the life of the bomber factory, there were 2,065,428 employee medical cases handled by the medical staff plus another 20,945 cases from contractor's workers. There were 96 amputations, most related to fingers and hands, and was the most severe type of medical treatment provided. Considering the dangers inherent in this type of manufacturing, especially with completely unskilled workers being pushed for more and more production, these numbers do not seem excessive. No records reflect any on-job deaths and Logan Miller commented in his oral reminiscences, "We never had one fatality through our own negligence." There was at least one fatal crash of a B-24 but that was after it had been accepted by the Army Air Forces.

Medical Facilities — Flight Operations: This department was headed by Dr. C.J. Clark, who was experienced in industrial management at the Rouge and trained in flight surgery at the Mayo Clinic. In July 1942 an aero-medical hospital unit was located in eleven rooms on the main hangar floor and staffed with 2 doctors, 5 nurses, 1 aero-medical technician, 6 first aid men, 1 secretary and 3 hospital utility men. A daily check of all flight crews was made to determine their flight status that day and physical examinations were made of the flight personnel every six months. In addition they prepared and trained airplane crews for altitude flights and use of equipment in flight (see chapter 6). It also served as a hospital for the hangar building and 1,500 operating personnel. At the time it was described as the first full time aero-medical unit set up for a flight department.

Plant Protection: Another area seldom thought about or discussed is the security of war-production plants and their employees and protection against sabotage, a very real concern in the early days of the war. Prior to the war, Ford had no formal plant protection department as we know it today. That function was under Harry Bennett and his men and was very informal. Like all areas of wartime employment there was no pool of trained protection personnel to call on. Initially a few men from the Rouge were assigned to Willow Run but as the building grew so did the need for protection. The answer was the same for all personnel needs in wartime. You take the best people you can find and train them. In January 1942 the Plant Protection Training School was opened at Willow Run. There was a lot to remember! The main building alone contained over three and half million square feet and twelve smaller buildings were scattered over 1,878 acres. As mentioned before, employees wore picture badges of three different designs with 14 color codes designating specific areas in the plant. The new security man had to be able to spot a badge and quickly determine if the man was where he belonged. The new security men had a lot to learn and as the plant grew so to did their numbers — 355 by mid–1944. Permanent assignments included 48 men and three patrol cars to airport duties and others to the security vault, Power House, armament cribs and the area where hundreds of thousands of gallons of gas were maintained. Others patrolled the gates, two parking lots for 15,000 vehicles each, acted as escorts for visitors, helped new employees and provided roving vehicle radio patrols.

While security prevailed at all war-production plants some areas were more secure and secret than others. At Willow Run it was instruments such as the Norden bombsight, radar, autopilots, etc. They were shipped to the plant under guard and locked in vaults. The vaults were guarded around the clock and access was by permit only, issued by Army Intelligence, and carefully checked requisitions were required. Each set of items was tagged for and tested on a specific plane on the assembly line, returned to the vault and then finally re-installed in that plane at the end of the line. Each move of these items was recorded and each item accounted for on a routine basis. With one plane an hour coming off the assembly line this was a cumbersome and time consuming task.

The security men wore uniforms consisting of a royal blue tunic and blue-gray trousers, and in February 1942 they were all armed and sworn in as auxiliary military police with the power of arrest. As such they were given pistol instruction and target practice and participated in military drill conducted by military personnel 2 hours a week. Similar Plant Protection Departments were established at all Ford war production facilities and this system proved to be the basis for Ford's Plant Protection Department following the war. In the Ford archives there are two archive boxes of photographs marked Sabotage but virtually all of the damage pictured is minor and looks more like carelessness. In any event there are no records indicating actual enemy sabotage was committed at any Ford facility.

Employment: Ford had originally planned to draw workers from surplus labor at the Rouge and other Detroit manufacturers as civilian production shut down. However, following the approval for Ford to build the complete plane their labor needs escalated.

Opposite: **This type of flyer was used in central and southern states to attract workers for the Willow Run plant. While many derogatory remarks were made about workers from these areas, they learned quickly and turned out more aviation production than any other plant (author's collection).**

Ford Motor Company
Bomber Plant
Willow Run   -   In Detroit Area
WILL EMPLOY
Men and Women

1. To Train for Work in Aircraft Industry, or
2. Those Who Already Have Experience or Training.

Work In World's Largest Bomber Plant.

Essential Industry
Excellent Opportunity for Advancement
Women Paid Same Hourly Rate as Men
Modern, New Buildings.   Clean Work, Interesting
and Pleasant
54-Hour Week. $1\frac{1}{2}$ Pay for Over 40 Hours
Employer will Pay Transportation

REQUIRES: Age 18 or Older. Draft Deferred.
Physical Examination

Those now Employed in War Industry or Farm Work will not
be Considered Unless Eligible for Statement of Availability
Under W. M. C. Regulations.

APPLY IN PERSON
Monday or Tuesday
NOVEMBER 8 -:- NOVEMBER 9
United States Employment Service
SOMERSET   Fountain Square   KENTUCKY

 PATRIOTISM: It is urgent that Men and Women be
Procured to fill these Jobs. If you are already employed full time, consider it your duty to place this Ad-
vertisement in the hands of a person who might be Interested.

Recruiting became a major problem! The expected surplus labor pool from Detroit never materialized having been absorbed by the local industries suddenly flooded with their own war-production contracts. In addition many workers who were available chose not to endure the seventy miles a day commute to and from Willow Run. The new Willow Run Expressway to Detroit was not opened until September 1942 and even then it was not fully extended until early 1945. The institution of gas and tire rationing in December 1942 coupled with the initial lack of public transportation between Detroit and Willow Run made ride-sharing a necessity and when workers rotated shifts these schedules were frequently upset. Even though the company set up facilities in-plant to service employees' cars while they worked, all these other concerns tended to diminish the allure of the big bucks being offered. By early 1944 their were 35 daily bus trips from Detroit while private bus lines operated another 130 daily trips.

An examination of Willow Run employment statistics sheds additional light on the enormity of the employment problems Ford had to overcome. When production ended in June 1945, Ford had hired 80,774 people in the Willow Run plant, of which only 30,021 stayed over twelve months; 34,533 stayed less than three months with 12,197 quitting in the first ten days.[17] Terminations for military service accounted for 10,003 men and 317 women. Employees came from 175 towns in Michigan and every state and possession of the United States as well as seven foreign countries.

As labor became more and more critical, Ford recruiters fanned out throughout the central, southern and Midwestern states of Michigan, Texas, Kentucky, Tennessee, southern Illinois and Iowa. This was the area the War Manpower Commission approved for Ford to seek employees, although when necessary other areas were approved. The AMC report[18] shows that of the 32,330 workers hired between March and May 1943, 14,693 came from outside Michigan, over 8,000 from Kentucky and Tennessee alone. The image of these workers from the South has been negatively described by many as barefoot hillbillies or rednecks who had never seen indoor plumbing much less the inside of a factory. One report commented, "They soon learned that a 'rivet gun' did not need telescopic sights — that the 'oleo' on the landing struts of the B-24 was not edible, and a 'stock chaser' really did not need a couple of hounds and a horse. It was indeed a new experience to the majority of those new employees." Yet these people learned quickly and eventually produced airplanes at fewer man hours per pound than any other aircraft worker in the United States.

Housing: As you read on concerning some of the deplorable conditions faced by the workers flooding into the Willow Run area, keep in mind they are reflective of many defense plants that were located near small towns like Ypsilanti and Ann Arbor. Large numbers of workers were needed from other areas and neither the local, state nor federal governments were prepared to deal with this massive influx of workers from a social or physical standpoint.[19]

Unfortunately, as construction started at Willow Run, there was no simultaneous start of planning for the workers' housing. Nor was much if any thought paid to the need for drastic increases in water, sewer and other infrastructure facilities. As a result no proper housing, or schools, or hospitals, or shopping in any quantity or quality would be available until mid–1943. When thought was given to public housing, the threat of government housing was initially resisted by both local businesses and Ford, apparently concerned that it would create a municipality with taxing authority or generate new

Democratic voters in Republican dominated Washtenaw County. Also local authorities and residents feared a reduction in property values and a ghost town after the war. One option, and there was a rumor that Ford had such a plan prepared, was for a company town which, in any event, would have been abhorrent to the union.

This lack of even rudimentary housing facing many employees flocking in from distant towns in Michigan as well as from out of state created a huge morale problem that affected production efficiency. Ypsilanti, the nearest town, was a small village of 12,000 and unprepared for the hoards of people that would descend on it, nor was the larger city of Ann Arbor, with a population of 30,000, any better able to cope. All of a sudden, there was need for housing for tens of thousands of workers.[20]

Ford's Plant Protection Department canvassed all possible facilities in a 25 mile radius around the plant seeking apartments and rooms in homes to parking spaces for trailers. Stories and photographs of the living areas of many of these people reflect squalid huts, trailers, shanties and even their own cars; it was more representative of a third world country.

Henry Ford sold more of his remaining Ford Farm lands to the government in October 1942 which was turned into the Willow Lodge dormitories to house 3,000 single men and women. By December 1943 Willow Village was opened with 2,500 units of temporary family housing.

Employment peaked at Willow Run in January 1943 after reaching 42,331 with actual workers housed peaking at 5,119 in December 1943.[21] By that time major resourcing of B-24 assemblies was well underway, reducing total employment and the need for additional housing. Fortunately, in the case of Willow Run, after the war Willow Lodge and Willow Village served as homes for veterans using the GI Bill to attend the University of Michigan.

Hours, Wages, etc.: A ten hour shift was the norm from September 1941 until May 1942 when it dropped to 8 hours six days a week. In February 1943 the plant went to two 9 hour shifts working a 54 hour week from March through August 1944 when production peaked and schedules were cut back.

Wages at Willow Run were higher than the average in the aircraft industry with the lowest rate of 95 cents an hour for janitorial type personnel. The highest was $1.80 an hour for toolmaker leaders. The average rate for assembly line workers was $1.15 an hour until July 1944 when it was raised to just under $1.20. Higher wages were one effort to overcome a degree of poor worker morale caused by situations previously discussed.

Cafeteria and dining facilities were provided for office employees while lunch wagons, which traveled the plant, provided meals for workers who could then eat in 24 lunch rooms scattered throughout the plant. And lastly, each employee was offered the use of a plot of ground for a victory garden, an idea strongly advocated by Henry Ford.

Key Personnel: In addition to Charles Sorensen, Mead Bricker, Logan Miller and others previously mentioned, Ford records also highlight the following key individuals:

Ed Bond — In charge of flight operations. Experienced pilot and former chief inspector, Ford Assembly Plant, Dallas, Texas.

E.D. Brown — Directed recruitment and employment. Twenty-five years with Highland Park and Rouge employment offices.

F.D. Bullock — In charge of material control and production scheduling. Material coordinator and production scheduler for 25 years with Ford.

Components of B-24 knock-down kit shipped to Consolidated Aircraft in Fort Worth, Texas, and Douglas Aircraft in Tulsa, Oklahoma (from the collection of The Henry Ford).

Hal Henning — Chief test pilot and Flight Superintendent in charge of airport. Experienced pilot.

S.D. Mullikin — Organized and headed all training at Willow Run. Long time instructor at Henry Ford Trade and Apprentice Schools.

Charles Patterson — Organized Tool and Die Department at Willow Run. Long time Ford Tool and Die manager. In 1944 he was appointed field superintendent of operations in the major Willow Run assembly department. He retired as a Ford Vice President.

Jack Reid — In charge of all purchasing at Willow Run. Many years experience as executive in Rouge Purchasing Department.

George Scarlett — In charge of tool coordination. Many years experience in machine and tool design. Along with William Pioch was responsible for the design and installation of Center Wing fixtures.

These were but a few of the men who made Willow Run work!

Other Assignments

Spare Parts: Production for emergency and normal spare part needs had keep pace with the flyaway and knock-down production and by early 1944 Ford was supplying 50 percent of all spare parts used in the bomber and 85 percent of all emergency spare parts shipments to overseas units. This volume of activity resulted in a new building of nearly

Two of these trailers were required for transporting one B-24 knock-down kit which was 80 percent of a complete plane. Using trailers reduced cost and time by one-third over rail shipments, freeing scarce rail capacity for other crucial production (from the collection of The Henry Ford).

500,000 square feet being erected at Willow Run to maintain an adequate inventory. Built of brick and steel it was equipped with overhead cranes and had a depressed track section capable of handling 22 railcars at a time. Orders for the smallest item to huge tail sections could be flown to any part of the world in hours. Employing 500 workers, up to 800 emergency orders were handled in a single day.

Specified in the initial contracts for B-24s was a provision for spare parts procurement amounting to 15 percent of the dollar amount of the contract. Ford's Field Service representatives assigned to the plants assembling the B-24 bombers analyzed their requirements, identifying slow moving or unnecessary parts, thereby reducing Ford's spare parts requirement to 8.75 percent. These actions resulted in the Army Air Force subsequently reducing the contract figure to 10 percent, resulting in a difference to the Army Air Force, from Ford alone, of over $50,000,000. In addition to complete bombers and knock-down units there were 455 sets of spare parts provided. These sets represented 80 percent of a complete plane or the equivalent of 364 additional planes.

Haulaways: The story of the transportation of these early knock-down B-24 kits to Fort Worth, Texas, and Tulsa, Oklahoma, is worthy of mention, for it illustrates the problems that were solved and economies generated by Ford in satisfying the country's

Traveling B-24 display for war bond drives conducted in major cities. Over one million visitors, including the author, attended this show on the Washington Monument grounds, Washington, D.C., in September 1943 (from the collection of The Henry Ford).

military needs. It was originally planned that these knock-down kits would be shipped by rail; however, rail shipments were costlier and railcars were desperately needed for other war-related materials. Not only would it require four railcars per bomber kit, but it would take more delivery time and the sudden impacts and shocks common to rail operations posed the problem of causing hidden damage to fragile airplane assemblies, damage that could later cause structural failure in flight.

Special automotive haulaway vehicles offered the answer. E & L Transport Co. of Dearborn, Michigan, an automotive transporter, designed a 63 foot trailer, said at the time to be the largest in the world. Two trailers would be required to haul each complete knock-down kit. Each bomber kit (80 percent of a complete bomber) was divided into three sections; one trailer carried the fuselage and rudders, while the other carried the wing assembly and other parts. Engines and other government-provided equipment were shipped direct by the other manufacturers. The trailers were pulled by specially designed Toreco tractors powered by two separate 100 HP 8 cylinder Mercury engines. With an overall length of tractor and trailer more than 75 feet and a loaded weight of about 50,000 pounds spread over eighteen tires, they were designed to negotiate all streets, curbs and underpasses between Michigan, Texas and Oklahoma while meeting all state axle-loading laws. Other state laws that conflicted with these oversize vehicles were waived.

There were 83 tractors and 85 trailers operated by two man crews who alternated 5 hour driving shifts. The cab was air conditioned and space provided for a rubber mattress for the relief driver. Each round trip took four days rolling 24 hours a day at an average speed of 40 mph. An average of 250 round trips were made each month with a record 375 round trips set in February 1944. Sixty of the company's drivers received merit awards for three or more years of accident free driving. The result was a 67 percent savings in time (4 days versus 12) and an estimated 67 percent reduction in cost, while, at the same time freeing the railcars to transport other critical war material. Ford continued to send knock-down kits to Consolidated in Fort Worth, Texas, until May 1944 and to Douglas Aircraft in Tulsa, Oklahoma, until July 1944. In addition to transporting knock-down kits, the haulaway trailers were also used to transport gliders from the Iron Mountain, Michigan, plant and B-24 bombers and gliders to war bond rallies in major cities in the United States.

War Weary Ladies: In 1945, with the war in Europe coming to an end, Ford was called on to handle 477 war weary ladies coming back from Europe. A crew of 1,000 men were retained at Willow Run after production ceased for preparing these ships for type "C" storage. These ships were flown to the U.S. by combat crews and turned over to Air Transport Command (ATC) at point of arrival. Within two hours of landing they were serviced and flown to Willow Run by pilots of the ATC. The initial contract called for combat stressed, but airworthy, B-24s to be stripped of all valuable government equipment such as bombsights, machine guns, photographic equipment, parachutes, life rafts, bombs, ammunition, etc., and then to pickle the planes for future use and storage at Willow Run. Oil was run through the engines and gas lines to prevent rusting. Hydraulic and brake systems as well as all other moving parts were checked, repaired and coated with suitable preservatives. After 371 of the 477 ships had been processed, it became obvious these planes would never be needed and the storage arrangements were canceled. Instead, all planes were put in first class flying condition and flown to a facility in Albuquerque, New Mexico. Virtually all of these planes ended up being scrapped or sold for insignificant amounts. Many of these ships had been built at Willow Run. One named "Red Ryder" had nine swastikas painted on the nose and another named "Knock-out" had flown 131 missions and had three Italian emblems painted on the nose. Today, there are sixteen B-24s still intact or under restoration but only two on flying status.

Miscellaneous: Ford developed mobile displays that showed a complete breakdown of the various systems of the B-24 including charts, schematic drawings and working mock-ups of many of the components. Complete in themselves they functioned as if they were actually parts of the ship. The units were sent to England where Army personnel were trained for front line maintenance. Five mobile units consisting of 17 panels each were built for the Navy. The first one went to England and the other four to naval training stations in the United States. Ford also provided traveling displays to aid in war bond drives in various cities where gliders and bombers were displayed in a manner so that people could actually walk through the bomber.

Ford also made baffle plates for the B-29 Superfortress's self-sealing fuel cells and solved a serious problem for the Hudson Motor Car Company, a prime B-29 contractor.

Ford-Built Consolidated Liberator Bomber

Watch The Fords Go By!

FLEETS of mighty bombers are coming from Willow Run! Fleets of giant four-engined *Fords* with wings and heavily armored bodies able to carry tons of bombs to the Axis!

These Ford-built Consolidated Liberator bombers are not only in production . . . *they're in volume production!* And they're leaving Willow Run in a steady stream for service throughout the world.

Never before Willow Run has anything so big and complex as this Liberator bomber been built on an interchangeable mass-production basis. Some said it couldn't be done . . . that frequent design changes would make mass production *impossible*. But army men knew that failure to produce aircraft in mass would prove disastrous. They knew that Victory demanded what

seemed *impossible*—and they relied on Ford to do it.

The army was right. What many thought *impossible has been done* at Willow Run!

There were difficulties such as manpower shortages, the training of inexperienced workers and the curtailment of transportation.

But today Willow Run is doing what Ford promised! The plant is producing bombers in volume . . . *and on schedule!*

At other Ford plants across the nation, fleets of *war models* are being delivered every day. These include M-4 tanks, M-10 tank destroyers, Ford-built 2000-hp Pratt & Whitney engines for which Ford has received the Army-Navy "E", and many other Victory models.

As you *watch these Fords go by* on their way to your sons and brothers at the front, remember that their quantity and quality reflect the feeling of the whole Ford organization that . . . *no effort short of Victory is enough.*

Ford Mass-Production Lines Deliver Fleets of Weapons

M-4 TANKS . . . PRATT & WHITNEY AIRCRAFT ENGINES . . . JEEPS
M-10 TANK DESTROYERS . . . AMPHIBIAN JEEPS . . . UNIVERSAL CARRIERS
CONSOLIDATED LIBERATOR BOMBERS . . . TRUCK AND JEEP ENGINES
TRANSPORT GLIDERS . . . ARMY TRUCKS . . . RATE-OF-CLIMB INDICATORS
TANK ENGINES . . . GUN MOUNTS . . . MAGNESIUM CASTINGS
AIRCRAFT GENERATORS . . . ARMOR PLATE . . . TURBO-SUPERCHARGERS

This list does not include other important Victory models now in production that cannot be named due to wartime conditions.

LISTEN TO "WATCH THE WORLD GO BY" FEATURING EARL GODWIN, EVERY NIGHT 8:00 P. M. E. W. T. ON THE BLUE NETWORK.

★ ★ Buy U. S. War Bonds And Stamps ★ ★

F O R D   M O T O R   C O M P A N Y

F U L L   P R O D U C T I O N   F O R   V I C T O R Y

Watch The Fords Go By, a Ford slogan since 1908, took on added meaning with this ad. *Detroit News,* May 23, 1943 (from the collection of The Henry Ford).

So large were the sections of fuselage skin surface of the B-29 that the only equipment in southeast Michigan able to roll them were at Ford's Willow Run plant. The sections rolled were convex pieces, 36 inches by 192 inches, tapering at one end.

The Liberator was used during the war by the air forces of Great Britain, Canada, Australia and New Zealand in addition to the United States. Additionally, because of the configuration of its fuselage, it was modified for use in transporting personnel, cargo and bulk gasoline and was especially useful in flying supplies over the "Hump," the Himalayas, in China. They also proved invaluable to the Navy for hunting submarines and serving as convoy escorts in the Atlantic Ocean.

The *Willow Run Plant Data* bulletin dated April 27, 1945, announced to all employees that all production would end no later than August 1945. The effect of employment layoffs was huge — 21,731 workers at Willow Run and another 9,000 at other plants producing bomber parts or assemblies, most of whom would not be needed by Ford for peacetime production.

As with all other war contracts Ford's objective was to build the best product at the lowest price. Ford's 1947 report to the Air Materiel Command states that the average price (including fee) for each B-24 produced in 1944 was $92,000 and $85,000 per plane in 1945. This report also states that the best information available from government data indicated that during 1945 Ford delivered B-24s to the Army Air Force from $10,000 to $30,000 less than its competitors.[22]

With Ford's highly automated machine and assembly line approach, they produced nearly fifty percent of all B-24s built. The final total showed Ford built 6,792 flyaways and 1,893 knock-down kits, a total of 8,685 planes of the 19,256 total planes built as well as spares that were the equivalent of 364 additional planes. The critics had finally been silenced! Willow Run was awarded the coveted Army Navy "E" for excellence in May 1945 and the final plane rolled off the line June 28, 1945. The plane was named the HENRY FORD, but at Mr. Ford's request his name was removed so all employees could share credit and sign on the plane.

The Air Materiel Command report summarized:

Willow Run's mass-production of B-24 Liberators was without precedent. There was no pattern of large-scale production in the aircraft industry to follow, and Ford staked everything on his belief that the mass-production techniques developed in many years of automobile manufacture could be applied equally well to an airplane, a washing machine — or anything.

Getting the huge plant into operation took considerable time and presented tremendous difficulties. But once in full production it turned out the promised bomber-an-hour with ease.[23] ... Willow Run, by that time was coasting. The plant could have produced over 600 planes per month had the Army needed them.[24]

A March 13, 1946, memorandum from the War Contract Termination Office stated:

[Ford] before the time of termination was in a position to deliver approximately three times as manyB-24s as were required by the Army Air Force: and accomplished at a cost far below the cost which the Army Air Force was purchasing similar airplanes from other manufacturers.

In October 1941, *The Dearborn Press* quoted Henry Ford as saying: "When the war is over we are going to retain the building we are erecting and construct airplanes on a mass production scale." He went on to describe his vision of the near future when there would be great fleets of airplanes capable of backyard landings. In November 1943 *Ford Times* quoted Henry Ford, "We have been planning for a long time to build a cargo plane at Willow Run after the war." A publicity release in July 1944 stated, "It is our plan to manufacture some product at Willow Run. It might be planes, of the cargo or passenger type, if we can get a design which is economical and safe enough. Or it might be tractors or other equipment." By September 1944, however, Henry Ford had decided that the best use for Willow Run after the war would be in the production of tractors. The matter was settled in 1945, when his grandson Henry Ford II, now President of Ford Motor Company which was in dire financial straits, declined to exercise the option to purchase the Willow Run plant. Henry Ford II told the employees, "The company regarded it as designed to meet a temporary need and just as expendable as a battleship."[25] To the obvious relief of their potential aviation competitors, Henry Ford II, being preoccupied with saving the Ford Motor Company from financial ruin, never entered the postwar aviation industry.

Late in the war Packard Motor Car Co. established laboratory facilities for testing turbine and jet engines at Willow Run and on November 1, 1945, Ford was directed to vacate the Willow Run plant as it had been leased to Kaiser Frazer Corporation for the manufacture of automobiles.[26]

In 1999, the Ford Motor Company donated $500,000 to the Imperial War Museum, Duxford, England, to assist in acquiring and restoring a Ford built B-24 bomber. It now resides with a number of other American combat aircraft in the museum honoring the United States airmen of the 8th Air Force who served from British bases in World War II.

B-24 Data: In researching specifications for this plane, almost every source listed different data for dimensions, weight, speed, bomb load and range, much of which was due to the various models that were not always stated. As a result the information used here is that contained in Ford's 1947 report to the government, which also failed to identify the model.

Ford Production	
B-24-E	490
B-24-H	1,780
B-24-J	1,587
B-24-L	1,250
B-24-M	1,677
(J, L and M models are variations of H)	
XB-24-K (converted D model not made by Ford)	1 (single tail)
YB-24-N	7 (single tail)
Total Flyaways	6,792
Knock-down — Fort Worth, Texas	939
Knock-down — Tulsa, Oklahoma	955
TOTAL	8,686

Plus spare parts for the equivalent of 364 planes.

B-24 specification (Ford records — model not stated)

Length	66' 4"
Height	18'
Wingspan	110'
Empty weight	36,500 lbs.
Fly away weight	49,900 lbs.
Maximum weight approx	56,000 lbs.
Bomb Load	8,600 lbs.
Gas capacity	2,720 gals.
Gas weight	16,320 lbs.
Engines	4 Pratt & Whitney 1,200HP
Crew	10 men
Machine Guns	10 (4 dual, 2 single .50 cal.)
Ammunition	4,648 rounds
Range: Combat	2,100 miles
Ferry	3,700 miles
Maximum ceiling	28,000 ft.
Bomb load	8,000 lbs. (400 miles)
	5,000 lbs. (800 miles)
	2,700 lbs. (1,200 miles)

Parts — 29,669 items composed of 152,235 parts.

Rivets — 519 difference sizes for a total of 313,237 rivets.

(Government supplied parts are listed as one part each regardless of composition.)

Other Specifications (non–Ford sources)

Cruising speed:	215 mph
Maximum speed:	290 mph

4

Gliders

While Germany had been prohibited from creating an air force by the terms of the Armistice ending World War I, they found that interest in aviation could be developed and encouraged by creating gliding clubs. Subsidized by the German government, by the 1930s these glider pilots had formed the basis of what would become the German Luftwaffe. The Germans made use of their glider expertise in the 1940 invasion of Holland and Belgium utilizing ten-man gliders to land troops 20 miles behind the lines. In May 1941 they again used gliders in their successful conquest of the island of Crete.[1]

The United States became interested in the usefulness of gliders following the successful German campaigns and they contacted the Waco Aircraft Company of Troy, Ohio, which had produced gliders since 1930. At the same time the government contracted with Waco to design and produce a military glider it announced plans for 27 glider pilot training schools. The Waco glider was designated CG-4A (CG stood for cargo glider) and was capable of carrying 15 men, or a jeep or a howitzer. The government soon realized additional production capacity was needed and 18 additional manufacturers were awarded glider contracts. Most of the companies were small airplane manufacturers, piano makers and other woodworking type businesses, none of which were accustomed to mass production methods. In March 1942 the Army, looking for more sources, approached Ford to also build the glider in its Iron Mountain, Michigan, plant.

Prior to 1940 a great deal of wood had been required in the manufacturing process of new automobiles, and this demand for wood and Henry Ford's desire for control over his raw materials led him to Michigan's Upper Peninsula in 1919.[2] Edward G Kingsford, a local real estate agent, Ford dealer and relative of Henry Ford by marriage, was asked to locate large tracts of timber that Ford might purchase. Ford's secretary, Ernest Liebold, wrote Kingsford "Mr Ford would like to get a block of land large enough to create a permanent supply of wood and that he would like to farm whatever land might be cleared to create a community and at the same time utilize the mineral rights." In the next few years over 700,000 wooded acres were purchased in and around Iron Mountain, Michigan. A power plant and a Model T body shop were established at Iron Mountain and employment in these plants created a large number of woodworking craftsmen. In following years, timber-harvesting and sawmills were established in four more towns in the Upper Peninsula.

By 1940, steel had replaced most of the wood required in the manufacturing of new automobiles with only the bodies of Ford's *Woody* station wagons needing any quantity of wood. This greatly reduced wood usage in cars had resulted in Ford's timber land dwindling to 250,000 acres by the beginning of World War II. With the attack on Pearl Harbor in December 1941 most of the plant was closed and unemployment in the area soared, forcing these trained craftsmen to seek jobs elsewhere. The only remaining work at the Ford plant, which required few employees, was making wood products: the large wooden shipping containers for B-24 bomber parts as well as the Pratt and Whitney engines. Also manufactured were wooden parts for jeeps, wood flooring, tables, shelving and a few other miscellaneous wood products.

Walter Nelson, Superintendent of the Iron Mountain plant relates, in his Oral Reminiscences, the problems in trying to obtain contracts for products the plant could produce. He had been in contact with the government concerning a war project for their idle Iron Mountain plant but the only contracts they had been offered were small, low cost wood products such as cots, lockers and boxes — nowhere near enough to keep a plant of their size busy. Andrew Higgins of New Orleans was just starting to build the plywood Higgins landing boats of D-Day fame and Ford began negotiating to be a second supply source. Nelson claims Ford was about to obtain a letter of intent for several thousand of these boats to be built at Iron Mountain when Higgins got wind of it and, through pressure by his congressman, squelched the deal with Ford. Higgins' facilities were not fully utilized and he didn't want Ford taking his design over. Ford's fall-back plan, which had no connection to woodworking, was to assemble the new all-metal amphibious jeep Ford was designing. They had taken steps to start assembly operations when they were approached by the Army to build the Waco glider. It was a perfect use for the Iron Mountain facility and the skilled woodworkers, not to mention a life saver for the local community. The glider contract required Ford to pay Waco a $20.05 licensing fee for each glider produced.

Specifications for the plywood components of the Waco glider called for Sitka spruce, none of which was available in the northern Midwest. The Army Air Forces decided to allow Ford to substitute poplar, birch or maple, which were in abundance in the Upper Peninsula, but in testing the spruce against the other three woods, Ford engineers found spruce to be the better selection and spruce was trucked in from the Pacific Northwest.[3]

Ford would be the first to build gliders by mass-production methods, as they had been the first to mass produce Eagle Boats in World War I and tri-motor airplanes in the 1920s. While the glider gives the impression of simple construction, there were over 70,000 parts consisting mostly of small wooden pieces that were glued together. The Army furnished engineering data and drawings prepared by Waco, but unfortunately the glider had not been engineered for mass production and Waco had never made full scale loftings or drawings. In addition the large surge of orders placed with Waco inundated their engineering department and prevented them from incorporating in their drawings many of the running changes made in the shop. Ford's first step was to make a full scale lofting of the glider, providing the accurate dimensions necessary for quantity production. In the process of lofting they corrected errors and re-designed the structure of many parts in order to simplify, improve and strengthen the ship. Many of these changes were later incorporated in the master plans used by all manufacturers. The impact of Ford engineers' work was shown by the fact that out of about 12,000 changes later issued, less than 1,000 pertained to Ford. In essence Ford drawings initiated many of the 12,000 changes.

While the plans were being re-drawn, Ford had to design, purchase or produce non-existing tooling and completely rework three of the Iron Mountain buildings for the new glider program. The three main buildings were cleared of 500 of the 650 production machines used for car production and the remainder modified for the glider job. It was also necessary to modify the air-conditioning system and install elaborate equipment to maintain temperature and humidity at points designated by the government to control the water content of the wood parts. Of the 1,029,280 square feet of floor area in the Iron Mountain facility, 391,680 square feet were utilized directly for the glider program.

Ford once again demonstrated that skilled workers, without previous experience in a specific field, could turn out precision work. Assembly operations were divided into eight components: nose, main fuselage, rear fuselage, tail and main wing segments and wing tips. This division was then used to estimate the time required to tool up and start production. Then jobs were broken down into simple operations for each worker.

Six months later in September 1942, the first Ford glider, a prototype built at the Airframe Building in Dearborn,[4] was towed into the air to be test flown by an Army glider pilot. At 8500 feet the glider was cut loose and for 15 minutes[5] was put through a grueling series of maneuvers. When the ship landed, the pilot reported it to be the best he had flown, the highest tribute possible.

The Iron Mountain plant, located far from any industrial base, provided (including the Sitka wood) 88 percent of the materials needed to produce the gliders. The only non–Ford items were instrument systems and control mechanisms supplied by the government and the steel-tube fuselage frame. Due to the lack of special steelmaking facilities at Ford's Iron Mountain plant, the frame was sub-contracted to the Lloyd Manufacturing Co. in nearby Menominee, Michigan. Ford personnel arranged to train and have Lloyd's men certified for aircraft welding as well as maintaining supervision over the building of the fuselage frames. The balance of the glider, excluding wings, was built up of wood ribs, struts and frames covered by cotton fabric with a plywood floor laid over a honeycomb-like sub-base for strength. The wings were built up of wooden ribs covered in a wood veneer and then covered again in cotton. Major assembly innovations included the use of gluing fixtures and infrared lamps allowing wood joints to be fixed together by gluing, reducing drying time in some applications from eight hours to ten minutes. Virtually all wood joints were fixed together by gluing with many being subjected to variations of this speed drying process. Army inspectors were dubious of Ford's gluing process but inspections found no faults or weaknesses. This process was passed on to the British for use in their Mosquito airplanes, which had a plywood stressed fuselage. Another area of improvement was in control cable assemblies. New assemblies were installed that eliminated 98 percent of the slow and costly hand splicing as well as improving assemblies and adapting them to the knock-down principle of the ship.

Because of the consistent high quality of these gliders, Ford was granted a Quality "A" Control Rating, which meant that Ford inspected its own work with only spot checks by government inspectors. In addition, Ford was appointed the prime engineering contractor, vested with the responsibility for making all revisions and improvements for all contractors.

While the first 100 CG-4A gliders were to be flight delivered from Ford Airport at Iron Mountain, the short runway and winter weather required them to be disassembled and trucked to Dearborn for re-assembly and flight testing. Following flight testing they

First Ford build CG-4A glider in a test flight at Ford Airport, Dearborn, Michigan. The test pilot reported it was the best he had every flown (from the collection of The Henry Ford).

were towed to their destinations to be used as training ships for the newly formed Army unit called the Air Commandos.[6] In early 1944 Ford cut a 150 foot wide path from the Iron Mountain factory to the Ford Airport located a mile away. Assembled gliders were then towed to the airport by tractor where a newly developed system by the Army used a C-47 airplane (military version of the Douglas DC-3) to snatch the gliders off the short runway. The planes snatched two gliders, picking one up on each of two passes over the field, and delivered them to various glider training schools. The balance were crated and shipped by rail or the haulaway trailers that had been designed for shipping the knockdown B-24 bomber kits. For rail shipping, the glider was divided into 20 sections. Each glider filled 5 crates and required two railroad flatcars to transport.[7]

Although the Army's contract called for test flights of only 5 percent (1 in 20), nearly all of the first 100 gliders built were flight tested before being delivered to the Army. As this represented more than 5 percent of the original contract, Ford was not required to flight test additional units. Army personnel at the training camps stated the quality of Ford gliders was such that the units had been found to stand up well under the minimum requirement of 500 hours of flight training operations without repair (nearly twice that of other contractors) and in most instances lasted 2,000 hours. Ford construction methods were so accurate that a Ford glider was sent to each of the other contractors to be used as a standard for interchangeability of parts. Ford insisted on assembling all remaining gliders as though for test-flight, and then dismantled them for crating. (This process, which was copied from their standard method of shipping trucks overseas, insured there were no missing parts.) Army personnel, at glider bases overseas, reported that Ford gliders were the only ones which could be readily reassembled. All contractors were subsequently required to do the same pre-assembly.

Material shortages delayed the delivery of the first Iron Mountain gliders until December 1942 when four units were built. January saw 17 completed, 44 in February, 78 in March and then an average of 127 a month until March of 1945 when three shifts working 8 hours each reached a peak of 216 gliders. Production ceased in August 1945.

The CG-4A could be towed at 120 miles per hour and had a gliding speed of 65 mph. It was 48 feet, 4 inches long with a wingspan of 83 feet, 8 inches and weighed up to 9,000 pounds loaded.

After the Allied invasion of Sicily, in which the CG-4A was used, the Army realized the need for a larger ship, one that could carry entire units. In June 1943, Ford received a contract for 50 of the semi-experimental larger CG-13A gliders capable of carrying 30 fully equipped men (later increased to 42) or two jeeps or a howitzer and one jeep with

First of the larger CG-13A gliders at Ford Airport, Dearborn, Michigan. The nose of the glider lifted up for quick unloading (from the collection of The Henry Ford).

crew and ammunition. The nose of the CG-13A glider was hinged so that on landing it could be raised and cargo quickly unloaded. Unfortunately in combat conditions many of these gliders landed with their nose against fences, stone walls or trees, drastically complicating the unloading process. Plans were on the drawing board for rear-unloading gliders at war's end. The first engineering sample CG-13A glider was also built at the Airframe Building in Dearborn and test flown in December 1943. The remaining units were built in the Iron Mountain plant. An additional 750 had been ordered but canceled by the end of the war in Europe.

The CG-13A could be towed at 200 miles per hour. Only slightly larger than the CG-4A, with a length of 54 feet, 4 inches and a wingspan of 85 feet, 7 inches the loaded weight jumped to 15,000 pounds.

Again, as with other Ford war production projects, contracted costs were substantially reduced as Ford engineers developed better and faster ways of manufacturing. As a result of production and design improvements the cost of building the small CG-4A glider dropped from $21,391 to $12,159 and the cost of the large CG-13A glider dropped from $62,202 to $30,276. Ford's costs were reported to be about half that of other contractors. Ford became the largest producer of gliders, building 4,202 CG-4A models (30 percent of the total) and 87 CG-13A models (73 percent of the total).[8] The success of Ford's glider production program is demonstrated by the increasing proportion of gliders built by Ford: 22 percent in 1943, 33 percent in 1944 and 50 percent in 1945. Towards the end of the war, contracts with most contractors had been canceled, leaving all production to Ford and Waco.

As well as the Sicily and Normandy invasion, gliders were used in the invasion of Southern France, the infamous Operation Market-Garden in the Netherlands and the crossing of the Rhine River into Germany as well as the China-India-Burma theater of operations and several operations in the Pacific theater.

The Iron Mountain plant and its 4,500 workers received the coveted Army Navy E award for excellence in production three times during the war, first in June 1944 then in February 1945 and again in September. At the June award Army Colonel E.W. Dichman stated "less than 3 percent of the 90,000 plants throughout the country are flying an 'E' award flag."[9]

Cancellation of the glider contract in August 1945 caused several severe post-war problems for the employees and the community. First was the one month reduction of the workforce from 3,378 on July 31, 1945, to 1,394 on August 31, 1945. Unfortunately it was not possible to use these workers to resume normal production as operations required the building up of stocks of lumber in the summer to provide inventory for times the loggers could not operate in the winter. Second, the remaining Ford workers having been paid government mandated wage rates based on aircraft production had to revert back to the lower wages normal for peacetime operations.

5

Aircraft Engines

The Rolls-Royce Controversy

In June 1940, Edsel Ford and Sorensen, with Henry Ford's consent, had accepted a contract from the government to produce, under license, 9,000 of the British Rolls-Royce aircraft engines but, much to Edsel's chagrin, this contract was quickly canceled by his father, causing a great deal of consternation and embarrassment to both Ford and government officials. It was reported at the time that Henry Ford, a pacifist, canceled the contract when he discovered that the contract for 6,000 of the engines would be directly between Ford and Great Britain. In answer to the outcry that Henry Ford was anti–English and his pacifist beliefs drove his decision, he explained that he thought the contract was with the U.S. government but found, instead, that it was a direct contact with Great Britain, a belligerent. He maintained that he was all for efforts to produce war materials for defense of the United States, which Ford Motor Company was already doing, but he would not deal with combatants. (In the late 1930s he had refused to sell any vehicles to Italy for its war in Ethiopia). Furthermore, Henry Ford pointed out, Ford of Canada and Ford of Britain were both using Ford facilities to the utmost for the defense of the British Empire. It wasn't until March 8, 1941, however, that Ford officials further explained in a *Detroit Free Press* article that Henry Ford's decision not to produce the Rolls-Royce engine was because he felt the engine was obsolete and he didn't want to appear to discredit the British engine, an engine his own company, Ford of Britain, was planning to produce. He never meant he would not produce war material for England. Henry Ford believed a new engine of his own design was a superior type that should be used in both British and U.S. military planes. Initial tests showed the Ford engine could develop between 1500HP and 1700HP verses the 1000HP of the Rolls-Royce engine. The Ford engine was later modified and became an outstanding tank engine (see Chapter 9).

Many critics have decried this explanation as a cover for Henry Ford's pacifism, and maybe rightfully so, but Ford (U.S.) had already accepted an aircraft engine contract from the French government. In June 1939 Ford had formed Fordair S.A., a subsidiary of Ford S.A.F. (France), to build 1,200 of the Rolls-Royce Merlin X aircraft engine.[1] Most of the production equipment had to be acquired in the United States and efforts were well underway when France fell to the Germans in June 1940. Having had a chance to see the details of the Rolls-Royce engine, Ford felt he could do better and it was at this time that he started work on his own airplane engine.

Pratt & Whitney Aircraft Engine

The Pratt & Whitney Aircraft Company had a long and very successful career in developing and producing aircraft engines, but by 1938 their domestic business had hit a lull and they needed to solicit foreign orders. Fortunately the French needed large numbers of engines and in mid–1938 purchased a license for their Automobile Talbot Company to produce the Pratt & Whitney R-1830, 1200HP Twin Wasp engine. However, the task proved to be more formidable than anticipated and by September 1939 the French had been unable to produce any engines. As a result the French ordered the engines direct from Pratt & Whitney. As Pratt & Whitney did not have the necessary capacity or funds to accommodate sizable orders, the French agreed to what amounted to a 10 percent surcharge on each engine to cover the additional investment in plant and equipment, allowing Pratt & Whitney to start production by early 1940. Before all the engines could be delivered, however, the Germans overran France and the British promptly took over the balance of the French order.[2]

Up to this point the whole air war had been carried on by airplanes with 1200 horse powered engines. Pratt & Whitney had recently developed the R-2800 engine, the first 2000 horsepower radial aviation engine. The R-2800 engine was a whole new design best illustrated by the comparison of its power to the Ford V8 engine as described by Sorensen. "This was a product, each of whose eighteen cylinders packs the power of one and a quarter Ford V-8 engines; which weighs roughly one pound per horsepower as against the V-8's seven pounds per horsepower."[3] Put another way it was like having the power of 22½ Ford V8 engines in the nose of a single engine plane.

The U.S. government was greatly expanding aircraft production in accordance with the President's demand but the lack of airplane engines proved to be one of the most serious bottlenecks. The government wanted both the R-1830 and the R-2800 Pratt & Whitney engines in volumes that Pratt & Whitney could not possibly handle. The answer was the same as when increased airplane production was needed — license production to the automobile companies.

With the potential productive capacity of the Ford Motor Company, William Knudsen, Chief of Defense Production for the U.S. government, was forced to ignore the embarrassment over the Rolls-Royce engine contract. He proposed in early August 1940 that Ford build the Pratt & Whitney 18 cylinder, 2000HP R-2800 radial aircraft engine for which Pratt & Whitney was the sole source. On August 20 Edsel Ford, Charles Sorensen, Mead Bricker, William Pioch and others visited the Pratt & Whitney plant in East Hartford, Connecticut, and discovered an intricate machine, much more sophisticated than any automobile engine ever built. While recognizing serious problems that they would have to overcome, Ford confirmed to the government that they could and would build the engine. Pratt & Whitney executive Edmund Eveleth commented, "They also recognized certain serious shortages. Mr. Sorensen called the Rouge to start a magnesium plant, and foreseeing the shortage of special alloy steels, called in the steel foundry people at the Rouge for that part of the job."[4] With a letter of intent in hand Ford engi-

neers descended on the East Hartford plant to observe and study Pratt & Whitney production methods. What they saw was a system whereby the engine stood still while a
group of experienced tool and die workers built up each engine — certainly not a system
conducive to mass production. What they found when they sought plans for the engine
is best described by Eveleth: "It was then that we realized that a great deal of craftsman-
ship and 'know how' of building the engines was not on paper, but in the heads of the
old-time Yankee machinists in our shop." Ford engineers determined that the requirements to mass produce this most intricate engine could not be met by any of Ford's existing automobile production facilities. This was the most complicated task Ford engineers
had been asked to undertake and the assembly line process had to be used if the needed
production was to be obtained. It would take a new building equipped with new and
many unique machines but, before all else, a complete set of plans had to be obtained.

On October 31, 1940, Ford received a firm contract for 4,236 of the R2800 engines
that required Ford to pay Pratt & Whitney a token fee of $1.00 for every engine pro-
duced.

Later, as production got rolling, Eveleth commented, "By close cooperation an aviation milestone was reached. The motor industries claimed they had never seen such a
perfectly engineered job, and the aircraft engine company claimed they had never seen a
new job tackled on such an enormous scale. At this point we all realized that we [Pratt
& Whitney] were the outstanding engineering firm and they [Ford, Buick & Chevrolet]
were the outstanding production firms to do the job." Nash-Kelvinator would later build
a small number of the R–2800 engines.

Eveleth relates in his manuscript the competition among the automakers:

> Ford [18 cylinder R–2800 versus Buick and finally Chevrolet, both making the 14 cylinder R–
> 1850] ... sent in the smallest number of men, 118 representatives for 192 visits and finished
> their first engine in 13 months. Buick, who of course was extremely interested in Ford's
> progress, stated they that they would do the job in less time than that of Ford. They sent in
> ... 202 representatives for 333 visits and they finished their first engine in 15 months.
> Chevrolet felt they were the last to jump on the band wagon, and they sent in 376 represen-
> tatives for a total of 510 visits. They stated they would complete their job in shorter time
> than Ford or Buick. Chevrolet's first engine was finished in 9 months.

Building: To determine the type of building needed Ford first had to determine how
they would assemble the engine and then decide the machines and fixtures that would
be needed. To that end they divided the engine into major sub-assemblies so that appropriate assembly lines could be designed. Six major groups were identified: front (nose)
section, main crankcase section, cylinders, blower section, intermediate rear section and
rear section. They then tore down and reassembled one of the R–2800 engines over seventy times until every movement had been charted and every stage in the assembly process
analyzed in order to find the most efficient way to perform every task.

Next they devised machinery and procedures to perform these tasks in progressive
operations. Nearly 9,000 machine tools were finally selected, and while some could be
obtained on the open market, many had to be designed and fabricated, a project carried
out by Ford's extensive Tool and Die Department that proved critical in initiating timely
production. These newly designed multi-purpose tools passed the parts from machine to
machine on conveyors until the part was completed and then conveyed to a sub-assembly line. The next step was to break down each component to its essential parts and

develop a job standard for each. These sub-assemblies, along with those supplied by other Ford locations or vendors, would then be delivered to the final assembly line at the time and place the part was needed by the worker.

With these specifications, architects proceeded to design the plant layout and determine requirements for the building. On September 17, 1940, ground was broken in the Rouge complex on one of the last remaining sites in the 1,200 acre Rouge complex. The first task was to drive 3,678 one hundred foot sections of steel pilings down to bedrock. Once the building was under construction protection from the elements was required to allow construction during the winter, which was a necessity in order to meet planned production schedules. As soon as several bays of steel structure were erected, scaffoldings were placed around the structure and then enclosed in more than 250,000 feet of moisture proof fiberboard and covered with tar paper. The temperature inside was then controlled by huge charcoal burners.

With additional orders expected from the government a temporary wall was erected at the far end of the building to save time in expanding when new orders materialized. Due to real concerns of possible air raids at the time, the factory was designed without windows, making it the first black-out plant. The main assembly facility was 1,400 feet by 360 feet with an adjacent engine test wing measuring 270 feet × 952 feet. The floor space eventually dedicated to this project, including out-sourced production, totaled 4,187,831 square feet.

Aircraft Engine Building showing wooden structure and weatherproof insulation installed around building to allow winter construction. It was considered the first black-out building as there were no windows (from the collection of The Henry Ford).

While the engine blocks were cast at the Rouge, many of the smaller parts and assemblies were sub-contracted to the village industry plants and other vendors freeing up space in the engine plant for more of the actual engine assembly work. When the original September contract was increased in November the temporary wall was removed, expediting the building expansion and the production schedule.

By April 1941, Mead Bricker had been placed in charge of the Aircraft Engine Division and limited production of parts was started. The first 951 engines were the R-2800-5 model rated at 1850HP. All others were rated at 2000HP.

Production: When the first engines came off the line on August 23 they were subjected to a grueling 150 hour dynamometer test. Having passed these tests the engines were taken to the Glenn L. Martin Company plant in Baltimore, Maryland, and fitted into a Martin B-26 medium bomber for testing. Performance was declared 100 percent satisfactory.

By the time the first engine was produced, the original contract for 4,236 was more than doubled to 10,317. This meant equipment designed to produce one engine an hour was obsolete as in many cases it was not practicable to just double the equipment to double production. That would have meant double manpower and space. Instead, new equipment was designed to double or triple production without adding manpower or space.

Production had reached 1,070 engines a month when in March 1943 the government increased the demand to 3,400 engines a month. Even with the additional space that was quickly added because of the temporary wall, and the farming out of sub-assemblies to the village industries, the near tripling of the order demanded more space and

The Pratt & Whitney aircraft engine was the most complicated and precise engine ever built by Ford. *Newsweek*, June 7, 1943 (from the collection of The Henry Ford).

equally as important more skilled manpower. The answer was farming out the fabrication of additional parts and sub-assemblies to Ford's larger branch locations around the country which had existing staffs of skilled workers. By the end of July 1943, 2,409 machines to produce sub-assemblies were moved from the Rouge plant to Highland Park, Michigan; Dearborn, Michigan; Kansas City, Missouri; St. Paul, Minnesota; Memphis, Tennessee; and Green Island, New York. This increased the floor space dedicated to engine production from 2,687,230 square feet to 4,187,831 square feet. Peak production was reached in August 1944 when 2,431 engines were produced by over 32,000 workers. By September Ford was geared up to produce 3,400 engines monthly, though actual requirement never exceed 2,431 units per month.

Ford Methods: Sorensen's call to the Rouge, during his visit to East Hartford, had started development of a magnesium foundry for the sole purpose of producing aircraft engine castings for the Pratt & Whitney engine (see chapter 7).

A major contribution to production and cost efficiencies was in centrifugally casting cylinder barrels, by the process described in Chapter 3, instead of the industry standard of forging. This system saved 35 pounds of high quality steel for each barrel produced and drove the price per cylinder down from $13.38 to $10.50. This process alone generated a savings of $2,989,302 on Ford engines produced during the war, not to mention the savings in high quality steel. The Army Air Forces were wary of this innovation until Ford proved its value in demonstrations, but Pratt & Whitney officials never adapted Ford's casting system. This also freed capacity at the Bethlehem Steel Corporation, which had been supplying the forged cylinder heads, to perform other critical war work. Another example of Ford's innovation was in cutting tools where standard high speed steel was used in 26 Fay Automatic Lathes to produce 1,800 engines a month based on the original government contract. When the order was increased to 3,400 engines it would have required 40 additional lathes costing $360,000. Ford engineers found that by using tungsten carbide tipped tools they could handle the increased production without the additional lathes. Another efficiency was the many new tools designed by Ford which were capable of performing, simultaneously, multiple functions reducing time and manpower requirements. One example was an operation on the cylinder sleeve where thirty-six single spindle back spot facing machines were needed with an operator for each. Ford engineers designed and fabricated a special machine, two of which eliminated the other 36 machines and their operators. A special process was developed using a water cooled arbor that reduced the time required to grind the thin walls of the cylinder barrel from ninety to twenty minutes and at the same time hold the barrel in round to .0005 inch accuracy. It was so successful that other aircraft manufacturers adopted it. These are but a few of the new tools designed by Ford engineers and toolmakers to solve new problems.

Due to the uniqueness of Ford production methods verses Pratt & Whitney methods, a new machining operation was required and developed for virtually every major part in order to assure the standardization required for mass production. All told there were 8,128 new machine tools designed by Ford engineers to use along with 844 existing Ford tools. Many of these tool designs were used by Pratt & Whitney, Buick and Chevrolet. There was great sharing of ideas and secrets among the companies which underlie Eveleth's comment, "Nobody in the world including none of our allied forces, and not even the German forces ever had the interchangeability that we had."[5] Pistons, cylinders, wrist pins, link rods, every common part was interchangeable in the engines built by all five companies.

Another improvement, obvious with hindsight, that saved hours of time on each engine produced, was developing a quick coupling device which eliminated the need to connect and disconnect all the wiring, piping and recording lines on each engine when being placed on the final testing cell.

Never the one to waste anything, Ford ran generators off the engines being tested. Each engine was tested for four hours and overall they generated enough power to meet over 95 percent of the electrical energy required for the entire building.

Field Service Operations: Due to the complexity of the engine, which was built up from 220 assemblies comprising 11,723 parts, it was necessary to not only train thousands of new employees but also to set up an Aircraft Service Department to train resident service representatives. The government contract required Ford "to follow the product from the final assembly line through airframe plants and to effect important changes on engines which had left the production line, no matter where they might be." A Ford field force of 50 men was trained in the fall of 1941 and assigned to ten airplane manufacturers using the Ford built Pratt & Whitney engine to insure changes were incorporated without delay. Their services were expanded to cover Army Air Forces bases throughout the United States and overseas. This program proved so beneficial that the Army requested the representatives to travel to its bases with Mobile Training Units to also train pilots and mechanics in the principles and operation of the engine. The presence of these Ford service representatives in the field were able, in many cases, to save disabled engines that the local mechanics, lacking the technical expertise, were unable to fix. Real life experience in the field also provided many ideas for changes in the manufacturing process that were passed on to the aircraft engine plant in the Rouge.

The Engine-Propeller Report was a monthly report sent to government inspectors showing the performance of various aircraft engine manufacturers. It measured their performance based on horsepower shipments and monthly shipments per employee and is another measure of how mass manufacturing techniques developed by Ford generated maximum production. Horsepower was the only logical comparison as different size engines were involved. The December 1944 report for the top six manufacturers (plus the second Pratt & Whitney plant) in total horsepower were:

	Employees	Floor Area Square Feet	Shipments Horsepower	Shipments Per Employee
#1 Ford (Michigan)	22,600	3,454,000	56,658,000	132
#2 Wright (Ohio)	29,200	5,310,000	54,228,000	44
#3 Pratt & Whitney (Connecticut)	27,400	4,991,000	42,101,200	66
#4 Buick (Illinois)	17,600	4,249,000	40,127,700	83
#5 Studebaker (Indiana)	14,800	2,861,000	39,761,300	129
#6 Packard (Michigan)	27,100	2,820,000	38,406,200	48
#13 Pratt & Whitney (Missouri)	18,900	3,903,000	6,800,000	26

(Of the 24 manufacturers rated, no others exceeded 92 shipments per employee.)

Results: In December 1942, the Army Air Forces assigned a Quality "A" rating which meant Ford engines were self-inspected with only nominal supervision by government inspectors. In March 1943, the first 1,000 per month production, it required 2,295 man-hours to produce each of 1,070 engines but by December 1944 through the end of the war it took less than 1,000 man-hours per unit. The best information available from government data in a 1947 report indicated that Ford delivered Pratt & Whitney engines to the Army Air Forces at $1,000 to $5,000 less than competitors in 1944 and at $4,000 to $8,000 less in 1945. On March 12, 1943, the Aircraft Engine Division was awarded the Army Navy "E" for excellence.

The aircraft engine plant employed over 32,000 workers at its peak, over 5,000 of whom were women, and built 57,851 engines.

The Ford engines produced at the Rouge were used in the Curtiss C-46, Douglas A-26, Martin B-26, Northrop P-61, Republic P-47 and Lockheed B-34 airplanes.

Pulse Jet Engine

In June 1944 the Germans started raining V-1 missiles, called buzz bombs, on Great Britain. These V (for vengeance weapons) flying bombs were 25 feet long and powered by a pulse jet engine. The engines were designed to fly for two hours with enough power to drive the plane and a 1,800 pound bomb load at 400 mph. Like the Kettering Bug in World War I, when the engine stopped the craft plunged to the earth. The weapon had a number of advantages: it was cheap to build without use of critical materials, could be easily launched en masse regardless of weather, and difficult to spot because of its fairly high speed and low altitude. Conversely there were drawbacks: fixed launch sites and targets meant their flight path was predictable and vulnerable to attack, poor accuracy limited their use to large targets such as cities, and slow speeds allowed them to be shot down when spotted by fighters or anti-aircraft batteries as well as allowing the fighter pilot to tip them over by building up air pressure between the wingtips of the V-1 and the fighter plane.

While they were very inaccurate, with only about 25 percent reaching their targets, they created havoc on a war-weary London with reports of 5,000 fatalities among the 46,000 casualties. Reaction from the Allies was swift. Based on Ford's participation in the experiments with the Kettering Bug in World War I and the recognized success of their engineering and mass production capabilities of precision equipment like the gun director, Ford was asked to recreate this engine. By early July, Ford was given the specifications contained in a sketchy five page Allied Command report which vaguely described the construction details of the German V-1 robot engine which had been obtained only by observation of the first 100 bombs reaching London. But on July 13, 1944, 2,500 pounds of salvaged German V-1 missile parts arrived at Wright-Patterson Field, outside Dayton, Ohio, from Great Britain. With the arrival of these parts Ford engineers hurried down to Dayton to examine the badly mangled engine parts of a V-1 dud that had impacted the earth at about 400 mph. On July 15 Ford was awarded a contract for the design, development and fabrication of 25 intermittent jet type engines to be used with a robot aerial bomb, code named MX-544. Republic Aviation Corporation was contracted to build the airframe.

Production: Due to time constraints, separate facilities at the Rouge could not be used and, as this was a secret project, production of parts without labels was spread around

Jet pulse engine being tested at Rouge. It was similar to the ones the Germans used in the V-1 bombs launched against London. Sandbags in the background were for noise reduction but excessive sound and shattering sound waves destroyed them (from the collection of The Henry Ford).

different departments in the Rouge. As the parts became available they were funneled to a central area for assembly. In three weeks, the first Ford jet engine was successfully operated at the Rouge plant. A 300 mph wind tunnel was erected behind the aluminum foundry for testing, causing excessive noise and shattering vibrations. The impact actually lowered the efficiency of the operators and employees in the main building and was unbearable to people in the surrounding neighborhood. Ford first built sandbag barricades to dampen the whine of the engines, but they were disintegrated by the intensive vibrations and pressure impulses of the engine. Silencers were finally designed that allowed for testing without the resulting turmoil. By October 1944, an assembly line had been set up in the government owned aluminum foundry and the first three engines built.

Designated PJ-31-1, these three engines were tested and accepted by the Army Air Forces, eliminating the necessity of building the other 22 units. These units led to an initial production order for 3,000 engines. With Ford's turbo supercharger project finished, almost the entire supervisory and engineering department was transferred to the jet engine project. During production a number of improvements were made. Some of the more important ones: air valves were improved providing increased durability — German valves lasted 7 minutes, Ford's lasted 2 hours under greater power output; grid bars were die cast instead of being milled, increasing power and engine life while reducing cost; the fuel metering device was improved through a redesigned unit providing more accurate controls; and stainless steel valves replaced steel valves, increasing engine performance while reducing costs.

Still lacking was instrumentation for measuring the actual performance of the engine in flight. Ford was sent an AT-23 airplane, a stripped down trainer version of the twin engine B-26 bomber, to modify into a flying laboratory for testing the engine in flight. Ford's testing part of the contract was canceled with the end of the war, but the modification of the AT-23 was continued so that Air Materiel Command personnel could conduct the tests. Ford engineers assisted in the establishment of a test launching site on the Gulf of Mexico which was within the area of the Army Air Forces Proving Grounds, Eglin Field, Florida. Ford also conducted one and three week courses for Army Air Forces personnel in operation and maintenance of the engine.

The American version of the V-1 was similar to the German unit with two main exceptions: launching and guidance. Most German units were ground launched from a fixed site and used hydrogen peroxide and potassium permanganate to launch and obtain

Air Force B-17 carrying the JB-2 with the Pulse Jet engine for airborne launch. It was intended for use in the Pacific but the Japanese surrendered first.

minimum speed for operating the pulse jet engine. The United States opted for an air-borne launch and added a radio-control guidance system.

Production efficiency quickly reduced assembly to 104 man-hours per engine from 161 man-hours for units made in the first month of full production. With the increased production expected this performance would have greatly improved.

These engines were designed to be used to power three types of missiles: the Army Air Forces' JB-2 and JB-10 and the Navy's Loon, with the JB-2 and Loon being substantially improved versions of the German V-1 buzz bomb. The Loon was designed for launching from submarines.

While reaction to the new weapon was positive there were concerns. The weapon was wanted *if* there would be no significant reduction in current production of bombs and artillery shells. An early estimate indicated a reduction in the production of artillery shells by 25 percent and bombs by 17 percent and just as important they would require 25 percent of Allied shipping capability to the European Theater of Operations.[6] In addition early testing showed great inaccuracy. Guidance problems developed as described by Donald Lopez in his book *Into the Teeth of the Tiger*: "Fighter planes were required to follow them until they crashed in order to shoot them down if the guidance system malfunctioned, as it often did, and the buzz bomb turned back towards land."

The importance attached to this secret weapon by the Army Air Forces is attested to by the fact that, subject to testing the tactical use of this bomb against Japan, Ford was asked to submit facilities requirement data for building 100 units a day, quickly revised to 500 units a day and once again revised to 1,000 units a day! However, only 2,378 engines were actually produced by the time the contract was canceled on August 14, 1945 (VJ day), and none were ever used in combat. Indications are some were used in Alaska as target drones for the new Air Force jet fighters. The nearly complete wind tunnel was shipped to Wright Field.

6

Other Aviation Contracts

Aircraft Distributor

Within a month after Pearl Harbor, a flaw was found in Republic Aviation's new P-47 Thunderbolt fighter. Despite all its power it was unreliable at altitudes over 32,000 feet due to repeated failure of the Pratt & Whitney R-2800 engine. Unable to find the cause of the failure the government, in January 1942, asked Ford, which was one of the manufacturers of the engine, to find a solution. The task was turned over to Ford engineer Emil Zoerlein, who decided that since the engine of the P-47 couldn't go into the stratosphere, the first step in solving the problem was to recreate the stratosphere at sea level. The answer was building a small altitude chamber (40 by 50 inches) which could simulate ascents to 60,000 feet in five minutes. In simulations they found the engine performed flawlessly at sea level but the hard rubber distributor heads were set afire at the higher altitudes. Air is the best insulator at sea level, but as altitudes increase, air density decreases, weakening the distributor's insulation quality to the point of failure. This failure resulted in a short circuit that burned out the rubber distributor head and caused the engine to fail.

With the problem identified, Ford engineers replaced the hard rubber heads with melmac, a plastic made of melamine resin and asbestos that would not burn. While it worked in the test chamber the real test had to be in the air. Charles Lindbergh thoroughly tested the new distributor in a P-47 at 10,000 feet over the previous limit raising the functional ceiling to 42,000 feet. While the immediate problem with the old distributor was being solved, Ford engineers were developing a new and larger distributor and magneto that provided an operating ceiling of 60,000 feet. However, as the original distributor, as improved, operated in the desired ceiling range and required only minimal production changes, it was selected as the critical need was for immediate production. The improved distributor was turned over to the Army Air Force on April 6, 1942, and installation was immediately ordered on all existing Thunderbolts. The distributor was used on all other Pratt & Whitney R-2800 engines being built as well on the Allison and Curtiss Wright 2,200 horsepower engines used on the Boeing B-29 Superfortress. As this distributor was required for all high-altitude aircraft, Ford granted free licenses to other manufacturers.

Aircraft Ignition[1]

Late in February 1943, Ford was given a contract to test a new ignition system developed by General Electric. Contract terms required Ford to test the system in the Pratt & Whitney R-2800 engine for a minimum of 55 hours at not less than 35,000 feet. Flight testing with the Ford built R-2800 engine in a P-47-D Thunderbolt involved Charles Lindbergh and other Ford pilots flying 31 flights and resulted in obtaining valuable data on the operation of various types of ignition systems at extreme altitudes. Lindbergh reached a height of 36,000 feet during the first flight and, in 20 hours of additional flight time over 35,000 feet, he reached a maximum altitude of 43,020 feet. Following the successful testing, the new General Electric system was adopted for the R-2800 engine. Lindbergh gained a great deal of high altitude performance data as a result of these tests which he was later able to use in providing valuable advice to Army Air Force fighter pilots when he visited them in the Pacific war zone. During the course of these flights Lindbergh also developed a valve system allowing the emergency transfer of oxygen from the regular supply in the aircraft to emergency jump bottles without changing masks.

Aircraft Generators[2]

In early 1942, Ford was in discussion with the Army Air Force regarding the manufacturing of dynamotors, an instrument to transform direct current of a given voltage to direct current of another voltage. Suddenly there was an urgent need for increased production of the P-1, a 200 ampere aircraft generator that supplied electrical energy for twenty-four volt aircraft systems, and Ford was asked to produce the generator instead of the dynamotor. Three different units were being built by General Electric, Westinghouse and Delco-Remy, all slightly different, but all had been approved by the Army Air Force. They were standard equipment on the Consolidated B-24 Liberator, North American B-25 Mitchell, Martin B-26 Marauder bombers and the Northrop P-61 Black Widow fighter as well as several other aircraft.

Ford had been building automotive generators for many years and, though the P-1 was much larger and more complicated, decided that the men at the Ypsilanti, Michigan, plant, who had built automotive generators in the past would be the best to handle the contract. Sixty percent of the plant would be turned over to generator production with the remainder dedicated to parts for the Pratt and Whitney engine and other items. Ford engineers, after tearing down and examining each of the three generators, selected the General Electric generator as the one to build. Although it was the more expensive and difficult to build it seemed the better generator from the standpoint of performance.

Ford engineers found the procedure for General Electric to produce these generators was to have workers build each component with one man performing most of that operation. Ford devised new procedures and methods which incorporated speed and efficiency. A progressive assembly line was set up, jigs and fixtures designed and hand operations were replaced with machines wherever possible.

A training program was established and 500 new employees hired, over half being women, none of whom had any previous factory experience. Eleven handmade generators were produced by December 1942 before the assembly line process was in place. In January, with the line in place, production jumped to 1,000 units and continued to increase until a peak of 4,000 units was reached in November 1943. The last of the P-1 generators came off the line in December 1944 and in February 1945 production was switched to a larger R-1, a 300 ampere generator. Only two pounds heavier than the P-1 it supplied 50 percent more energy.

Again, Ford methods and procedures reduced the man-hours to build each generator from 57 hours in June 1943 to 18 hours in December 1944. One major change was in welding the leads. Because the R-1 operated close to the melting point of tin, solder could not be used. Other manufacturers used a very complicated Taylor-Winfield welding machine costing over $50,000. Ford developed a special brazing machine which did the work as well or better at a cost of only $600.00.

Once again Ford reduced costs to the government. The P-1's initial cost of $273.62 in April 1943 was reduced to $93.95 by July 1944. Similarly the cost of the R-1 dropped from $233.43 in January 1945 to $143.18 when production was curtailed in April of the same year.

The Ypsilanti plant produced 76,166 P-1 generators and 11,223 R-1 generators and for their outstanding performance they were awarded the Army Navy "E" for excellence on three different occasions — April 8, 1944; November 25, 1944; and June 30, 1945.

Turbo Superchargers[3]

The supercharger was critical to high performance aviation as it allowed airplane engines to operate in the thin air of high altitudes with the same efficiency as if it were at ground level. In actual tests, an aircraft engine which developed 1,000 horsepower at sea level generated only 300 horsepower at 35,000 feet due to the decrease in air density. Just as oxygen allows air-crews to function at high altitudes, turbo superchargers enable aircraft engines to fly higher by compressing the rarified atmosphere to sea level density so that carburetors can function efficiently. The turbo supercharger performed the same function as any other supercharger, the difference being in the way it is driven. The turbo unit is driven by engine exhaust gases, while the non-turbo unit uses gears and belts driven by the engine crankshaft, which reduces usable horsepower.

In January 1942 there was such a demand for the General Electric B-2 turbo supercharger that Ford Motor Company was asked to build 4,000 a month at a cost of approximately $2,000 each. Following a visit to the General Electric plant in Lynn, Massachusetts, to inspect their manufacturing process, Ford submitted a letter of intent to the government. The government responded by placing an order for 40,000 units with an expenditure authorization of $41,400,000. With a contract in hand Ford found space in the Pressed Steel Building at the Rouge and by September the first shipment of 17 B-2 units was made.

The turbo supercharger was a precision machine built to precise specifications. Most of the parts had to withstand temperatures of 1,500 degrees Fahrenheit and the rotor or moving part of the unit had to be balanced to withstand vibrations at 31,000 revolutions per minute. Ford engineers developed an assembly line process and a number of major innovations to obtain volume production. One change was the compressor box which was made of cast aluminum, a critical alloy. Ford designed a box of comparable quality and weight using low-carbon steel, thus saving many pounds of scarce aluminum in each engine. Another aluminum saving improvement was stamping the compressor casing out of cold-rolled deep-drawn sheet steel which was readily available in the Ford mills instead of cast aluminum. The total process eliminated the need for expensive machinery for finishing the aluminum castings which saved time in the assembly process. In addition over three million pounds of aluminum were saved as a result of these innovations. Another 45,209 of these low cost steel compressor castings were also supplied to Allis-Chalmers.

As in other jobs requiring precision standards, workers had to be carefully selected and trained. The actual assembly operation was handled by women who represented about 45 percent of the 1,100 total workers. By October 1943 production of the B-2 units were completed and production began on the improved B-22 unit. Fifteen thousand of the B-2 units and 37,281 of the larger B-22 units were produced for use in B-17 Flying Fortresses and B-24 Liberator bombers before termination of the contract in October 1944. The first units cost $3,500 but by August 1944 the cost had been reduced to less than $750. One of the reason cited for the termination of this contract was the urgent need for using the facility for the production of jettison fuel tanks described later.

Rate-of-Climb Indicators[4]

The rate-of-climb indicator was a finely engineered instrument that was produced and assembled at Pioneer Instrument Company, a division of Bendix Aviation Company. An indication of the precision needed is the fact that 75 percent of the Pioneer workforce was made up of watchmakers. Due to the urgent necessity of this item and Ford Motor Company's performance in producing the precision made gun director, they were approached in early 1942 to build 30,000 rate-of-climb indicators at a rate of 3,000 a month. In order to enter production as quickly as possible, assistance and some instruments were required from Pioneer. Unfortunately, Pioneer management apparently looked on Ford as a competitor and reportedly were somewhat reluctant to assist Ford. This reaction in wartime, even though Pioneer couldn't build enough of the instruments to satisfy the critical demand.

The indicator consisted of 147 separate parts weighing 24 ounces and was assembled piece by piece by highly skilled watchmakers. With only two watchmakers available, Ford used them as foremen and resolved the lack of skilled help, as usual, by the mass production of parts and the assembly line process for construction. Due to the fineness of the work, many of these workers were women who, it was believed, were better able to handle the precision assembly that was required. For example, one ceramic tube had to have a $3/1000$ inch hole drilled into it and it was found that women, mostly, had the necessary lightness of finger. Because of the sensitivity of the parts the work area had to be completely air conditioned to maintain a constant temperature. Also affecting the mechanism were the particles of dust from workers' clothes and as a result special smocks were required. Many innovative manufacturing steps were taken to reduce the number of parts and procedures implemented that reduced assembly time. As a result, high quality, watch-like mechanisms were, for the first time, mass produced on an assembly line.

The job was placed with Ford's Manchester, Michigan, plant with the first indicators being shipped in December 1942. The 3,000 monthly rate was never reached and in October 1943 with only 5,360 units shipped the contract was canceled. No reason was found in the records for the cancellation.

Altitude Chamber[5]

As the Army Air Force required that all B-24 bombers be flight tested at an altitude of 35,000 feet, Ford Motor Company developed and built one of the most advanced altitude chambers in the world for simulating temperature and altitude changes in flight, something that could not be done simultaneously at any other facility. In addition it provided research facilities for both engineers and doctors. With plans approved in May 1942, material shortages delayed the completion until February 1944.

The test chamber, designed by Ford engineers and located in the main hangar, could simulate pressure and temperature changes at any rate up to an ascent of 5,000 feet a minute and at any rate of descent to 25,000 feet a minute. Cooling could be reduced from a plus 70 degrees to a minus 70 degrees in 8 to 12 minutes. This approximated climbing from sea level to 60,000 feet at the rate of 5,000 feet a minute.

The chamber, fitted with chairs that could be vibrated to simulate flight conditions, could accommodate 14 men and was used to test the ability of men to withstand extreme cold and loss of atmospheric pressure in the stratosphere. The chamber was equipped with all equipment available in an aircraft which provided training that allowed the B-24 crews to experience actual flying conditions while learning their reactions in meeting emergencies at high altitudes as well as monitoring their medical status. In addition it tested generators, converters, automatic pilots, hydraulic systems and gyro-instruments.

The test chamber was turned over the Army Air Force and transferred to Wright Field, Ohio, in September 1944.

Quick Change Engine[6]

In late 1943 Ford was requested to design, develop, and test a quick change power plant, with a minimum number of changes, that would be adaptable to airplanes then in service. Specifications called for the removal and installation of an identical power plant in 45 minutes. An additional 15 minutes was allowed for planes equipped with turbo superchargers. Ford engineers started development work immediately but a P-47-D Thunderbolt test unit was not delivered until February 1944. In order to meet specifications the cowling had to be redesigned and a new type engine mount developed along with new electrical, hydraulic and control connections.

The task was accomplished with a redesign that added only 32 pounds versus an expected 75 pounds and took only 8.5 minutes to remove the engine and place it on a stand and 15.2 minutes to install a new engine. A complete power plant was exchanged in 23.7 minutes compared to the 40 hours then required to change a similar engine in a normal airplane. Unfortunately the task wasn't completed until July 1946 — too late to assist the war effort and with the dawn of jet engines the system was probably never utilized.

Jettison Fuel Tanks[7]

In late 1944 jettison fuel tank availability became critical due to an increasing need for fighter escorts on long distance bombing raids in the Pacific Theater of Operations. Because the need was so great and shipping space was at such a premium, a knock-down version was vital and the Army Air Force was striving to find a manufacturer to not only produce a knock-down tank, but to do so quickly. While Ford of Australia and a number of companies in the United Sates were producing the standard tank, for various reasons, they were unable to deliver a knock-down version.

On October 1, 1944, Ford was asked if they could design, develop and produce a knock-down, 310 gallon jettison fuel tank, 13 feet long by three feet in diameter, for use on the Lockheed P-38 Lightning, Republic P-47 Thunderbolt and Northrop P-61 Black Widow fighter planes. Fortunately, Ford's Pressed Steel Building in the Rouge was just finishing a contract for the turbo supercharger and the freed-up space was suitable for building the fuel tanks in the quantity needed. On October 10, 1944, a contract was issued for 20,000 tanks with another 22,381 ordered three weeks later. Originally designed to hold four knock-down tanks in a crate which was designed to act as a bench for assembly, the tank was redesigned so that ten tanks could be shipped in each crate. The very large presses required to make the 13 foot half shells from aluminum were very scarce, but fortunately such presses were available at the Rouge. Production requirements were

Four jettison fuel tanks packed four to a case to save shipping space to the Pacific Theater of operations. These were urgently needed to provide extended range for fighter planes protecting B-29 raids over Japan. The packing case was designed so that it could be used as an assembly bench (from the collection of The Henry Ford).

300 units per day. By February 1, 1945, 70 fixtures and 290 dies had been designed and built and two weeks after that 60 hand made tanks were shipped direct to China from Dearborn. Only 17,000 tanks had been made by July 15, 1945, when the capture of Iwo Jima in the Pacific diminished the need for the long range fighter escort and the contract was canceled.

As an indication of Ford's efforts to expedite production on this rather small contract, there were over 32 sub-contractors involved in providing parts and producing the tank.

7

New Foundries and Smelters

Steel Making Facilities

Henry Ford, pursuing his desire to complete the vertical integration of his automobile manufacturing empire, started planning for steel making in 1920 and by 1925 the first hot steel was poured in the Rouge. Rolling mills were erected and Pressed Steel and Upset buildings followed. Ford was using 1,000,000 tons of steel a year in the production of cars and trucks and within two years they were producing half of it themselves. As a result, when defense spending intensified in late 1940, Ford had available for war production $43,000,000 worth of buildings, machinery and equipment for open hearth and steel mill operations. Because of this Ford provided a substantial portion of its own steel requirements for war contracts and was able to provide additional quantities to other manufacturers. But even with the existing Rouge facilities additional capacity, especially in specialty metals, was required as the war progressed.

During World War II Ford produced 1,777,517 net tons of pig iron, the Electric Furnace produced 127,937 net tons of steel and the Open Hearth produced 2,524,156 net tons of steel. In addition the new steel foundry for armor plate produced another 100,117 net tons of steel.

Armor Plate Foundry[1]

Ford's tank contract provided for the government to supply pre-fabricated hulls and turrets as well as engines. Unfortunately armor production, like engine production, was not able to keep up with government demands so neither the hulls and turrets nor bulk armor plate was available to Ford. But fortunately, the Rouge facilities outlined previously lent themselves to this type of production: main and jobbing foundries, rolling mill, coke ovens, blast furnaces, etc. While a new steel foundry and armor plate building were being erected by Ford to provide for the tank contract, Ford used its existing facilities to start armor plate production. The making of bulk armor plate was very labor intensive in the heat treatment and forming process. The quenching of the hot plate, to ensure its ballistic qualities, resulted in warping of the plate as it cooled, which then required straightening. This was a difficult, expensive and time consuming process requiring heavy presses which were critically scarce. Ford engineers were able to develop a new and innovative production method which, by simultaneously quenching and straightening the steel, prevented the warping of the armor plate and reduced the manufacturing time from 2 hours to a few minutes. The Ford method tightly locked the hot steel plate in presses that prevented any movement and then forced water onto the plate through multiple holes bored into presses at the rate of 700 gallons per minute. Cooling in two or three minutes, the steel plate would not warp and could then be immediately processed. This process saved so much time that Ford's cost of armor plate was reduced to a little more than three cents a pound when all other makers were charging 35 to 50 cents a pound. Even with a government ordered cutback in orders in 1944, the net cost was still less than four cents a pound. The process saved so much money for the government that it sent auditors to check Ford's books to verify the figures.

This armor was also used by Ford for jeep floors and the light armored and utility command cars. In addition, at the suggestion of Charles Lindbergh, who felt bomber pilots ought to have more protection against .50 caliber machine guns and 20mm cannons, a new, thinner armor offering more protection from explosive shells was developed and 5,400 seats were produced to protect B-24 bomber pilots. Following the cancellation of the tank contract in early 1943, Ford continued to produce armor plate to fulfill its own needs and provide surplus armor plate to others as directed by the government.

In March 1943 the Army Ordnance Department tested 1, 1½ and 2 inch rolled homogeneous armor plate from seven companies. Ford armor plate was the only armor plate successfully passing all tests.

Lieutenant General L.H. Campbell, Jr., chief of Army Ordnance, wrote in *The Industry-Ordnance Team* in 1946:

> The company converted some of its great peacetime automotive steel producing capacity from sheet steel to armor plate and, in the process, made an outstanding contribution to the science of fabricating armor plate.

Aluminum Foundry[2]

Cylinder Heads: When Ford agreed to produce the Pratt & Whitney aircraft engine in 1941, Sorensen realized they would need more aluminum than the market could supply. He immediately started work on an Aluminum Foundry and as result the foundry, 840 feet long by 300 feet wide, was completed and producing by December 1942.

This Aluminum Foundry, considered at the time one of the finest in the nation, was built in the Rouge for one specific purpose—making aluminum cylinder heads for the Pratt & Whitney R-2800 aircraft engine manufactured by Ford. A vast array of conveyors, in continuous motion, carried the cylinder head through each department and process, from raw material to finished product without once leaving the conveyor system. And through all these stages extreme tolerances had to be maintained. It employed about 4,000 workers with 40 percent being women. The factory[3] was laid out and tooled to provide the greatest number of cylinder heads at the lowest possible cost. Because the productivity of the foundry so far exceeded expectations the third shift was eliminated in November 1943. A major contribution to production and cost efficiencies was in centrifugally casting cylinder barrels as described in chapter 3. In addition to the productivity, costs were reduced about 17 percent and 553,968 cylinder heads were cast by the time the foundry was closed in June 1944.

Tank Engine: To speed production of aluminum castings for the cylinder block head and oil pan for the M4A3 tank engine, a new foundry was built in the former Lincoln plant paint shop and loading dock. By borrowing three furnaces from the Rouge, the new foundry started production in July 1942. This dovetailed with the tank assembly line already operating in the Lincoln plant and eliminated the need to purchase castings from outside suppliers.

Magnesium Smelter[4]

With the greatly increased defense production before World War II magnesium, produced only by Dow Chemical, was identified as a critical light metal and the government needed production from five more plants. As most of the magnesium alloy to be produced was destined for building the Pratt & Whitney aircraft engine, Ford agreed to construct a magnesium smelter. On January 16, 1942, with a letter of intent in hand, the first piles were driven into the ground for the foundation of the new building in the Rouge complex. Much like the airplane engine building, the frame of this building was also wrapped like a package so that construction could continue through the winter months. Plans called for a building 800 feet long by 160 feet wide with 48 furnaces. An increased production schedule required the width of the building be increased to 280 feet and the number of furnaces increased from 48 to 96. The furnaces were 19 feet high, 16 feet wide and 18 feet long. The smelter processed raw materials into magnesium alloy for use in the new magnesium foundry also under construction. On May 10, 1942, the first magnesium was produced and by June 19 three furnaces were in operation.

As most smelting required immense amounts of electrical energy not available in most places, including the Rouge, a committee of the National Academy of Science had proposed an alternative smelting method called the ferrosilicon process which allowed ingredients to be heat processed by either gas or by much reduced amounts of electricity. Theoretically it could also be put into production and start the flow of this vital alloy almost immediately. However, the ferrosilicon process was based largely on theory. One of the first steps was converting the Ford cement plant to magnesium production. Ford's facility was the first of five magnesium facilities planned by the government and as a result Ford engineers had to develop many new methods before the process could be used in the manufacture of magnesium. Dolomite limestone was reduced to a lime mixture for forming into briquettes. The briquettes were the raw material that the smelter process would turn into a magnesium alloy. Production increased month by month, reaching a peak production of 1,000,870 pounds in February 1944 just a month before the smelter was closed. By war's end nearly 9,778,525 pounds of magnesium was produced.[5] Having met the national emergency for additional magnesium production, the smelter closed in March 1944.

Magnesium Foundry[6]

After examining the new Pratt & Whitney engine at the factory in Hartford, Connecticut, Sorensen recognized the need for increased magnesium production as well as aluminum. He immediately called the Rouge and, along with the order to start building an aluminum foundry, had them also start building a magnesium foundry. The magnesium foundry was built on four floors of the north end of the iron foundry, but separate from the iron process. The sand molds for casting were prepared on the third and fourth floors and then conveyed to the second floor where molding and casting operations were done. The first floor was for core-making, baking facilities, heat treating furnaces and other miscellaneous activities. Again Ford developed improvements included a new way of welding the material as well a method of salvaging scrap that resulted in 85 percent of scrap being recycled. Research into magnesium casting resulted in a 50 percent reduction in the molten magnesium formerly required. The foundry made 26 castings for the Pratt & Whitney aircraft engine and 23 for the B-24 bomber. The foundry produced a total of 12,106,871 pounds of magnesium castings.

8

Wheeled Vehicles

Jeeps[1]

In 1937 and 1938, the American Bantam Car Corporation, makers of a compact car, loaned several of their units to the Pennsylvania National Guard for use in their summer maneuvers. Based on their favorable reaction Bantam started corresponding with the U.S. government about the use of similar vehicles for the Army. The Army had been exploring the use of small vehicles and on July 10, 1940, invited bids from Bantam, Ford and Willys Overland Motors for 70 Light Reconnaissance and Command Cars, with an 80-inch wheel base, ¼ ton, 4 × 4 vehicle with a weight not exceeding 1,275 pounds. The bid weight was way too low to produce the vehicle as specified and along with other lesser problems was quickly amended. Final specifications raised the maximum weight to 2,160 pounds and required a maximum speed of at least 55 mph on the road with fuel consumption allowing travel of 150 miles on one tank of gas. Ford declined to bid because the size of the contract would not justify the amount of developmental engineering required. Bantam, whose bid was higher than Willys', won the bid as they promised a quicker delivery date — 70 days verses Willys' 170 days. On July 25 they were awarded the design bid and a contract for the vehicle and delivered the first unit in late September 1940.

In October Ford was again solicited for a bid and, having been given plans to the Bantam vehicle by the Army, began to realize the potential. They reconsidered their decision not to bid and built two prototype vehicles as did Willys. One of the two Ford units submitted was designed and built entirely by Ford and one contracted out to the Budd Company for a body. The Budd unit was rejected by the Army in favor of the Ford design. This small vehicle became known as the Pygmy.[2]

After the 70 Bantam production units and the Ford and Willys prototypes had been tested the Army Quartermaster made numerous revisions and then split a 1,500 unit order between Bantam, Willys and Ford for 500 units each in order to have three models and three sources of supply to consider. Final specifications for these units differed slightly from the initial test units and while the vehicles from all three companies looked somewhat similar they could not be considered standardized.

This initial order was increased shortly thereafter to 1,500 units for each company and on November 9, Ford submitted a bid quoting $975 per vehicle with a $50 discount if paid for within 30 days of delivery. Changes increased the final cost to $992.59 per vehicle.

On February 5, 1941, "General Charles Bonesteel started the wheels rolling on Ford production when he drove the first speedy, bug like unit from the assembly line."[3] The first 500 units were assembled by March 19, 1941, but because of strikes at the Rouge plant and the frame supplier's factory the last of the 1,500 vehicles wasn't produced until May 7, 1941.

Additional orders rolled in —1,000 units on May 2, 1941, with 33 of these units to be diverted to the Brazilian government and 403 to the Netherlands East Indies. June 30, 1941, saw an order for another 1,150 units to be shipped to China, 144 to Great Britain and 6 sent to a Polish training camp in Canada. An additional 50 prototype 4 × 4 (all wheel steer) units were ordered on June 26, 1941, but in trials were deemed "too maneuverable, especially when the units were being used in large groups and in close formation." All of the units were built with the Ford tractor engine and were designated GP models. Early Ford jeeps had the script letter "F" stamped on the rear panel until they and Willys were ordered to drop company identification for uniformity among manufacturers.

Following the 1,500 unit order for each of the three manufacturers, Bantam was eliminated from further consideration even though they were responsible for the preliminary design. This was a blow to Bantam as, while they understood they would never be the sole source of supply, they certainly expected to share in the contracts. According to testimony in the Truman Committee hearing on national defense the decision was made because "Bantam was too small and weak (financially) to handle the order."

While the Army was completely satisfied with the Ford and Willys vehicle the Quartermaster Corps, wanting a standardized unit, decided to buy nearly 20,000 more units from Ford "because they believed the company was the most dependable source of supply and its product had the most suitable features." Using only one source would guarantee a standardized unit which would not only keep spare parts to a minimum but would also facilitate repairs and maintenance. However, it was deemed contrary to government policy to give all the business to Ford when there were other suppliers.

The answer to the all or none basis was a standardized unit that all successful bidders would produce. The Ford unit was powered by a 30HP, 119 cubic inch 9N tractor engine and the Willys with a 139 cubic inch Go-Devil engine. The Willys unit was favored because it provided slightly better performance, but made their total unit 107 pounds over the bid specification of 2,160 pounds. By reworking the body Willys was able to meet the maximum weight limit.

While the Ford design had already been approved they were asked to adopt the Willys unit with the more powerful engine. Ford offered to increase the power of the tractor engine by enlarging the bore, which would have allowed Ford to go into large-scale production immediately. However the Quartermaster Corps wanted complete interchangeability of parts. Ford acquiesced and spent $1,125,000 just to retool to produce the Willys engine with overall retooling costs approximating $4,000,000. Because of the acute shortage of outside tool and die facilities, making the project even possible for Ford was the availability of their Tool and Die Department at the Rouge.

A meeting was held with Ford, Willys and the Ordnance Department to select the best features of each design. As a result the Ford design was adopted for the following

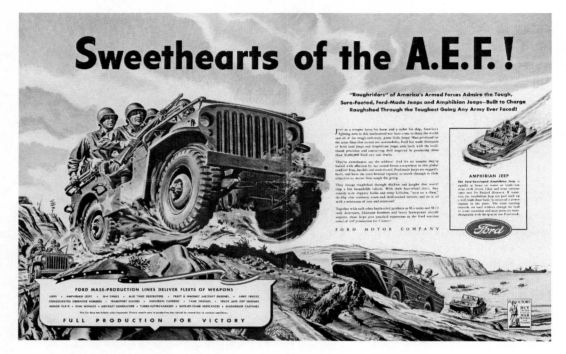

The first jeep came off the line in November 1940, making it the first wartime product made by Ford. *Saturday Evening Post*, September 4, 1943 (from the collection of The Henry Ford).

parts: complete hood which was flat and could double as a field table, cowl, dash, rear panel tire carrier and front floor reinforcements. The remainder of the body was the Willys design which consisted of the frame, sides and floor, which were practically identical to Ford's. Problems developed with the Willys frame that proved difficult for them to resolve so Ford was tasked with designing a new frame that was interchangeable with the Willys body. The axle and transfer case were provided by Spicer Manufacturing Company and the Transmission by Warner Gear Division, Borg-Warner Corporation and other outside purchases included steering gears, drive shafts, tires, frames, wheels and brakes. Overall purchases from sub-contractors accounted for about 43 percent of the material cost of the Ford built vehicles. The Ford unit had a 15 gallon fuel tank which gave it a cruising range of 300 miles at the maximum allowable speed of 65 mph.

The manufacturing processes was also improved by Ford. One notable example was in casting instead of forging the steel crankshafts. Casting the crankshaft was not only a great time-saver but reduced by 25 percent the use of steel that was lost when forgings were trimmed. The jeep was equipped with a 6 volt electrical system and when, in the fall of 1943, the Army Signal Corps wanted a 12 volt system so the jeep could be equipped with a radio, Willys suggested mounting an additional 6 volt unit which would have increased the weight of the vehicle and taken up more space. Ford engineers responded with a jeep equipped with a 12 volt system that could be converted into a kit for instal-lation. It was more complicated than it sounds as a 12 volt generator mount had to be devised with a suitable drive, the frame reinforced and an electrical suppression system installed. This was all done within a month. Numerous other engineering contributions

Ford GPW model, with the Ford built Willys engine. It was produced at six Ford assembly plants. GPW designated: G = government vehicle, P = 80" wheelbase, W = Willys engine (from the collection of The Henry Ford).

made included a direct control center gearshift, cowl-hinged hood, tubular frame windshield, protected headlights, gun-base mounting and so on.

On October 16, 1941, contracts were issued to Ford and Willys for 15,000 units each of the new standardized jeep.[4] Using the Willys designed, Ford made engine, production was scheduled for 300 units a day. By December 29, 1941, another contract was awarded for 63,146 units. May 16, 1942, saw another order for 23,158 units and on July 30, 1942, another 78,454 units were ordered and increased by 46,447 units on June 10, 1943, and increased again by 26,536 units on November 15, 1943. The final contract for 65,432 units was received May 29, 1944, but only 25,137 were built by the time the contract was canceled at the end of the war.

The Ford built units were designated as follows: GP for units built with the Ford engine under the first contract (G designated a Government vehicle, P designated an 80" wheel base reconnaissance car), GPW designated units built under the contracts for units using the Willys designed engine and GPA designated the amphibious unit known as the Seep, which is discussed below.

This new Ford GPW built in February 1941 was the first in a production run that would total 277,896, 43 percent of all jeeps built with the Willys engine. Ford produced jeeps were built in the following locations:

Ford Plant	GPW Units
Rouge, Michigan	21,492 + 4,458 GP models
Chester, Pennsylvania	18,533
Dallas, Texas	93,748
Louisville, Kentucky	93,391
Edgewater, New Jersey	1,333
Richmond, California	49,399
Grand total GP & GPW models	282,354

The jeep was virtually the only war contract on which Ford was not the lowest cost producer. Ford was geared for maximum efficiency and could produce vehicles far in excess of government orders. The Rouge alone could produce 6000 cylinder blocks a day and the Army's maximum order never exceeded 500. Compounding the situation, jeep orders were spread across five other plants which by themselves could produce 1925 units a day. The size of each order ranging from 1,500 to 78,454 units, staggered over 11 dif-

An experimental jeep nicknamed Swamp Buggy mounted a 37mm gun. This idea was later used to mount a 75mm recoilless rifle on a jeep (from the collection of The Henry Ford).

ferent time periods, and split at the government's request between six plants, precluded major investments in tooling for mass production. Production was split as a defense measure and to provide for quicker delivery time around the country and at the same time limit the burden on the nation's transportation system. The situation was further complicated for Ford by the need to shift jeep production in and out of various plants to make way for more urgent government work. None of the plants were ever able to even approach capacity production leading to much temporary tooling and inefficient use of labor. This piecemeal and staggered small unit order system prevented Ford from utilizing its mass production techniques which would have greatly reduced the per unit cost. Shipping parts to these five other locations added $5,708,000 to freight costs.

Total Ford production was 282,354[5] or 44 percent of the total 647,925 jeeps built during the war, a small fraction of the potential capacity offered by Ford, which could have built all of the jeeps produced in World War II in about four months. Willys, on the other hand, with only one plant with a daily capacity of 500 units, and the jeep representing 90 percent of its total government contracts, was able to maintain a high degree of efficiency throughout the war resulting in lower costs.

Ernie Pyle, the most famous of all World War II correspondents, summed up the jeep: "And the jeep — good Lord, I don't think we could have won the campaign without the jeep. It did everything, went everywhere, was faithful as a dog, as strong as a mule, and agile as a goat. It consistently carried twice what it was designed for, and still kept going."[6]

The jeep served the military through the Korean Conflict when it was replaced by the Ford designed and built MUTT in 1960. Officially designated the Military Utility Tactical Truck it was, although similar in appearance to the original jeep, a completely new vehicle and served until replaced by the Hummer in 1982.[7]

In March 1941, the *Detroit Free Press* went public with the Blitz Buggy nickname of these first vehicles off the line. But what was the source of the jeep name? In 1937, tractors supplied to the Army by Minneapolis Moline were called jeeps; however, most common suggestions are that it was a contraction for Ford's GP definition or the cute little Jeep character who had mystical powers and appeared in the Popeye cartoons in the late 1930s.

Amphibian Jeeps[8]

The Army had tried numerous methods, without success, of making the jeep capable of crossing deep water under its own power, in effect, a small amphibious scout car. In December 1941 the Army approached Ford and the Marmon-Herrington Company with a crude drawing which showed only the hull shape of the vehicle and fundamental ideas around which they wanted an amphibian type jeep designed. Ford's proposal was accepted as it was 400 pounds lighter. This was a brand new idea and Ford proceeded to lay out and design a vehicle and within 60 days the first of three prototype vehicles was made. Two were three passenger vehicles while the third, which was approved, could accommodate five men and equipment.

As a water-going, four-wheel drive vehicle was a new concept there were unique problems to be conquered. Among then was developing a method to seal the hull

Formation of Seeps in the Rouge River. Ford's ship, the MS *Benson Ford*, is in the background tied up to the Ford Rouge dock (from the collection of The Henry Ford).

openings without impeding the exterior mechanism. Next was to perfect an engine-cooling system that would work efficiently when hull openings were closed so the vehicle could operate in the water. Other tasks included fitting marine parts and systems into a land vehicle as well as developing inside framing to strengthen the amphibian hull while leaving room to access the engine and other mechanical parts. To insure the watertightness of the unit it was entirely seam-welded, requiring the development of a new welding structure and welding gun. To speed production they incorporated the jeep engine and as many jeep parts in the design as possible. That said however, the Seep, while somewhat similar to the jeep in size, was a completely new vehicle and three times as complicated as the jeep. It had a 15 gallon fuel tank giving in a cruising range of 250 miles with a top speed of 60 mph on land and 5.5 mph water speed in second gear.

The vehicle was first used successfully in the Sicily Campaign. It was of lesser help though in Europe due to the terrain where most rivers were in ravines which made it difficult for the vehicle to enter or emerge from the river. Many, if not most, were shipped to Russia where they seemed to work well in the vast plains of the Russian Steppe.

The Ford Photographic Department prepared a demonstration film,[9] at the request of the Quartermaster Corps, comparing the ability and agility of the Seep to the standard jeep. It shows the Seep traversing rough country as well as the jeep and in one case towing the jeep out of a depression the Seep had just crossed. Also shown are both vehicles, neck and neck, speeding 60 mph down the runway at Ford Airport.

Ford was the sole source for the amphibious jeep, nicknamed Seep, pictured at the Rouge factory. They were first used in the Sicily campaign (from the collection of The Henry Ford).

The Seep name some say was a contraction of sea jeep but there are stories from old time employees who claim to have watched some of the early test units entering the Rouge River and slowly sinking as water seeped through unsealed cracks, resulting in the nickname Seep.

Ford was the sole producer and built 12,778 of these amphibian vehicles by the time production ended in May 1943.

Armored Cars[10]

By the summer of 1941 the U.S. Army had little in the way of vehicles for mechanized combat similar to what the Germans were utilizing in Europe. Many pre-war news films in the theaters at the time show American troops in training using old cars and trucks with big TANK or ARMORED CAR signs on their side. In mid–1941 prototype armored car units were submitted to the Army by Ford for a six wheel drive unit designated T-17 and by Chevrolet for a four wheel drive unit designated T-17E1. Specifications included four main characteristics: 1. Low silhouette, 2. Quiet operation, 3. Long range 4. Good radio facilities. Also needed was 37mm gun in a closed turret and a full armored hull.

Ford received an order for 3,760 of the T-17 vehicles but the prototype weighed in at 30,000 pounds and was cumbersome and undergunned for its size and weight. This

Armored car T-17, weighing in at 30,000 pounds, proved too heavy for use as a scout type vehicle. Production stopped after Ford had built 250, just enough to use up the parts inventory (from the collection of The Henry Ford).

type of vehicle, designed to be used for scouting, was more like a tank on wheels. The Army favored tracked vehicles for units this heavy and quickly reduced the T-17 order to 250 units, just enough to use up materials Ford had on hand. Ford engineers, realizing the weight of the T-17 would cause a problem, had created a smaller, lighter version concurrently with working on the T-17, and suggested to the Army that it would be much lighter and offer more mobility. The Chevrolet T-17E1 version continued to be built for the British.

A new contract was issued for this smaller unit which was designated T-22. This new vehicle weighed in at 13,000 pounds, had less armor but offered greater mobility while retaining the 37 mm gun. The basic innovation of this vehicle was in making the armored hull serve as a chassis instead of building an armored body on a truck chassis. In the fall of 1942 all available armored cars were tested at the Aberdeen Proving Grounds, Aberdeen, Maryland, and at the Armored Forces Board, Fort Knox, Kentucky. After severe testing of all designs, Ford's vehicle with a 6 cylinder Hercules JXD engine,[11] Warner Gear Transmission and Timken Modified T-32 transfer case, was selected and designated M-8. Armor plate for these units was rolled at the Rouge plant Armor Plate Mill. The vehicle now weighed in at 16,500 pounds. The motor was cradled between two sets of power driven axles giving the rear end of the vehicle a four wheel drive. Engaging the

Armored Scout Car M-8, weighing just 16,500 pounds, replaced the heavier T-17. Ford was the sole source for this vehicle and build 8,410 units (from the collection of The Henry Ford).

front wheels created a six wheel drive vehicle. The M-8 could travel at 55 mph and traverse 60 degree grades. It was equipped with ⅜" and ¾" armor plate and a turret capable of revolving through 360 degrees. With various alterations by the military, the final version was tested by Army Ordnance at the Milford Michigan Proving Grounds. The experience gained in handling the production problems of the T-17 proved useful in insuring a smooth launch for the M-8. Ford simplified manufacturing of the vehicle by developing huge fixtures to hold pieces of the armored hull during fabrication. This fixture permitted the hull to be rotated into different positions to facilitate the welding process. An armor plate floor was designed by Ford and accepted as standard when combat experience determined the need for protection against mines. In March 1943 the first of the light armored scout cars came off the line. It had a 59 gallon fuel tank giving it a cruising range of 400 miles at a maximum allowable speed of 56 mph.

At the same time that Ford was ramping up for production of the M-8 Greyhound, a modified version, designated M-20 Utility Command Car or a troop carrier, was developed. In place of the turret on the M-8, it had a square crew compartment equipped with a .50 caliber machine gun mounted on a circular track. It had a 56 gallon fuel tank giving it a cruising range of 400 miles at a maximum allowable speed of 56 mph. Both of

Utility Command Car M-20 was a modified version of the M-8. Ford was the sole source and build 3,791 units (from the collection of The Henry Ford).

these units were intended to combine the speed and maneuverability of an automobile with the protection (and in the case of the M-8, the firepower) of a light tank.

Another variation of the M-8 was the T-69, an anti-aircraft unit with an automatic turret containing quad .50 caliber machine guns.

A major challenge was in export packaging of spare parts. Contracts called for sufficient parts to maintain the vehicles for a full year in the field. Parts were ordered and shipped in sets of 100 requiring more than 700 types of wooden boxes with a total of 1,500 boxes filling three carloads of spare parts per set.

There were 1,512 changes on the M-8 and 499 on the M-20 directed by the military, and handled by Ford engineers without interrupting the production run. Ford produced 8,410 of the M-8 armored cars 3,791 M-20 vehicles.[12] Ford was the sole source of these vehicles.

The primary producer of the M-8 was the Twin City plant, which built 6,397 units. This plant was initially selected as Minneapolis-St. Paul was located in a non-critical labor area. However skilled workers, especially welders, were lacking. An armor plate welding school was established and over 600 men trained during the course of production. The Chicago plant built 2,127 M-8 units and all 3,791 of the M-20 vehicles.

In June 1945 the government issued a contract for the production engineering of a new experimental armored car, the M-38 designed by Chevrolet, which terminated a month later with the end of the war.

In recognition of the Twin City plant's performance, it was awarded the Army Navy "E" for excellence on March 24,1945.

Military Trucks[13]

Prior to the first government specified truck contract in May 1942. Ford had produced approximately 40,000 standard 158 inch wheel base, 6 cylinder trucks, boxed for export as Lend-Lease shipments. During the war, at the request of the government, Ford developed many miscellaneous military vehicles — cargo, troop and weapon carriers. Pilot models were produced of many but most were never put into production. These exercises were not in vain, however, as they provided much design and performance information for use on the government designed trucks that were built in volume at a later date.

The new standard truck contract from the government, designated G8T, was a 6

Bomb Service Truck built for the U.S. Navy came with a winch as pictured or with a revolving crane (from the collection of The Henry Ford).

cylinder 158 inch, 1½ ton 4 × 2 truck chassis with cab, cab with platform and later with a stake body. They were basically standard Ford trucks modified to Ordnance needs at a cost of $300 per unit. Since all G8Ts with cargo bodies were to be exported Ford's Edgewater, New Jersey, branch, which was an assembly plant, was selected for several reasons. First was their location to ocean shipping and second was they had a seasoned staff readily available as they had been actively shipping Ford vehicles overseas for years. All trucks assembled at Edgewater were test run, disassembled, then packed for overseas shipment. This had been a peacetime procedure at this plant to insure that all parts of the truck were in the shipment. All crated trucks were shipped with a 56 page illustrated manual to insure that even the least qualified mechanic could successfully reassemble the trucks. Stake and tractor trucks were produced at the Dallas, Texas, plant. In the summer of 1945, due to a critical shortage of trucks on American farms a number of these trucks, already crated for overseas shipment, had to be uncrated, reassembled and 80 × 144 inch bodies installed. Ford then shipped the trucks as directed by the Department of Commerce.

Due to the critical steel needs, Ford engineers designed a stake body using 400 pounds less steel than the peacetime models saving over 28,000 pounds of steel.

This was one of the few government contracts that did not require extensive modification of a Ford plant. Unfortunately, like the jeep, these savings were offset by the fluctuations in orders. At one point 50,000 units of a 66,000 unit order were canceled four months after the order had been placed and material procurement nearly complete. Of 179,484 vehicles ordered only 77,604 were actually produced.

One of the more distinctive military trucks was the one and one-half ton GTBS cargo truck configured as a bomb service truck and built for the U.S. Navy. Ford produced 7,053 of these vehicles in two configurations — winch equipped and revolving crane.

There were a great many other varieties of Ford trucks built in smaller quantities for the military: 134", 156", Ton-and-a-half pickup trucks, ton-and-a-half low silhouette cargo trucks, etc.

Fordson and Moto-Tug Tractors[14]

Henry Ford's popular Fordson tractor that he had been building since 1917 was built in Ireland and Daghenham from 1929 until 1938. The old Fordson had a fatal tendency to occasionally roll over on the operator when plowing and Harry Ferguson had developed a hydraulic system that prevented this type of accident. In 1939, while Daghenham continued with the Fordson tractor, Henry Ford and Harry Ferguson made a handshake deal for Ferguson to produce a new 9N model Ford tractor in the Rouge and market it as a Ford Tractor — Ferguson System.[15] With food on the high priority list of wartime needs, the new tractor was urgently needed. With wartime restrictions the 9N was modified by changing the rubber wheels to steel and elimination of starters and generators and designated a 2N. Between 1940 and 1945 188,505 Ford-Ferguson tractors were produced at the Rouge.

In 1941, the Mercury Manufacturing Company of Chicago, makers of industrial tractors, approached Ferguson to purchase the tractor engine and transmission for a new industrial tractor. Finding it too expensive, Mercury ended up selling the rights to the

Moto-Tug, built for use in shipyards, docks and airports, was low enough to fit under the wings of the B-24 bomber. Powered by the Ford tractor engine, it was build by Ford-Ferguson (from the collection of The Henry Ford).

new tractor to Ford-Ferguson in November 1942. Named the Moto-Tug, it was designed for use in shipyards, docks, airports and on aircraft carriers. The Navy Department responded with a contract to Ford-Ferguson for a pilot run of 50 units, later increased to 500. Ten were diverted to Willow Run where, under daily use, it was found too light for some uses. As a result several models were produced with the main ones being the BNO-25, weighing 3,600 pounds, and the BNO-40, weighing 5,700 pounds. The Moto-Tug was lower than a standard tractor so it was more maneuverable and able to operate under airplane wings. The front and rear bumpers were made of armor plate to withstand expected hard usage.

Other government agencies wanting the vehicle had to order through the U.S. Navy and 3,025 Moto-Tugs were produced. The tools, dies and fixtures for fabricating all parts cost $25,000 and these tools along with all the parts were shipped to E.E. Shatz, a Ford tractor dealer in Columbus, Ohio, where they were assembled at the rate of ten per day. There are no records as to whether Shatz significantly increased his production capacity to produce the total 3,025 units or if another vendor was obtained.

Civilian Type Vehicles

The last civilian vehicle to be produced, a blue, Super DeLuxe Fordor Sedan, came off the Rouge assembly line on February 10, 1942, and was immediately followed by the first Ford (GPW) jeep. This last car was officially the 30,377,509th vehicle built by Ford since 1903. However, the government allowed a very limited additional production of civilian cars from parts already produced.

Passenger cars ordered by the government, with, in most cases, only minor changes, were basic civilian vehicles finish in an olive drab, lusterless, enamel paint. The only exception was 104 Tudors ordered for the Justice Department finished in black. While there were a number of small orders throughout the war, most were covered by nine contracts:

12,177	Fordor sedan for U.S. Government
138	Fordor Mercury for U.S. Navy
200	DeLuxe Station Wagons for U.S. Navy
3,500	4 × 4, ½ ton pickups for U.S. Government

In most cases the units were built at various branch plants. However all contracts required pilot models for inspection and were built at the Rouge, which gave them a chance to iron out any assembly problems. Necessary parts were then produced at the Rouge and shipped to the appropriate branch for assembly.[16]

In order to keep Ford vehicles running, massive parts replacement shipments were made to the armed forces around the world from the Rouge. All parts were packed to protect them from water corrosion in the event of submersion during invasions and landing operations. Spare ready-to-run engines were given a break-in run to insure they would operate immediately on arrival and then packed in waterproof boxes.

Despite its contributions in so many ways, Ford received orders for only 387,737 vehicles for the armed forces out of total of 2,665,196 produced by all manufacturers. Some attributed this to payback by Knudsen for being fired by Henry Ford years earlier, but apparently all other manufacturers felt they too had been shorted.[17]

9

Tracked Vehicles

Tanks and Tank Destroyers[1]

By the summer of 1941, the Army was in the process of developing a new tank to replace the M3 model medium tank, called the General Lee, whose deficiencies would be highlighted on the battlefields of North Africa in 1942. Its air-cooled radial engine kicked up such a cloud of dust that it nearly blinded the tanks following behind. Also, the tank had a very high profile and was entirely riveted, with battlefield reports reflecting very poor ballistic protection. When hit with heavy shocks, rivets were destroyed, resulting in the heads popping off inside the tank, causing casualties by spraying the crew with the equivalent of small arms fire. In addition, under combat conditions, the effective life of these engines averaged less than 100 hours.

In August 1941 government representatives approached Ford about the urgent need for manufacturing facilities in light of the impending war crisis, in particular tank production. As the tank design had not been firmed up, Ford engineers, along with other auto manufacturers were sent to the Ordnance Department's Aberdeen Proving Grounds in Maryland to offer technical production suggestions and help complete the drawings. One immediate result was that tanks would be produced with welded hulls. By October 1941 contract negotiations started, during which Ford was actively developing tools, jigs and fixtures for a tank production line in the Lincoln plant. Agreement was reached in December and a contract issued in the amount $38,365,949 for facilities and 400 M4A3 Sherman tanks. The contract continued in force until November 1945 with many additions and amendments. The contract covered medium tanks M4A3, three inch gun motor carriages M10A1, mounts for 75 and 76 mm guns, bogie brackets, tank engines, various armor castings, and reconditioning of tank engines.

The original government tank contract with Ford was for assembly, specifying that engines, armored hulls and turrets would be provided by the government. Problems developed immediately as the Navy had priority on the specified diesel engines leaving none available for the Ford contract.[2] As a result Ford was requested to develop their own engine for use in the tanks they would produce. Similarly there was insufficient availability of prefabricated hulls and turrets, which were also to be furnished by the government, nor was there available armor plate to produce them. To execute the contract Ford would not merely assemble the tanks but they would also have to design and make the

Wood pattern model of a tank. Ford engineers used this system to design assembly line procedures to build cars and adapted it to build the Sherman M4A3 tank. The turret is shown facing to the rear (from the collection of The Henry Ford).

engines as well as produce the necessary armor plate and then fabricate the hulls and turrets.

Once the designs were finalized the drawings were given to the Ford pattern makers to build a wooden tank. Wood bucks were commonly used in car design by 1940 and, with a vehicle of this size so different from the cars they had been producing, it was a logical thing to do. A rough wooden substructure was formed and then clay slabs applied. Shapers would then shape the clay to specified dimensions to form a full size tank. Each part would then be carved in wood and when all the wooden parts fit, machining experts would determine how to make the proper tooling to produce the part. The final step would be setting up the production line for ease of assembling the parts by unskilled workers.

While nearly a duplicate (except for engines) of the tanks then being built by General Motors (M4A2) and Chrysler (M4A4), Ford engineers developed several innovations, among them improved interior accessibility permitting quicker and easier servicing of the engine and substituting three castings for the 27 separate pieces formerly required for the 75mm main gun mount. Being hampered in obtaining parts for the gun mount

76833·A·6·23·42

Sherman M4A3 medium tank equipped with the Ford designed GAA V8 tank engine became the standard tank for the U.S. Army after the invasion of North Africa (from the collection of The Henry Ford).

from outside vendors, over 50 parts, including the intricate elevating mechanism, were re-sourced to Ford facilities: 7,987 of these gun mounts were produced for the Ford tank as well as tanks made by other manufacturers.

In May 1942 the first of the new Ford tanks, designated M4A3, built with hulls and turrets made of Ford armor plate and powered with the first of the new Ford GAA tank engines, described later, rolled off the line at the Highland Park plant. Initially tanks were subjected to 100 mile shakedown tests at a new track built adjacent to the Highland Park plant. With improving quality, shakedown tests were finally reduced to 25 miles. In all there were 2,060,256 square feet of floor space located in the Rouge, the Lincoln Plant and the Highland Park plant dedicated to tank production.

The M4A3 tank weighed 68,400 pounds, carried 175 gallons of gasoline and could travel 130 miles at a maximum allowable speed of 28 mph. The tanks were originally equipped with a 75mm turret mounted cannon (with 97 rounds of ammunition), carried one .50 caliber and two .30 caliber machine guns and were operated by a five man crew.

By October 1942, with a contract for the M10A1 tank destroyer, a parallel production line was set up in the Lincoln Plant — one for the M4A3 tank and the other for the

Twin assembly line at Highland Park plant to build the M4A3 tank (right line) and M10A1 tank destroyer (left line) (from the collection of The Henry Ford).

"The Toughest Fords Ever Built" gave new meaning to the Built Ford Tough slogan. *Saturday Evening Post*, June 5, 1943 (from the collection of The Henry Ford).

The M10A1 tank destroyer was identical to the tank with the exception of the superstructure (from the collection of The Henry Ford).

new tank destroyer, a vehicle using the same chassis and engine as the M4A3 tank. The main differences were the upper hull structure and a more powerful 76mm cannon. The turret for this gun was protected by three inch armor on the front, two inch armor on the sides and rear and one inch armor on the top. This unit weighed 63,000 pounds, carried a 192 gallon gas tank allowing it a range of 160 miles at a maximum allowable speed of 28 mph.

By mid–summer 1943 it was determined the numbers of M4A tanks needed could be handled by two of the three manufacturers and, as the government had more investment in the General Motors and Chrysler facilities, it would be less expensive to terminate the Ford contract. Although tank production ended in September 1943, Ford would continue building the GAA tank engine and producing armor plate for other manufacturers through the end of the war. Ford produced 1,690 M4A3 tanks and 1,038 M-10A1 tank destroyers.

Ford Tank Engines[3]

Ordinarily, it would take about three years to develop the required tank engine, but Ford engineers, having been exposed to the plans for the British Rolls-Royce airplane engine, had undertaken work in mid-1940, at a cost of $2,000,000 without the benefit of a Government contract, to develop a more powerful gasoline fueled V12 aircraft engine.

In the next 18 months they developed an engine with a supercharger rated at 1,500 horse-power. This compared to the 1,000 horsepower Rolls-Royce Merlin engine Ford was preparing to build in its Manchester, England, plant at the time. The Ford engine was cleverly designed by Ford engineer Cornelius Van Ranst.[4] Called a brilliant design, it had a cylinder block and crankcase cast in one aluminum unit resulting in lightness and dura-bility that later proved itself in battle. But, by the time the new Ford engine was devel-oped, the government needed a new tank engine more than it needed the new airplane engine, no matter how good it was. Van Ranst quickly redesigned this V12 engine into a 450HP V8 engine and after extensive testing it was accepted by the government. Early negotiations for the M-4 tank were for a unit with a nine cylinder air cooled engine, but by September 1941 the Ordnance Department began looking at Ford's V8.

Ford used its experience in casting over 8,000,000 car crankshafts and flywheels to do the same with this tank engine, instead of the generally accepted practice of forging, with corresponding savings in labor and material. Of great importance in quickly meet-ing production goals was the fact that much existing automotive machinery could be used as was or with slight modifications. At peak production 82 percent of the automotive equipment at Lincoln was used for this engine. The engines, after being cast at the Rouge, were moved to the Lincoln Plant in Detroit, Michigan, where 26,979 of these tank engine were completed during the war.

The Ford engine was not only a great deal simpler to repair than the others but it also raised the operational life of the average tank engine from 100 hours to 400 hours without the need of changing engines.[5] To simplify maintenance and combat service, the entire engine was designed as five sub-assemblies, each constituting an independent unit. This reduced the time required for training mechanics, increased the availability of tanks on the front line by drastically cutting servicing time, and minimized the variety of parts required by service depots.

It "was widely held to have been the best all-around engine produced for the M4 series tank it powered."[6] The Ford engine became the standard engine for all M4A tanks and M10A tank destroyers made by Ford and later by other manufacturers. From a prac-tical standpoint it was important that similar model tanks be sent to the same combat areas to simplify the replacement parts inventory in the local repair depots. Early M4A1 tanks were powered by the Continental R975 nine cylinder engine licensed from Wright but, due to aviation needs, production capacity was limited. General Motors M4A2 tanks were powered with two 16 cylinder diesel motors set side by side and rated at 220 HP. Most of these were used in the United States for training or sent to Russia. The Chrysler M4A4 tanks were fitted with five 6 cylinder automotive engines mated to a single drive shaft and rated at 370 HP. Most were used for training in the United States or shipped to Great Britain. Following the North African campaign, where the General Lee tank was used, the M4A3 tank became the standard for the Army.

There were six variations of this tank engine[7]:

• GAA 450HP V8 liquid cooled standard engine.

• GAF 450HP V8 liquid cooled engine similar to GAA but with slight changes adapt-ing it to a low silhouette tank.

• GAN 450HP V8 liquid cooled engine similar to GAF but with changes to accommo-date a GE 500KW generator and controls to propel a low silhouette, all electric tank.

• GAY Experimental 450HP V8 liquid cooled engine similar to GAA but altered for use with the English tank.
• GAB Experimental 700HP V12 Liquid cooled engine for use with the English tank.
• GAC Experimental 700HP V12 liquid cooled engine for use with the American tank.

The GAF model engine, listed above, was used exclusively in the M26 General Pershing heavy tank that reached the European battlefield in February 1945.

Peak production of the Ford engine reached 1,287 engines in November 1944. In addition to producing tank engines, a reconditioning line was set up that salvaged 1,648 engines during the war.

Universal Carriers[8]

The Universal Carrier, or Bren Gun Carrier as it was more commonly called, was very popular with the British Army. It was a full tracked, amphibious, lightly armored vehicle for carrying infantry, machine gun and mortar crews through small arms fire. Ford of Canada had been producing the Universal Carrier but could not meet the quantity

British and Canadian manufacturers could not produce enough Universal Carriers for the British army. Ford and U.S. Army Ordnance engineers substantially redesigned the unit and Ford built them in the Somerville, Massachusetts, plant (from the collection of The Henry Ford).

demanded by the British Army. In February 1942 Ford was requested by the U.S. Government to build and ship, under the Lend-Lease program, the Universal Carrier based on a sample vehicle and British War Office plans. In testing the sample vehicle at the Army's Aberdeen, Maryland, Proving Grounds a number of unsatisfactory characteristics were noted and the U.S. Army Ordnance Department and Ford engineers made a number of changes to improve performance, simplify its design, and expedite its manufacture. Some of the most important changes were lengthening the vehicle to change the center of gravity to prevent the vehicle from tipping over backwards on grades of 60 percent, redesigning the steering system to the type used on all United States tanks, changing from a riveted hull to a stronger, all-welded, watertight hull, replacing the 90HP Ford V8 engine with a 100HP Mercury engine specially adapted for this vehicle, and adding an extra bogie wheel on each side to increase tire life. In addition the exhaust system was rerouted to the inside of the hull with the pipes out the top which increased the ground clearance and allowed for operation in deeper water. After the redesign work was approved a contract was issued for 21,000 units, designated T-16, to be produced in the nearly idle Ford plant in Somerville, Massachusetts, which became the sole source of this vehicle. A test track was built within the plant area. The vehicle had a 23.8 gallon fuel tank which gave it a cruising range of 95 miles at a maximum allowable speed of 30 mph.

Somerville was an ideal choice as all units were to be shipped to Britain and the Ford plant was located just outside the Port of Boston. None of the machinery at the plant was suitable for work on the vehicle, making it necessary to gut the building of all Ford equipment. There were also other challenges. Somerville was an assembly plant and the new vehicle included much fabrication, especially welding. There were no welders available in the Boston area so three workers were sent to the Rouge for a welding course and then returned to Somerville to act as instructors. A 15 day, 120 hours training course in welding eventually trained 524 workers.

Much of the fabrication of parts was sublet to local vendors, rather than being done back at the Rouge, to have quicker availability and lessen the demand on the national transportation system. As Ford produced only 20 percent of the total vehicle, Ford engineers and production men maintained close contact with suppliers to insure quality and assist them in quickly resolving problems.

During July 1943, the first full month of production, it took 537 man-hours to produce each of the 579 units. In the peak production month of June 1944, it took 321 man-hours to produce each of the 1,040 units. In January 1945, major design changes were made creating a new model designated T-16 EL. The old unit was elongated, and front and back bogies were relocated along with the relocation of many other items. Ford built a total of 13,893 Universal Carriers by the time production ended in May 1945 with peak employment of 17,693 workers. Following this performance Secretary of War Robert Patterson congratulated Ford "for accomplishing more than what once seemed reasonable or possible." The Somerville plant was awarded the Army Navy "E" for excellence on July 20, 1944.

With the war in Europe winding down the contract was terminated early and Ford was negotiating a contract for 10,692 M-29 Cargo Carrier for the Somerville plant when the war ended.

Prior to the order for the Universal Carrier Ford had developed new track-links for the British built unit which were breaking when the vehicle reached high speed, causing serious injuries to crew members and necessitating repairs under fire. Ford used a special malleable cast steel it had developed for automotive production and, with a different method of heat treating, produced over 7,000,000 of these much improved track links.

10

Other Contributions

Gun Directors[1]

Even before the Japanese attack on Pearl Harbor the United States recognized a growing threat of Axis air attack from hidden bases in Mexico, Central and South America, or of planes operating off aircraft carriers along the coastlines of the United States.

Existing coastal protection in the United States consisted almost entirely of fire control systems designed for large caliber guns. Mounted in fixed positions, they were designed to fire in one dimension on naval vessels traveling at comparatively slow speeds. The existing fire control systems were hand operated plotting boards and other devices that became obsolete with the threat of fast, high-flying airplanes operating in two dimensions. New equipment had to be mobile and plotting time had to be drastically reduced.

Sperry Gyroscope Company had designed a rudimentary machine by early 1934 and by 1940 they had developed and built a sophisticated gun director. The complex mechanism of this machine quickly determined the target's position (height, distance and direction) projected and translated the target's future position into firing data for the guns and then fed the firing data to the guns. The actual firing unit for use against low flying aircraft was composed of pods containing either four 50 caliber machine guns or four 37 mm cannons.

> The lightning calculator in the gun director is machined to limits of one ten-thousandth of an inch and is capable of performing mathematical calculations in five seconds which would require five hours if tackled by 15 mathematical experts.[2]

Designated the M-7 by the Army, this gun director was extremely complicated consisting of over 11,000 parts with tolerances so close and mechanism so intricate that there were no gauges exact enough to measure some of the parts. It included 276 aluminum die castings, 721 gears, 380 nickel alloy shafts, 549 ball-bearing sets and 39 instrument dials. As a result, the few Sperry units produced had been made by highly experienced technicians who had fit each part and assembly by hand. Mass production had never been attempted by Sperry and no one was equipped to build units in the numbers that was suddenly needed by the U.S. Army.

The Ordnance Department, doubtful that the director could be mass produced at all, approached Ford on this project in August 1941 with the faint hope that, due to Ford's

The gun director was a highly sophisticated, Sperry designed and hand built anti–aircraft weapon needed in quantity. Ford designed a precision manufacturing and assembly line process to build units in quantity until development of an electronic based unit made it obsolete. The unit above is a large type for use on shipboard (from the collection of The Henry Ford).

demonstrated record of mass production at very high quality levels, they might be up to the task. The chief of U.S. Army Ordnance advised Edsel Ford that they had been selected because of the company's mass production experience, adaptability of existing equipment and the energy and resources of Ford management. While Ford's experience in building automobiles and engines was not applicable to mass production of a mechanism this fine, they accepted an order in October for 400 of these gun directors built to Sperry specifications.

Six floors of four buildings in the Highland Park complex, which conveniently were unoccupied at the time, had to be completely reconditioned with some, where directors were tested and adjusted, being temperature controlled. The next step was obtaining the labor needed for such delicate assembly.

The shortage of skilled labor dictated the development of standard type machines that could be operated by unskilled workers and, like all Ford assembly line processes, the job was broken down into many simple steps so no one person had too complicated a job. Then a school was established that would eventually train nearly 5,000 unskilled workers. As serious as training workers was the fact that no tools for this work existed. As a result one of Ford's greatest contributions was in the development, design and production of tools, dies and fixtures and processes that could make parts to the extremely fine dimensions demanded for quality mass production. The Sperry worker had to select parts from a group that was supposed to be identical until he could find one that fit the assembly he was working on. Ford's first task was to build director parts so uniform that all similar parts were interchangeable. But, even with these precision tools, some parts still had to be visually inspected. Many small parts were produced at Ford's Village and Branch operations and some critical items such as bearings were contracted to outside vendors. As in other contracts Ford personnel assisted vendors in getting production started and working with their employees until they were able to meet Ford production and quality standards.

Shortly after receiving the M-7 contract, which was a heavy unit designed for use with land batteries of anti-aircraft guns, they received a contract for a smaller M-5 director for use on naval ships.

One of the many machines developed by Ford engineers was the critical range and azimuth disc. Attempts by others to manufacturer these discs in quantity always produced many defective pieces. Ford machinery overcame the problems eliminating much waste and provided discs to Sperry. Ordnance reports indicated that when Ford assemblies were placed in gun directors produced by other manufacturers they helped increase the efficiency of the instruments, confirming the quality of Ford's mass production of these precision assemblies. Another problem was the fact that completed units shipped into extremely cold climates impaired the delicate mechanism. Ford engineers solved the problem by adding a heating system in the director which, with some suggestions by Sperry and the Army, was made standard in all future units.

The gun director, basically a defensive weapon, was made obsolete by the increasing superiority of allied air power and with the development in November 1942 of a new electronic type of detector using radar which could locate aircraft at night and in any type of weather. Production on the M-7 started in August 1942 and ended in May 1943. M-5 production started in November 1942 and also ended in May 1943. The final tally showed 802 M-7 and 400 M-5 gun directors being produced.

Interior view of a gun director showing the complexity of the unit with over 11,000 parts, many of which were of extremely fine dimensions (from the collection of The Henry Ford).

A side benefit of the contract termination was that the trained personnel in the production of the Gun Director were, due to their organizational and management experience, assigned to positions of leadership at a critical time in the development of the B-24 bomber project.

Tire Plant[3]

The Ford Tire Plant was opened in the Rouge in January 1938 as another step in Henry Ford's effort at total vertical integration. Like all other Ford manufacturing efforts the plant was designed for mass production with the use of unskilled labor. When opened it was considered to be the world's most advanced tire plant, utilizing new equipment and production methods, mostly designed by Ford engineers, to produce 16,000 tires a day. The efficiency of the plant was demonstrated by the fact that the time consumed from raw material to finished product was less than five hours while contemporary tire plants took two to four days. Not only was this the most efficient plant in the use of manpower and electricity, but also the only tire plant in the world where daily visitors could go through without fear of soiling their clothes, a tribute to Henry Ford's obsession with cleanliness in his factories.

By 1941 the plant was dedicated to producing tires and tubes for the Ford jeeps it was making, but in late 1942 the government directed Ford to dismantle and ship, under the Lend-Lease program, most of the tire making machinery to Russia, which was in need of truck tire making equipment. The United States had all the capacity needed to utilize available tire making materials and Russia was in desperate need of this type of machinery. In September 1943 the tire plant was sold to the Treasury Department and 4,500 tons of equipment and 50 machines, 60 percent of the total plant, was shipped to Russia. Later, reports indicated the machines were never used by the Russians. The balance of the equipment was shipped to other tire manufactures as directed by the Treasury Department.

In the four years of operation the plant turned out almost 8,000,000 tires for cars, trucks, and tractors and another 320,766 tires and 257,139 tubes for jeeps.

While dismantling was underway, conversion to other war production was progressing and in July 1943 work started on tail assembly items for the B-24 Liberator bomber being made at Willow Run. When the tire making machinery was fully disposed of, they made stabilizers, elevators, fins, rudders and ailerons for the tail section along with rear decks and canopies for the B-24 as well as flaps and nose and main landing gear. Of particular concern was the highly stressed landing gear assemblies, described in chapter 3, as these had to bear the entire 32½ tons of the bomber during each landing. Also produced were distributors for the Pratt & Whitney R-2800 engine and for the engines used in the B-29 bombers. A two week school was set up in the plant and more than 6,000 men and women were taught riveting and assembly. At the peak of war production about 5,200 workers were employed.

While not specifically named, they shared in the Army Navy "E" award made to the Aircraft Engine Division for their work in making molded aircraft distributors which were supplied to Allison, Dodge, Pratt & Whitney and Curtiss-Wright. They boasted: "Not one lost production day since Pearl Harbor due to strikes or work stoppages."

Ordnance Modification Depots[4]

Ford plants at Chester, Pennsylvania, and Richmond, California, in addition to building jeeps, also served at depots for overseas shipments of tanks and other vehicles. Specifically they received, stored, prepared, modified and packed over 25 different types of equipment from spare parts to motorcycles, cars, amphibious tractors, armored cars and tanks.

Two types of work comprised most of the ordnance depot's operation. The first was modifying Army vehicles and various items of equipment to match the environment of the theater of operations for which they were being readied.

A few of the tank modifications give an idea of the scope of their responsibility: installation of a flamethrower mechanism on tanks, conversion of tank recovery vehicles into prime movers, conversion of M-4 tanks into mine exploders, modification of tank turrets, installation of additional armament, radios, periscopes, compasses and appropriate small arms.

The second type of work consisted of preparing vehicles and other items for shipment overseas after modifications had been completed. This was a more complicated job than merely packaging the item. Preparations for shipment required extensive operations designed to give complete protection for items while they were in transit. Vehicles and components were cleaned with chemicals and coated or sprayed with various rust preventatives. Tanks were dehydrated and sealed by the Blue Freezing operation to prevent rust. Finally each item shipped was stenciled with an identifying number.

Chester Ordnance Depot— This Ford plant was operated as the largest Army Ordnance Depot in the United States. With a building of 700,000 square feet and sixty-two acres of land it operated as a Ford car and truck assembly plant and as a parts depot serving the surrounding area. In February 1942 the government issued a contract for the use of the Chester facility as a modification and shipping center for military vehicles and other ordnance. Most Ford operations were removed and Ford engineers designed and modified the facility for government needs and within months military vehicles began to flow in and out of the depot. In addition, the Chester branch produced 18,533 jeeps as well as operating a service to overhaul and repair tanks shipped in from various proving grounds.

An early task assigned to this depot in July 1942 was processing 600 M3 General Lee medium tanks in time to participate in the battle of El Alamein in North Africa. It required the replacing of all engines and changing all the armor plate. The entire process was accomplished in three weeks.

The Chester Ordnance Deport was awarded five Army Navy "E"s: September 1942, August 1943, May and December 1944 and June 1945. At the award of the fourth Army Navy "E," Army Lt. Gen. Lewis E. Campbell, Jr., chief of Army Ordinance, remarked that Chester was "the grandest operation in our entire military Ordnance effort."

Richmond Ordnance Depot— With 576,000 square feet of buildings and forty-eight acres of land this plant had also been a car and truck assembly plant. In July 1942 the government issued a contract for the use of the Richmond facility as a modification and shipping center for military vehicles and other ordnance. As with the Chester operation Ford engineers had the facility modified and within months vehicles began to flow in and out of the depot. In addition to the Ordnance operations the Richmond branch also produced 49,399 jeeps.

The Richmond Ordnance Depot was awarded four Army Navy "E"s: July 1943, Jan-

uary and October 1944 and May 1945. In addition, in January 1944 they were given the
Crosier Gold Medal Award for Meritorious Service.[5]

In 2004 this abandoned Ford facility was dedicated as the Rosie the Riveter / Home
Front World War II National Historical Park.

Squad Tents[6]

During the war, the government ran out of sources for producing additional canvas
protective coverings of numerous types. All available factories were at their limit, forcing the government to seek production from manufacturers that might be able to adapt
some of their machinery to meet this urgent need.

Ford Motor Company on being advised of the need suggested that the Trim Department at the Highland Park plant might be of use. The Trim Department was already
equipped with sewing machines, cutters and other material fabricating machines as well
as skilled employees with experience in producing automobile upholstery.

In January 1945 Ford was given a contract for 12,000 squad tents (later raised to
21,500) with all materials to be supplied by the government except the brass or zinc grom-
mets which would be purchased by Ford. Seventy-six thousand square feet of floor space
was cleared on the fourth floor of the Highland Park "A" building, an assembly process
laid out, and a number of new machines installed. Each tent was 32 feet 8 inches long,
16 feet wide and 12 feet high and large enough to house nine Ford size cars. Many improvements in sewing techniques and types of thread were suggested along with the improving the pattern design that reduced the yardage required for each tent from 250 yards to
231 yards. All the Ford recommendations were approved by the Quartermaster Corps.

Some difficulties were encountered as they started production. While the workers
were skilled upholsterers, fabricating canvas was an entirely new skill. Ford representatives were sent to several tent manufacturing companies to study their methods so Ford
workers could duplicate them and, where possible, improve on them. Also Ford machines
were designed to handle heavier thread than that used on the canvas tents and all had to
be changed over. Even when changed over more machines were needed to handle the volume required by the contract. One unexpected problem developed when the Ford employees heard that workers in other factories doing the same type of work were being paid on
an incentive basis and threatened to quit unless they received the same benefits. Apparently nothing came of this protest. After acceptance by Army inspectors, the tent was
folded and rolled into a protective cover then placed in a burlap bag for shipment. A
completely packed tent weighed 250 pounds.

With the war ended the contract was canceled in September 1945 with 107,803 tents
produced.[7] The man-hours required to produce each tent fell from 161.6 hours for 203
tents in March 1945 to 27.5 hours for 1,433 tents at the end of the contract.

Marine Operations

In 1919, after the court battle with the Dodge Brothers, Henry Ford acquired 100
percent of the stock of the Ford Motor Company and in succeeding years pursued his

goal of vertical integration of his automotive empire so that he could control the availability of nearly all materials required to produce a car. This included the acquisition of not only the raw materials but also the means of transporting these materials to his factories. The result was, among others, the acquiring of vast tracts of lumber in the Upper Peninsula of Michigan along with coal mines in Kentucky and West Virginia. Acquiring these sites led to the purchase of the Detroit, Toledo and Ironton Railroad to transport coal in 1920 and development of Ford Marine Operations to carry ore and lumber products to the giant Rouge factory in Dearborn, Michigan.

One of the more important raw materials was iron ore from Minnesota for Ford's steel making facilities in the Rouge plant. Because of the need for this ore and other materials the Ford maritime fleet was launched.[8] In 1923 construction began on two new 612 foot long ore carriers to carry iron ore from the Mesabi Range in Minnesota and wood products from Ford facilities in the Upper Peninsula of Michigan to the Rouge Plant. The two new ships, the M/S *Henry Ford II* and the M/S *Benson Ford,*[9] named after Henry Ford's two oldest grandsons, were launched in 1924. They were the finest ships on the Great Lakes at the time and were powered by 3,000 horsepower diesel engines when virtually all other ships on the Great Lakes were coal-fired, steam-powered vessels. The owner's quarters on the M/S *Henry Ford II* included two master staterooms and two smaller staterooms finished in mahogany and other fine wood inlays and could accommodate eight guests. The ship was outfitted with the finest trimmings such as nickel chrome plating for the railings, switch gear, steering wheel, portholes and other items. The crew's quarters were finished in English oak. The M/S *Henry Ford II* was Henry Ford's favorite ship which he used for his summer trips to the Upper Peninsula, making the scheduling by Ford's Marine Operations often dependent on Mr. Ford's plans.

In 1925 Henry Ford purchased 199 World War I surplus merchant ships that had been in storage since the end of the war. The stipulation was they were to be scrapped, so as to not hurt United States shipbuilders by flooding the market with inexpensive ships. Ford paid an average of $8,530 per ship to be scrapped and by paying a premium to the government he was able to salvage and recondition 26 of these ships for use in his emerging maritime fleet.[10] The first two reconditioned surplus ships for the fleet were the S/S *Oneida* and the S/S *Onondaga.* Ironically, both would be torpedoed during World War II ten days apart in the same location.

Also, in early 1925 the M/S *East Indian,* built in Japanese shipyards in 1918 and acquired by the United States in World War I, was purchased by Ford and fitted with the same diesel engines installed in the M/S *Henry Ford II.* Too large for the St. Lawrence River canal system, the *East Indian* was used for ocean trade, becoming the first Ford ship to circumnavigate the globe in 1926.

In the first half of 1942, German submarines sank over 300 merchant ships, most off the Atlantic coast. While the government had started compulsory chartering of private shipping in early 1941, the success of the submarines accelerated these requisitioning activities. The Ford maritime fleet stood at 31 vessels in early 1941 of which 28 would be chartered, or sold, to the U.S. Government. Ten ships had been turned over to the government by January 1942 and rest by the end of year. All charted ships were manned by their original crews and officers and all Ford seamen were enlisted in the U.S. Merchant Marine.

Ford's Merchant Fleet 1941	
M/S ships (diesel)	9
S/S ships (steam)	2
Tugs	6
Barges (World War I)	13
(The government restored them to their original deep sea configuration)	
Lighter	1

Only the M/S *Henry Ford II*, M/S *Benson Ford* and the tug *Dearborn* remained in Ford service, hauling materials for wartime production.

Five of the Ford ships were sunk by German submarines early in the war and another 5 foundered, most due to severe storms. Sunk: M/S *Lake Osweya*— torpedoed in February 1942, 250 miles east of Boston, Massachusetts (39 men lost). The ship was loaded with ammunition and a British ship in the area reported a large explosion. No wreckage was found. M/S *Green Island*— torpedoed in May 1942, south of Grand Cayman Island (no men lost).[11] S/S *Oneida*— torpedoed in July 1942, off the coast of Cuba (6 men lost) and S/S *Onondaga*— also torpedoed in July 1942, off the coast of Cuba (15 men lost). M/S *East Indian*— torpedoed in November 1942, off the coast of Cape Town, South Africa, was the last Ford ship lost (55 men lost). One grim story came out of these losses. Most seamen lost from torpedo attacks can only be presumed dead but the death of Capt. George Hodges of the S.S. *Onondaga* was confirmed when body parts and his initialed ring were found in a shark caught in the area.[12] Insurance on the Ford chartered boats escalated in 1942. For example the daily rate for the M/S *Green Island* in January 1942 was $40 a day and over $1,000 a day by May. At the time Ford was receiving charter fees of only $762 a day!

In addition to the Ford owned ships, Henry Ford's 138 foot long yacht *Truant*, purchased in 1935, was turned over, in July 1941, to the Navy for the duration of the emergency. Navy records indicate it was returned to Ford in late 1943. The ship's disposition is unknown. Also, Sorensen's private yacht, the 47 foot *Helene II*, was requisitioned by the government in 1942.

During the war, Ford had chartered other Great Lakes ships to carry Ford's raw materials and following the war all the Ford ships chartered to the government and the tug *Dearborn* were sold. Ford's fleet was enlarged in the next few years with the addition of four large steam-turbine-powered ore freighters. All Ford Motor Company marine operations ended in 1989.

Timber, Mining and Charcoal[13]

As previously discussed, by 1941 Ford owned about 250,000 acres of timberland in Michigan. The facility was originally opened as a sawmill to produce the many wood parts for his Model T automobile. A town named Kingsford followed with many Ford built homes for employees. Additional logging communities and sawmills were established in the Upper Peninsula at L'Anse, Alberta, and Pequaming. Pequaming and L'Anse also had port facilities to move wood products to the newly created Rouge plant outside of

Detroit. A power plant and a Model T body shop were established at Iron Mountain and as production got underway it became apparent that a use had to be found for the large quantities of scrap wood being generated. A wood distillation chemical plant was opened to salvage a number of chemicals from the scrap wood as well as produce charcoal, which would prove to be a major wartime product.[14]

By 1944 Iron Mountain was producing 75 percent of all the nation's charcoal, a regulated wartime product, required for essential uses. Nearly all perishable foodstuffs transported by rail or truck in the U.S. cold zones were protected against freezing by the Ford developed charcoal briquette as nearly all of these vehicles were equipped with charcoal heaters. In addition Ford charcoal was used by shipyards, foundries and metal refineries for preheating molds. The benefit of the Ford briquette was that it burned hotter, longer and at a uniform temperature versus the uneven temperature generated by raw stick charcoal.[15]

The Ford sawmills had a capacity of producing 450,000 board feet of lumber a day and during the war they produced about 152,000,000 board feet of lumber. One-third was used in making glider parts and shipping crates for Pratt & Whitney engines and miscellaneous wood products such as flooring and tables. The balance was diverted as directed by the government.

In addition, Ford operated one iron ore mine and leased another, both of which produced about 250,000 tons of iron ore a year. Ford also had an investment of over $7,000,000 in coal mines in Kentucky and West Virginia.

Precision Gauges

While Ford did not produce gauges under government contract they were critical to the mass production of wartime goods. In 1902 Charles E. Johansson (1864–1943), born in Sweden, received a patent for measuring instruments, universally known by the nickname "Jo blocks," and eventually recognized as the universal gauging standard by the Encyclopedia Britannica. These gauge blocks are rectangular pieces of fine tool steel precise up to 8 millionth of inch (.000008) and so perfect that two blocks can be wrung together (sliding one onto the other), and stick as if magnetized. They cannot be separated by pulling them apart, only by sliding one off the other. Two 100 pound weights have been supported by two of these blocks so wrung together.

While a number of smaller sets of gauges were available, the standard set of Jo blocks contained 81 blocks ranging in size from .1001 inch to 4 inches, making 120,000 measurements possible. They have been credited with making mass production possible and Ford was quoted as saying they were the backbone of their expansion. In 1915, the U.S. War Department made them the standard for civil and military firms producing war materials.

In the 1920s, Johansson's company was in financial distress and in 1923 Henry Ford hired Johansson and purchased his company. The Jo block sets were also available with jigs and fixtures that along with the blocks can define any measurement. Of more than 10,000 gauges designed and built by Ford, more than 95 percent were made available to other companies engaged in the war effort. Every manufacturer used either these Ford produced gauges or others during the war for references in the setting of their measur-

Two Johansson Gauge Blocks, held together by friction only, could support these two 100 pound weights. The measuring gauges were essential for precision mass production (from the collection of The Henry Ford).

ing instruments. As mentioned in earlier chapters precise measurements were critical to Ford and other manufacturers for their mass production efforts.

Rubber Plantation

Because of restrictions placed on crude rubber supplies by the British, whose Asian facilities controlled two-thirds of the world supply, Henry Ford and Harvey Firestone had to look for other sources. Thomas Edison was unable to come up with a substitute from local plants and as a result Henry Ford started a rubber plantation, named Fordlandia, in Brazil in 1927 while Firestone started one in Liberia. By 1941 Fordlandia contained over 3,600,000 rubber trees and with the Japanese taking control of the crude rubber supplies in Asia, Ford's plantation offered hope that they could supply some of the national war needs. In spite of the estimated $20,000,000 invested in Fordlandia, the first harvest in 1942 was a meager 750 tons. Yields in following years were not much better and the rubber plantation became one of the first failing enterprises to fall to the severe expense reductions enacted by Henry Ford II after the war.

Inventions and Patents[16]

Ford developed over 350 patents during the war relating to nearly every phase of its war production from jeeps, tanks and airplanes to metallurgy and chemicals. These patents, in addition to all the still useful patents Ford had generated since 1903, were shared with other war producers without payment of royalties. In addition Ford held many permanent, royalty-free licenses (licenses purchased outright in lieu of fees) obtained from pre-war agreements, the value of which was passed on to the government on Ford produced goods. One major item was in metallurgical patents, which were the result of Ford's pre-war development and used throughout the industry. They were patents relating to the steel alloys Ford had developed which allowed the production of steel castings having the equivalent or superior qualities of items made by the forging process, saving a great deal of time and material versus forging. A major wartime developed patent passed on to others was the method of flat-quenching armor plate in the straightening process described in Chapter 7 — again, a great time saver. Another wartime patent, shared with the British, was the high-speed method of gluing wooden glider assemblies, reducing hours of drying time to minutes.

Two other pre-war patents made available to all without fee are also worth mentioning. When building the Ford Tri-Motor airplane in the 1920s Ford developed a caster type of tail wheel (patent #1,642,699) still used in World War II. Of more importance was the radio beacon (patent #1,937,870), allowing planes to fly from point to point in all sorts of inclement weather and was the basis of all blind flying. The entire aviation radio range system was built around this development. It should also be noted that all Ford patents related to airplane manufacturing from 1925 to 1932 were made available to all interested parties without payment of royalties.

Miscellaneous

Other war production items of lesser importance were:

1) One hundred fifty pieces of 105mm gun barrels for $171,850. In January 1942 Ford was asked by the Ordnance Department to set up and operate a centrifugal casting plant to cast, rough-machine and heat treat 25,000 gun barrels of assorted sizes. In March they were authorized to develop and manufacture a machine capable of simultaneously casting six tubes for the 105mm howitzer. By July the extreme shortage of

electric-furnace steel of aircraft alloy jeopardized the gun barrel project and in August it was canceled.

2) Five hundred pieces of 75mm projectiles for $13,838. Ford was asked to produce projectiles by the centrifugal casting method but lacked the capacity to produce them in quantity. They did, however, develop the method for the government and then supplied engineering data and blueprints to another supplier and provided engineering assistance to get that supplier started in production.

3) Produced 1,648 Model GAY tank engines, a variation of the standard Ford GAA tank engine, for the British. In addition 17,670 V8 engines and 17,639 axles were converted for British use.

4) Produced over twelve million dollars worth of coke, charcoal, oil, tar, and ethel acetate and other chemicals and by-products from the Iron Mountain and Rouge plants.

11

Ford Facilities

New war contracts were assigned to Ford plants depending on their current contracts and their abilities to handle the new production task. The increase of orders for the Pratt & Whitney engine required enlarged plant facilities and employees. Willow Run, on the other hand, had sufficient facilities but faced extreme problems in staffing. An alternate solution to both problems was found in outsourcing of parts assemblies to Ford's other plants and village industries that had available facilities and experienced factory employees.

In addition to Ford's four major plants — the Rouge complex, Highland Park, the Lincoln plant and Willow Run — there were 11 branch plants, 3 non-assembly plants and 18 village industries active in war production as well as non-traditional sources such as timberlands, sawmills, iron mines, coal mines and other smaller operations. An additional 15 branch plants were leased or sold to the government for other war related production: Leased — Buffalo, New York; Denver, Colorado; Houston, Texas; Long Beach, California; New Orleans, Louisiana; and Omaha, Nebraska. Sold — Alexandria, Virginia; Atlanta, Georgia; Charlotte, North Carolina; Cleveland, Ohio; Des Moines, Iowa; Milwaukee, Wisconsin; Norfolk, Virginia (repurchased after the war); Seattle, Washington; and St. Louis, Missouri. Ford's remaining manufacturing empire provided a total of 23,341,000 square feet of factory space for war production.

Ford also maintained their 32 sales and service offices throughout the country to assist dealers in meeting the increasing demands of the civilian population in maintaining their aging vehicles. In addition, they aided the many dealers who were sub-contractors for overhauling local vehicles for the Army and Navy.

Following are the Ford Motor Company facilities dedicated to war production and the products they produced. Items listed are not, in all cases, all inclusive of what each plant produced during the war as contracts shifted from time to time as needs changed.

Main Plants

Rouge Manufacturing Facilities: Had in place for use in varied defense production: open hearth and blast furnaces, coke ovens, strip and rolling mills, iron foundry, steel mill, pressed steel plant, tool and die building, assembly line and ore docks.

Rouge Aircraft Engine Plant: Built 57,851 Pratt & Whitney engines and was awarded the Army Navy "E" for Excellence.

Rouge Ferguson: Built 102,183 Ford Tractors with Ferguson System.

Rouge Tire Plant: Built 320,766 Jeep tires and tubes, B-24 bomber: entire tail assemblies, canopies, nose and main landing gear and flaps. Also built airplane distributors for B-24 and B-29 bombers.

Rouge Other: Built 4,458 GP model and 21,492 GPW model jeeps, 12,778 amphibious jeeps, 553,868 Pratt & Whitney cylinder heads, 52,281 aircraft engine superchargers, 26,979 V8 tank engine castings, 2,411 pulse jet engines, 17,008 jettison fuel tanks. Also established an aluminum foundry, magnesium smelter plant and foundry and new armor plate plant that produced over 100,000 tons of steel as well as fabricating tank hulls, gun mounts and turrets. Also built military trucks of various configurations and passenger car parts for the military.

Dearborn Airport and Airframe Building: Located on the old Ford Airport built in 1925. This was the old airplane building where Ford Tri-Motor airplanes were built from 1926 to 1931.[1] With the recession and rapid decline in aircraft production the plant was closed and the airport turned into the Dearborn Test Track. With the advent of World War II the airport was reopened to handle much of the air traffic caused by war work in the area. The airplane building was used to train workers and build parts for the Willow Run plant and later build and flight test the prototype GC-4A and GC-13A gliders.

Highland Park: Built 1,690 M4A3 Sherman Tanks, 1,038 M-10 Tank Destroyers, Pratt & Whitney engine parts, 1,202 gun directors and 9,498 squad tents.

Lincoln Plant: Built tank parts and 26,979 tank engines, and B-24 parts. The 1250HP Pratt and Whitney engines for the B-24 bomber were received from Pratt & Whitney for engine dress up and then shipped to Willow Run.

Willow Run: Built 8,685 B-24 Liberator bombers. Also filled most spare parts orders from around the world. Awarded the Army Navy "E" for Excellence.

Branch Plants

Chester, New Jersey: Ordnance Depot Modification and Processing Center for tanks and other vehicles for overseas shipment and built 18,533 jeeps. Awarded the Army Navy "E" for Excellence 5 times.

Chicago, Illinois: Built 2,126 M-8 Armored Cars and 3,791 M-20 Armored Cars

Dallas, Texas: Built 93,391 jeeps, 5,899 G8T Cargo Trucks and 314 G8TA Cargo Trucks.

Edgewater, New Jersey: Built 71,350 G8T Cargo Trucks, 5,951 GTB Cargo Trucks, 4,292 GTBS/B/C Bomb Service Trucks, 776 GTBA Service Trucks and 1,333 jeeps. Also processed trucks for overseas shipment.

Green Island, New York: Produced parts for Pratt & Whitney engine, military vehicles, P-1 aircraft generator and gun director.

Hamilton, Ohio: Produced parts for Pratt & Whitney engine and for B-24 bomber as well as dies and fixtures for many applications.

Kansas City, Missouri: Built parts for the Pratt & Whitney aircraft engine: cylinder heads, cylinder barrels and cylinder muffs.

Louisville, Kentucky: Built 93,391 jeeps, 1,442 GTBA Cargo Trucks and 2,750 GTBC Bomb Service Trucks.

Memphis, Tennessee: Built parts for the Pratt & Whitney aircraft engine: rocker arms, piston rods, rough prop shafts, counterweights, piston pins and gear parts.

Richmond, California: Ordnance Depot Modification and Processing Center processed tanks and other vehicles for overseas shipment. Also built 49,399 jeeps. Awarded the Army Navy "E" for Excellence 3 times.

St. Paul, Minnesota: Built 250 T-17 Armored Cars, 6,397 M-8 Armored Cars and Pratt & Whitney aircraft engine pistons, cam supports, pump assembly, gears and tractor bearings. Awarded the Army Navy "E" for Excellence.

Somerville, Massachusetts: Built 13,893 Universal Carriers for Britain. Awarded the Army Navy "E" for Excellence.

Upper Peninsula

Iron Mountain, Michigan (1921–1952): Built 4,202 CG-4A model and 87 CG-13A model gliders. Fabricated wooden parts for gliders and also provided wood products such as shipping cases for gliders and Pratt & Whitney aircraft engines, hardwood flooring, tables and other small wood items for other plants. In addition to building gliders, the Iron Mountain complex contained a chemical and wood distillation plant, opened in 1924, that provided numerous chemical products and charcoal. Ford Airport, opened in 1931, was located nearby. They were awarded the Army Navy "E" for Excellence three times.

Sawmills and timberlands located along Lake Superior that serviced Iron Mountain[2]:

L'Anse (1922–1954): timberlands, sawmill and dock facilities.
Pequaming (1923–1942): timberlands, sawmill and dock facilities.
Alberta (1936–1954): timberlands, sawmill.
Big Bay (1943–1951): sawmill.

Village Industries

In the early 1920s Henry Ford started to decentralize a small part of his mighty mechanized empire by locating small plants in rural areas surrounding Detroit and in neighboring counties. They were all located alongside waterways to obtain power by using water wheels and as a result they are commonly referred to as the hydro plants. They were small operations designed to allow the farmer to tend his crops and animals when necessary and work in the Ford plants in the offseason. Peak peacetime employment ranged from 19 workers at the Saline and Brooklyn plants to 1,200 workers at the Flat Rock plant although Ypsilanti would be the largest of these plants during the war. There were 21 of the village industries operating during the war with all but three[3] involved in war production. In their efforts to reduce their enormous post-war losses Ford closed all but two of the plants by the mid–1950s. Northville, Michigan, the first to be opened in 1920, was the last of the village industries to close in 1989. Dates of plant operations are in parentheses.

Brooklyn, Michigan (1930–1967): Produced 49 types of bushings and bearings for the B-24 bomber as well as machining a number of Pratt & Whitney engine and glider parts. Also made horn rings for Government trucks.

Clarkston, Michigan (1942–1947): Machined gears for Gun Director and produced parts for the B-24 bomber as well as drill bushings and die buttons. Nearby schoolhouse was remodeled for sewing jobs: safety straps for jeeps, and web straps, covers and seat cushions for military trucks.

Dundee, Michigan (1936–1954): Produced parts for Pratt & Whitney engines, tanks, vehicles and gun directors and handled all bronze coatings for all parts made there.

Flat Rock, Michigan (1923–1950): Produced lamps for tanks, trucks, armored cards, universal carrier and electrical junction boxes for B-24 bombers.

Hayden Mills, Michigan (1935–1948): (now known as Tecumseh) Machined 82 different parts for B-24 bomber.

Manchester, Michigan (1941–1957): Built 5,360 rate-of-climb indicators, ammeter gages and small assemblies for B-24 bomber.

Milan, Michigan (1938–1947): Produced ignition coils and cam plates for Pratt & Whitney engines and truck, tank and amphibian jeep parts.

Milford, Michigan (1938–1948): Produced 18 parts for Pratt & Whitney engine, 170

This **Dundee, Michigan, plant was typical of the small Ford village industries, all located by river ways to take advantage of hydropower. They proved instrumental in spreading the workforce and producing small parts for the large war machines (from the collection of The Henry Ford).**

different bushings and spacers for B-24 bomber, glider parts and parts for trucks and engines

Livonia, Michigan (Newburgh Plant) (1935–1948): Produced nearly all drills used in Ford's war effort and machined 13 parts for Pratt & Whitney engine.

Northville (City), Michigan (1920–1989): Produced valve guide bushings and machined 67 parts for Pratt & Whitney engine and rate of climb indicator.

Northville, Michigan (Waterford Plant) (1925–1954): Produced precision gages.

Plymouth, Michigan (Phoenix Plant) (1922–1948): Produced voltage regulators and generator cutouts for trucks and armored vehicles and wired junction boxes made at Flat Rock for B-24 bombers.

Plymouth, Michigan (Wilcox Plant) (1923–1948): Produced taps and machined parts for Pratt & Whitney engines.

Saline, Michigan (1938–1947): Produced soybean oil for paints and plastics and machined parts for Pratt & Whitney engines.

Sharon Mills, Michigan (1939–1947): Produced light switches and starter switches for trucks and assisted Ypsilanti plant in winding generator armatures.

Westland, Michigan (Nankin Mills Plant) (1921–1947): Produced special tool and die work and all engraving work and defense experimental work.

Willow Run, Michigan (Hydro) (1941–1944): Machined 56 parts for B-24 bombers.

Ypsilanti, Michigan (1932–1947): Built 87,390 generators for trucks, tanks, armored cars, Pratt & Whitney aircraft engine, gun director and P-1 aircraft generators for various aircraft. Awarded Army Navy "E" for Excellence three times.

Other: In addition to the above established plants, Ford had a $7,000,000 investment in coal mines and also operated iron ore mines which produced 250,000 tons of iron ore. Had 250,000 acres of timber lands and sawmills in Michigan's Upper Peninsula. They also had timber tract in Kentucky and coal mines in Kentucky and West Virginia. During the war 152,000,000 board feet of lumber was produced. Over 50,000,000 feet was used at Iron Mountain for glider parts and crates and other wooden products used by Ford plants. The balance was diverted to outside consumers at the direction of the government.

At war's end plants had to be reconverted for civilian production. In the case of Ford's main plants, reconversion of the Rouge cost $14,000,000 while costs for Highland Park and Lincoln were substantial but not recorded. The cost in reconverting the branch plants was $12,332,000 while the cost to reconvert the village industry plants was just over $1,000,000 as all war contracts they received were able to be handled with relatively modest changes to their existing layouts.

12

Training and Service Schools

In view of Ford's unrelenting efforts to reduce redundancy in mass production it is amazing to find "no concerted effort was ever made to coordinate educational activities at all plants in the Ford Motor Company system." As a result many of these schools appear to overlap and the numbers of graduate civilian and military students and student hours are scattered throughout Ford records. Training courses were conducted for as few as the one man trained for the Norwegian Air Force to the thousands of workers and Army and Navy personnel trained to produce, use or maintain the various weapons built by Ford as well as the Navy School, complete with barracks and hammocks for the sailors, established at the Rouge for training naval personnel in numerous skilled-trades jobs. In one record training might be called the Airplane School and in another the B-24 School, which may or may not be the same as the Aircraft School. Some records show only total numbers while others itemize the courses offered and the numbers of workers and military attendees. Most of the schools have been sorted out from Ford records for this chapter, but it is not a precise accounting — it is more an overview and summary of the many schools. You will find additional specialized schools described in other chapters.

The Ford training programs developed in World War II were built on the foundation of the very successful Henry Ford Trade School and the Ford Apprentice School established many years before. Prior to the start of hiring thousands of unskilled workers to produce more and more items that were outside their normal production systems, Ford's experience with mass production told them massive new training programs would be needed. Compounding the problem was the lack of professional instructors in total and specifically for many specialized skills that would be needed. The worker training programs were most active in the early years of the war when the bulk of the unskilled, and sometimes uneducated, men and women were being hired. Along with the need to train workers in assembling the parts and servicing the machines it was also vital to train supervisory personnel and the military personnel who would have to service, maintain and repair the many war machines they would be called upon to use.

Henry Ford Trade School and Ford Apprentice School

As the war in Europe crept close to the shores of the United States in the late 1930s, Ford had at its disposal the nucleus of two systems for training workers. First was the

Henry Ford Trade School for impoverished and orphaned boys, many the sons of World War I veterans, and second was the Ford Apprentice Trade School for training men as journeymen in the skilled trades. These were two of the most comprehensive training programs for developing skilled workers of any manufacturing company in the United States and many graduates of these schools would be instrumental in Ford's being able to meet the demands placed on it by the many and varied war production contracts it was awarded.

Ford's education and training systems trace their beginnings to the Valley Farm project started by Henry Ford in 1911 to improve the life of about a dozen boys and was oriented to agricultural pursuits. It switched to educating boys in the mechanical arts when it was transferred to the Highland Park plant in 1916. It evolved into the Henry Ford Trade School designed to train youths in tool and die work and in 1930 was moved to the new Rouge plant. By the time it closed in 1951 it had graduated over 8,000 boys. While not required to do so, many graduates accepted the opportunity to work at Ford and thus were available to help Ford in its wartime efforts.

The Ford Apprentice School was started informally in 1915 with a small group of men hiring an instructor, on their own, to teach them mathematics after hours. Henry Ford heard about it and was so impressed that he hired the instructor and furnished a classroom to continue the work with a first class of 15 men. Its value was quickly recognized and the school grew to the point that it became a permanent training program for employees to qualify as journeymen in the various skilled trades.

In 1941, the apprentice school operated out of the tool and die and the "B" buildings, both in the Rouge. With the advent of the war, branches were started in Highland Park and Willow Run in 1942. Under the standard apprentice School program a total of 2,022 students completed the requirements during the war, amassing over 16,000,000 hours. Other specialized training courses were conducted: 500 foremen were trained under one program, and other programs generated 1,125,000 training hours by non-apprentices taking individual courses such as the one in which 275 women were given 29,000 hours of training in machine operations and 5,300 more were trained as riveters on the B-24 bomber. Additionally, in 1942 when courses were set up at Highland Park, workers were trained on the extreme complexities of the gun director and, when Pratt & Whitney engine and B-24 bomber assemblies and parts were transferred to Highland Park, another 10,000 workers were given 3,000,000 hours of training. Another was the program for training workers for the fine precision needed in building the turbo supercharger.

Many of the early graduates of both of these schools were the backbone of Ford's Tool and Die Department, and had been privileged to learn their trade at the largest such facility in the world at that time. With an investment of over $14,000,000 (over $196,000,000 in 2006 dollars) in buildings, machinery, tools and equipment, it contained the finest precision machine tools available. These tool and die men used their experience and the resources of the department to make precision machinery and tools that were either new designs or just unavailable due to extremely high demands placed on all tool and die facilities during the war. With all the new production challenges Ford faced, many critical production problems were quickly resolved by these highly skilled tradesmen.

Other Training

Aside from the basic courses offered in the trade schools, there were vast new training needs generated by new products Ford was to build. Schools were needed for assembly, maintenance and repair for airplanes and airplane engines, tanks, armored cars, anti-aircraft gun directors and everything else Ford made for the government. Industrial arts teachers, tradesmen and almost anyone with a technical leaning were recruited as instructors. In establishing all of these training courses, instructors had to develop their own syllabuses as well as training materials for the students. Most of these early instruction and training aids were eventually formalized and produced as manuals for instructors and students who came on board at later dates. Along with the vast expansion of training programs for the unskilled workers, foremen were needed to insure organized and systematic production. This created a need for a formal foreman training program to fill immediate as well as ongoing replacement needs.

Some courses were highly specialized, as in the case of a Norwegian sergeant given a 26 hour course to enable him to maintain Royal Norwegian airplanes based in England. Or the 30 American and Canadian servicemen trained in operating the amphibian jeep on land and water so they in turn could train others. In addition, many groups outside Ford utilized the training facilities or materials.

Training schools were urgently required for military personnel as well. While workers needed to learn the necessary assembly skills to produce war material, the military personnel needed to learn how to use, maintain and repair the engines, tanks and airplanes the workers were producing. Although there are no final or total statistics, one can imagine the numbers of schools and hours of training needed for over 145,000 workers, their replacement and all the military personnel to acquire the needed skills.

JEEP SCHOOL

The first of the Ford war-driven schools, operated from December 1940 to January 1942, were to train Army personnel in the handling and maintenance of jeeps. One thousand one hundred seventy enlisted personnel were given two weeks of classroom and two weeks of laboratory training. Noon meals were served to the trainees at cost, but all other expenses, including transportation to and from their quarters at Fort Wayne (west side of Detroit) were absorbed by Ford. In later contracts, training expenses would be spelled out.

SEEP SCHOOL

The use of this new type of amphibian vehicle necessitated special training for personnel and Ford established a school at the Rouge plant for 30 American and Canadian servicemen. They observed the manufacturing and servicing problems with the vehicle and learned to operate the Seep on land, in the water and in various terrain and weather conditions. The men were then sent to various theaters of war to train additional personnel.

NAVY SERVICE SCHOOL

The most formal and outstanding contribution in the training of military personnel by Ford Motor Company, or any other company, was that of the elaborate Navy Service School established in late 1940.

In December 1940 ground was broken for the Dearborn Naval Training School in the Rouge on land Ford leased to the Navy for $1. Forty-five days later commissioning ceremonies were held, turning the school over to the Navy. At this time Rear Admiral Chester Nimitz's comments included:

> Cognizant of our needs, Mr. Henry Ford offered the Secretary of the Navy the facilities of the renowned Henry Ford Trade School to help meet the Fleet's demand for trained men. To meet these needs he has made available, at no expense to the government, administration buildings, barracks and mess halls fully equipped to accommodate 1,200 or more enlisted men of the Navy. This school is a most important practical contribution to national defense. ... In addition Mr. Ford has agreed to supply the instructors — another important contribution as it relieves the Navy of drawing on its already insufficient number of trained officers and men for this purpose.

Located within the Rouge complex the facility was designed to house 2,000 naval personnel. Ford furnished the original buildings consisting of eight 250 man barracks where men slept in hammocks, mess hall and galley, recreation building, steam and power generating plant, administration building, athletic field and theater and later a fire engine.

Naval barracks built at the Rouge to house sailors attending the Navy Service Schools. Henry Ford built the entire complex and turned it over to the Navy for $1.00 a year. Ford also provided instructors, relieving a critical training problem for the Navy (from the collection of The Henry Ford).

Ford also furnished 91 instructors, initially from the Henry Ford Trade School, 14 clerks and machine tools and equipment necessary for training. Classrooms, library, and laboratory space were provided in the Ford Apprentice School, located in the Aircraft Building and also in the "B" Building where the Henry Ford Trade School was housed. A model sub-chaser engine room, housed in a realistic hull, was also located in the "B" Building.

The ship's company comprised 246 naval officers, enlisted men and WAVES (women sailors came on board in January 1944). Enrollees were selected from the naval training stations around the country where, after completing basic training, they were given a month of preliminary mechanical training. Following this training men were selected for a definite trade to study when they got to the Rouge Plant, where they usually spent 90 days in intensive training.

The men were taught to be electrician's mates, carpenters, storekeepers, pattern makers, machinist's mates, metalsmiths, shipfitters, boilermakers, molders, aviation machinist's mates and motor machinist's mates. Later on, diesel engine courses were taught even though Ford had never produced diesel engines. While there was a four month specialized training program for Navy machinist's mates most other courses were shorter and men would be assigned to other Navy facilities for advanced training while still others, requiring lesser training, would graduate with a rating in various specialties and be given a permanent assignment.

In late 1944 the school was converted into a radar training station and the Navy took over all instruction responsibility. During the period the Navy Service School was operated by Ford 22,303 men graduated after receiving nearly 8,500,000 hours of training.

WILLOW RUN

With the start of airplane manufacturing, very basic training was mandatory. This was an area of production completely unfamiliar to Ford and with the hiring of thousands of unskilled laborers (the local skilled labor pool was nearly at full employment) to build a very complicated machine, training was a concern necessitating immediate action. Early on, Ford knew they would face immense problems as many of the new employees came predominantly from the middle and north central states and most with little or no manufacturing experience. Initially, workers were trained at the Rouge Plant but, as soon as practical, training was moved to Willow Run. Courses were conducted on all phases of airplane manufacturing from assembly, welding and riveting and inspection to blueprint reading, flight mechanics, pilots, copilots, Army and Navy specifications and supervision. Early on problems developed stemming from basic courses covering far too much for the assembly line worker. They confused the unskilled trainee and took too much time teaching him more than he needed to know. As a result more specialized courses were developed that resulted in better work and more satisfied workers.

In July 1942 a building for the Apprentice School was completed at Willow Run, connected to the main plant by an overhead ramp. A year later it was staffed with 165 teachers with 3,800 employees being trained. All classes were conducted in three 1 hour periods for the convenience of the employees, many of whom were attending on their own time. Overall there were 26 subjects taught with the greatest number of workers, 21,977, being trained as welders. By the end of the war an estimated 120,000 civilians were trained in as little as a day or as long as several weeks. An additional 60,000 Army and Navy personnel were also trained.

AIRCRAFT (ENGINE) SCHOOL

Setting up training programs for the manufacture and assembly of the highly sophisticated Pratt & Whitney R-2800 engine was critical as this was a unique challenge to Ford's attitude that anything could be mass produced. Everybody connected with the program had to be trained and the first school was established in July 1941 to train workers in four categories.

The first group was trained for the actual manufacturing operation that included the need for precision, differentiating among various metals and the use of the general and precision tools. The second group was trained for assembly operations by way of classroom instruction and actual practice on test panels. The third group, destined to test and inspect the parts as well as the entire engine, required a thorough understanding of scientific recording instruments including the use of the slide rule, which was in constant use. The final group was an apprentice system to train workers in aircraft engine mechanics according to the type of work that would be assigned. In addition special courses were established for supervisors and foremen. Courses were also set up to train B-24 bomber inspectors and machinists for their assignments. Also, assembly workers, machinists, welders, inspectors and supervisors were trained in the production of the turbo-supercharger, which required a very high degree of precision.

At the same time, an Aircraft Engine Apprentice School was established to train workers and Army and Navy personnel in the repair and maintenance of the Pratt & Whitney R-2800 engine. Training was also offered to train workers for the B-24 Liberator contract. In addition to assembly type instruction, courses were offered in mechanical drawing, mathematics, engine mechanics, metallurgy and electrical systems. A B-24 crew course trained 21,283 men on the Pratt & Whitney R-1830 engine. When the school closed in 1945 an additional 5,270 civilian and Army Air Force students had been trained on the Pratt & Whitney R-2800 engine.

AIRPLANE SCHOOL

Originally established in the Airframe Building at the Ford Airport in 1941, it was later moved to Willow Run. By war's end 52,284 students had completed training is such fields as Army-Navy specification, flight mechanics, hydraulics, lofting, radio, rigging, riveting and welding. Instructors also served as an emergency pool of supervisory employees.

By June 1942 the Airplane School was also responsible for the training of Army Air Force mechanics for front line maintenance done in the field. Following basic training, qualified men were selected for basic mechanics school and on completion were sent to an airplane factory school for advanced training. They learned everything from patching bullet holes and changing engines to replacing damaged or missing landing gear. By late 1942 a twenty-eight day course had been developed covering airplane structure, hydraulics, electrical, landing gear, propeller, engine, supercharger and flight inspection and maintenance. It was an amazing amount of information to be learned so quickly. By late summer 1943 there were 1,600 students attending courses in two shifts with 240 mechanics graduating every four days. Five thousand military personnel completed a 5 week training course on Pratt & Whitney engines.

This school, with the Ford instructors, was later transferred to the 3509th Army Air Force Base located in five hangers on the eastern edge of the airport at the site of an abandoned airfield. Here the students had 65 R-1830 engines and 12 B-24 bombers to learn on. When the school closed in June 1945 a total of 21,283 mechanics had graduated.[1]

Airplane Flight School

Separate from the Airplane and Aircraft Schools and production, the Flight School was established to train men as inspectors, servicemen and as members of flight crews. They formed the Flight Test Department whose task was to inspect, repair and test fly the ships before they were turned over to the government. Included in the department were 10 senior pilots, each with over 10,000 hours of flight time. Students were given a 12 week course divided between classroom and practical work on the bombers and had to achieve a 90 percent average in order to pass and qualify as staff for the Flight Test Department.

Tank and Tank Engine School

A tank engine school was organized at the Lincoln Plant in September 1942 and continued until June 1945. It was designed to train Army and civilian personnel in the repair and maintenance of the Ford built M-4A3 tank, M-10A-1 tank destroyer and the Ford GAA tank engine. Some were given further training on the M-8 and M-20 armored cars. Fifteen thousand square feet of space was assigned for the school alongside the tank engine assembly line in the Lincoln Plant. Each student had to disassemble and re-assemble an engine and as a final test had to install it in a tank and then drive it over the test track. Thirty instructors were rotated through Army camps to get hands-on experience in maintaining the tanks under diverse training conditions. As part of the government contract many of the civilian personnel trained served as Ford service representatives and visited 53 Army camps in the United States and overseas locations assisting the Army in the operation, maintenance and repair of tanks, armored cars and other Ford built vehicles. During the school's existence 1,566 Army personnel and over 5,542 civilian tank and tank engine service men were trained.

Gun Directors

Another school was required by accepting the contract for the production of the gun director. Ford had no experience in building an item of this precision and complexity but set it up on a modified assembly line. Tolerances were so close that individual inspections still had to be made on many parts. Trained under the Apprentice School system, few records on the school have been found but it did train nearly 5,000 unskilled workers.

Civilian Vehicle Service

With the end of new car and truck production for the civilian market, maintaining service for existing cars became of extreme importance for the Ford Motor Company and its dealers. Service was needed not only for civilian vehicles but also those vehicles operated by the numerous small military camps and posts throughout the United States. Ford's 32 branches remained staffed with service personnel to assist dealers in normal activities as well as aiding the many dealers who were sub-contractors for overhauling local vehicles for the Army and Navy. In addition local branch service personnel conducted 2,685 days of training at 30 different Army camps across the United States.

MANUALS

A little recognized responsibility was the group tasked with the job of compiling, printing, and then revising the endless stream of operating and maintenance manuals and parts catalogs and then distributing them, literally, throughout the world. All government contracts required some combination of technical and instruction manuals, parts manuals and special tools manuals. Manuals were needed for 16 types of vehicles, B-24 bomber, gliders, Pratt & Whitney aircraft engine, M4A3 tanks gun directors and squad tents among others. Total cost for Ordnance manuals alone was $309,951.

13

Foreign Operations

Following its incorporation in 1903, Ford established its first foreign outlet when Ford of Canada was incorporated in 1904. The first overseas sales were made in Britain but, while they were made shortly after Ford was organized, it wasn't until 1908 that a Ford sales outlet was established in London, followed by a manufacturing plant at Trafford Park near Manchester in 1911. With the growth of Ford over the years a new plant, duplicating Ford's Rouge plant on a smaller scale, was opened in Dagenham, outside of London, in 1931.

Records of wartime activities in Ford's foreign operations, similar to those compiled by Charles LaCroix for Ford (U.S.), are non-existent. In fact there are few if any war production records available for any of Ford's foreign operations with the exception of the booklet *Ford at War* by Hilary St. George Saunders. While by no means as detailed as LaCroix's effort, it does detail the important phases of Ford's war efforts in Britain and nicely describes the working and living conditions of Ford workers in wartime, a subject LaCroix never touched on.

British Empire

FORD OF BRITAIN

Ironically, following the first bombing of London by the German Luftwaffe in 1939, the first war-related reactions by Ford of Britain were based on "urgent instructions from the authorities to make arrangements to immobilize the factory should the enemy invade our shores. It seemed an odd way to begin a war."[1] One direct result of the impending war hearkened back to Britain's experience in World War I when the food supply was seriously jeopardized by German submarine actions. Following that war much of the farming created by wartime needs in Britain became unprofitable and more and more farms were abandoned and turned into a more profitable use as pasture lands. In 1939, at Ford's suggestion, the government agreed to purchase three thousand Fordson tractors that Ford would stockpile at Ford dealers around Britain to be released to farmers in case of war. Ford agreed to repurchase the tractors if not needed. As an afterthought the government paid the farmers £2 an acre to encourage them to plow up their pastureland, something they had been loath to do, and plant crops. This bonus proved sufficient to allow farmers to buy their tractor direct from the Ford dealer. The government's foresight was fully vindicated as Britain's imported food requirements were once again imperiled by German U-boats which sank 327 merchant ships in the Atlantic during the first half of 1942.[2] The availability of these tractors and the bonus helped to get over six million additional acres of land in production by the end of the war. The tractor count in Britain increased from 55,000 in 1939 to 140,000 by 1944, 85 percent of which were Fordsons.

The main Ford plant in Dagenham, opened in 1931 on 66 acres, was located on the River Thames, just east of London. Although on a much smaller scale, it replicated the Rouge plant in Dearborn, Michigan, in its steelmaking, tool and die department, assembly and other areas. In urgent cases Ford (U.S.) had critical tools flown across the ocean by bomber to save time and to avoid the risk of the U-boats. At the time World War II started, the plant was capable of producing 120,000 vehicles annually along with 200,000 tons of pig iron from its blast furnace, 400,000 gallons of benzole, 250,000 gallons of coal tar, slag from the blast furnace was used to make tarmacadam, and 10,000,000 cubic feet of gas was recovered from its coke ovens.

Ford V8 Engines: The first military contract was issued to Ford in 1939, and while minor in total dollars it was of great importance. The contract was for the Dagenham built Ford V8 engine to be used to power anti-mine rings fitted to bombers to neutralize the magnetic mines laid across British harbors by the Germans. They were also quickly installed in merchant ships for the same purpose. Neither the Fordson tractor or V8 engine production placed any burden on Ford, which continued producing civilian vehicles, uninterrupted, until April 1940.

Dagenham's V8 engines, in addition to the anti-mine use, were used by the Royal Navy to power their motor torpedo boats that harassed enemy shipping in the English Channel. Twin V8 engines also powered many of the assault craft used in early commando landings in occupied Europe and in the invasion of Normandy in 1944. In addition they were used to power the winches of the barrage balloons along with a great many more mundane war-related tasks.

Airplane Engines: The most important aircraft engine produced by Britain during World War II, was the Merlin V-12 engine built by Rolls-Royce. Even with two engine plants at Derby and Crewe, the Air Ministry realized that Rolls-Royce could not produce enough engines for the coming war. In October 1939 the Air Ministry asked Ford if they could build 400 of the Merlin engines a month. With a positive response from Ford a site search for a new factory was started and in March 1940 construction was started in Manchester, England, for the new Ford aircraft engine factory. An early problem for Ford was the same one Ford (U.S.) faced in building the B-24 bomber and Pratt & Whitney aircraft engine. The Rolls-Royce engine, comprising 10,000 parts, was virtually hand built by experienced craftsmen individually fitting many of the parts. One example was that while the Rolls-Royce blueprints called for four different screw thread-forms on each engine, their craftsmen applied their own modifications meaning there could be many more different thread-forms used on each engine. In reviewing the plans for the Merlin engine, Ford engineers found the design tolerances allowed by Rolls-Royce far greater than Ford allowed for their own automobile engines.[3] Ford reworked the engineering drawings to provide for the much finer tolerances required for making interchangeable parts, which was essential to their mass production on an assembly line.

Ford sent a team of 190 men to the Rolls-Royce plant to learn how to make every part. The team then set up Ford's aircraft engine assembly line where each unskilled worker would be required to assemble or fit only one or two parts. As Ford would have to do later in the United States, they had to start from scratch to find employees for the new factory as well as obtain the necessary but scarce machinery. In wartime England the employment task was greatly magnified as most of the labor pool was already occupied in producing war material but, like Ford (U.S.), they did not need skilled labor. They could quickly train the average person to do simple repetitive tasks. In the end women were the answer. Women made up 43 percent of the 17,316-person workforce in Manchester. Much of the special machinery came from Ford's own tool and die shop at the Rouge-like plant at Dagenham outside London. Some of the more specialized machines came from Switzerland through Nazi occupied France. The Swiss claimed that, as neutrals, they had the right to trade with all belligerents.[4] The Germans, who also depended on the Swiss for precision instruments, were hard pressed not to honor their claim.

Each part would be tested before assembly and each assembly tested before installation in the engines. Completed engines were tested to their design limits, torn down and each assembly retested and examined for faults, then reassembled, sealed and shipped. Ford's performance was truly outstanding, manufacturing over 34,000 engines and, starting with the first engine delivered in June 1941, not a single one failed the stringent acceptance test of the Royal Air Force.

Production targets called for 400 engines a month costing £5,640 each. By September 1942 the target was exceeded and, due to Ford innovations and production methods, the cost per unit was reduced to £1,875. By mid–1944, monthly production exceeded 900 units a month at a cost of just under £1,200 each. Most of the Ford engines were MkXX models used primarily in the Avro Lancaster and Handley Page Halifax bombers, Bristol Beaufighter, Bolton Paul Defiant, and Hawker Hurricane fighters. Variations were used in the Avro Lancasterian and York Transports and de Havilland Mosquito fighters.

German bombing raids on the factory started on December 23, 1940, and while only a total of 125 bombs fell on the factory with casualties of 3 dead and 8 wounded, many bombs fell nearby, destroying many of the homes of the workers. In spite of this, production was never seriously affected.

It was at this same time that the Manchester plant was under construction that Henry Ford canceled a contract to build 6,000 Merlin engines for Britain in the United States. Once again, as in World War I, this caused a serious public relations problem for Ford's British management. As in World War I, however, the management was able to separate the negative image of Henry Ford from that of the company, due mainly to Ford of Britain's war related production.

Military Vehicles: Not as dramatic, but certainly as important to the war effort, was the vehicle production from the Dagenham plant. Months after the war started Ford was still on a 40 hour week building civilian vehicles and would continue to do so until April 1940. No significant war production orders had been placed with Ford's Dagenham factory due to its obvious location just east of London and the genuine fear that its production capacity would be an early target of the German bombers. In spite of the opinion that nothing could be done to hide the factory, Royal Air Force experts developed a plan to paint a picture on the roofs of the various buildings, making them appear from the air as a vast marshland with tracts running through them. Within months of the scheme being applied an aerial photograph, highlighting the camouflaged Dagenham plant area, was recovered from a downed German airplane. In any event less than 200 bombs fell on the plant during the war and while the casualties amounted to 5 killed and 24 injured, like Manchester, no serious production interruptions occurred.

Nothing but small orders were forthcoming until the appointment of Winston Churchill as Prime Minister in May 1940. In spite of Churchill's snatching Ford's two top managers, Percival Perry for a senior position in the Ministry of Food and Patrick Hennessy for the Ministry of Aircraft Production, both of whom would be knighted for their efforts, the mighty Dagenham machine began churning out war materials. By June 1940 large contracts had been received by Ford for special military vehicles, primarily trucks, followed by orders from the Royal Air Force for tractors to haul bombs. Conversion to military production accelerated, hampered only by the delay in acquiring the necessary machines Ford was unable to produce themselves, shortages of critical materials and the hiring and training of personnel. The later problem was tempered, as it was in Manchester, by the decision to hire women for factory work, something Ford had never done. By the end of the war 10 percent of the 34,000-person workforce at Dagenham were women. Ford's efforts were greatly aided by the help of over 450 sub-contractors all over Britain.

In addition subsidiary plants or shadow plants, as the British called secondary operations, were established. Ford built so many parts for the universal or Bren gun carrier that an old factory, built in 1777, was established in Leamington for the sole production of steel tracks for several types of tracked vehicles. Tracks for these vehicles, made of malleable iron, tended to wear out and Ford provided a special crankshaft steel that increased track life substantially. About 6,000,000 of these new tracks were produced.

Early in 1939 Ford established training courses for drivers of these army trucks as they realized they would be operating in many difficult conditions and in places where repairs and spare parts were not available. A course at Dagenham was started that lasted from one to three weeks and included many soldiers from the occupied countries of Europe. By the invasion of Normandy on June 6, 1944, Ford had trained over 12,000 members of the military as well as making over 9,000 visits to military bases giving lectures and instructions to many more army drivers and fitters.

A serious problem considered by Ford engineers was the waterproofing of vehicles as experience in the North Africa and Sicily invasions resulted in many vehicles being stalled and abandoned on or near the beaches due to water damage to the engines. With the upcoming invasion of France this became a critical consideration. Ford engineers found a compound called Trinadite that, spread all over the electrical equipment, kept water from vital parts. Tests were successfully made by running a vehicle 200 miles, then entering the sea and running submerged for over a mile. Very few failures were reported on the beaches of Normandy on June 6, 1944.

As well as making vehicles, over 12,000 jeeps, trucks and universal carriers shipped from the U.S. and Canada were reassembled by Ford, aided by many of their Ford dealers. Also, 26,000 overhauls of existing models and engines were carried out by the Lincoln car depot.

General: Unlike wartime manufacturing in the United States where air-raid tests were routinely conducted, actual air-raid warnings and air attacks were a way of life in Britain. Imminent raid warnings by spotters along the coast caused the workforce to seek shelter with a resultant loss of production. However, as the spotters became more sophisticated in their interpretations of the direction the bombers were taking, the down time decreased. Even so, the alert was sounded twelve hundred times subjecting the workers to spending 2,154 hours under threat of air attack. This does not count those times in 1944 and 1945 when V-1 and V-2 bombs fell unannounced.

Ford had built the only automotive owned blast furnace at Dagenham in 1934 and it continuously produced 500 tons of iron a day through April 1944, when it was shut down to reline the interior surface. Production at Dagenham produced a number of by-products, one of the main ones being Tarmacadam, a product manufactured from the slag produced by the blast furnace. It was used in the construction of the runways at 56 airfields in Britain. Along with Tarmacadam, other by-products included toluene for explosives, xylene for varnish, sulphate of ammonia and benzole gasoline (similar to the benzene made by Ford [U.S.]).

By war's end 360,546 wheeled vehicles had been produced at Dagenham, including 10,000 universal carriers and 136,811 Fordson tractors. The value of war production at Dagenham, including 93,810 new engines, 157,010 reconditioned engines and untold spare parts, totaled £556,979,194. Geary in his *Ford Military Vehicles* states the grand total of all Ford's overseas operations was 606,390 vehicles.

Civilian Aid: When the German air raids became extreme and overwhelmed the

Henry and Edsel Ford donated 450 emergency food vans to provide hot meals for Londoners who were homeless or whose utilities had been destroyed. They served over 81,000,000 meals during the war (from the collection of The Henry Ford).

capacity of the mobile canteens of the YMCA, Salvation Army and others to feed those made homeless or whose utilities were inoperable, Henry and Edsel Ford established a trust fund to purchase a fleet of 350 fully-equipped emergency food vans, each of which could serve 800 hot meals to the needy following bombing raids. The trust fund was enlarged by the advance sale of these vans to Ford Motor Company at the estimated postwar equity value of the vans. These funds and further donations raised the fleet to 450 units which were stationed throughout England and served over 81 million hot meals during the war. The canteens were garaged and maintained free of charge by Ford dealers.[5]

Ford of Canada

Ford of Canada controlled, through subsidiary companies and direct dealers, the sale of Ford products in India, Asia, Australia, New Zealand and South Africa. As a result of Japanese advances in the late 1930s most of the Asian countries were quickly overrun and unable to provide war material to the Allies. The remaining companies made substantial contributions.

FORD OF CANADA

Canada produced 380,000[6] wheeled vehicles of fifty different types, 47,000 of which were armored vehicles.[7] Ford of Canada was the single largest source of vehicles for troops in the United Kingdom. German General Rommel of North African fame issued an order in December 1941, "For desert reconnaissance only captured English trucks are to be employed, since German trucks stick in the sand too often."[8] Most of these captured trucks were Ford built so it was praise indeed for Dagenham and Windsor. They also produced components for aircraft including replaceable cylinder barrels for engines.

Ford of Australia— Its biggest war effort was in designing and building landing craft, lighters (small boats for unloading large freighters), cargo boats and other marine items for the war in the Pacific. It also produced 35,146 motor vehicles and a vast array of other military goods such as aircraft drop tanks, Bofors guns and parts for howitzers as well as an extensive reconditioning operation for United States aircraft engines.

Ford of New Zealand— It produced 10,423 wheeled vehicles, restored 1,117 war-damaged jeeps, produced millions of grenades, mortar shells, other munitions and miscellaneous war products.

Ford of India— It produced 134,007 wheeled vehicles.

Ford of South Africa— It produced 34,869 wheeled vehicles.

Malaya— It produced 15,199 wheeled vehicles until overrun by the Japanese.

Other Overseas Operations

In 1941, Ford established reserve against income to provide for the expected loss of investments in the following companies:

France	$2,692,381
Germany	$8,034,049
Japan	$4,771,325

These reserves totaled $15,497,755, virtually none of which was recovered after the war.[9]

Ford of France— As did most of the other Ford companies in Europe, Ford of France produced war materials until overrun by the Nazis in 1940. The French company built trucks, airplane engine parts, and parts for a 20-mm anti-aircraft gun.

Ford of Italy— Ford had been nearly regulated and taxed out of business in Italy in order to protect Fiat from foreign competition and the decision to slowly wind down Ford operation had been made. Because Ford production in Italy was virtually eliminated, Ford of Egypt had been providing vehicles for Mussolini's army. When Italy attacked Ethiopia orders for Ford vehicles jumped to 4,767 in 1935, a sixfold increase over the previous year. Reports that bombs and poison gas were being used against the Ethiopians outraged people and Henry Ford, in line with his principle not to sell to combatants, imposed his own sanctions by canceling deliveries of 800 units, already paid for, and refusing delivery of any more vehicles. This was a month before the League of Nations imposed their partial sanctions and it remained in effect even after the League backed down. This was quite unpopular in Italy and, with increasing sanctions, Ford ceased all operations in Italy in 1940.[10]

Ford of Japan— Ford organized a branch operation in 1925 and attempted to begin manufacturing in 1935. That next summer they applied for a license to assemble vehicles but provisions of the law provided licenses would be available only to Japanese companies. Ford tried to negotiate a partnership with Toyota and failing that did negotiate a buyout with Nissan. That fell through when other laws forbade Ford to transfer large sums of money to Detroit. The military wanted all foreign vehicle makers out of Japan and all Ford operations were slowly strangled to the point that they ceased all business December 8, 1941.

Ford-Werke of Germany— By late spring of 1941, with the German conquests in Europe, Ford facilities in eight countries (France, Belgium, Netherlands, Denmark, Finland, Italy, Hungary, and Romania) came under the complete control of Hitler.

"American influence over the Ford-Werke plant decreased after the outbreak of the European war in September 1939 and ceased altogether in 1941."[11] "In December 1941 Ford-Werke fell under the direct authority of Germany's Reich Commissioner for the Treatment of Enemy Property."[12] German Ford production was now controlled by the Nazis, but it was less than a quarter of Dagenham, which produced more vehicles than Germany and all the other occupied countries combined.

In the late 1990s Ford Motor Company (U.S.) was accused in a class action suit charging that forced and slave labor was knowingly used in its German factories during the war. The suit was dismissed by a federal judge in 1999. But in 1998 Ford had launched an extensive worldwide investigation of these charges by independent researchers, unfettered by any restrictions and with access to all Ford Motor Company records worldwide. In addition one of the two overseers of the project had lost three grandparents in the Holocaust.[13] This research resulted in a 208 page document published in 2001 entitled *Research Finding About Ford-Werke Under the Nazi Regime*. It covered the labor, management and financial situation of Ford-Werke from the late 1930s through the end of World War II.

Due to the severe shortage of labor in Germany, exacerbated by the Nazi social policy of keeping women out of the workforce, virtually every industrial company operating in Germany during World War II used foreign and forced labor to some degree. The workers were recruited, by the German government, as voluntary workers from German allies, forced civilian workers from occupied countries, prisoners of war and in mid–1943 inmates of concentration camps. Obtaining any employee including German nationals, required an application be made to the government detailing the company's needs based on Government orders received.[14]

Records on employment are very sparse but available data indicates that at the Ford Cologne plant in 1943 and 1944, upwards of 40 percent of the estimated 5,000 employees were foreigners. About one-third were prisoners of war, mostly Russian, while another third were Russian civilians.[15] Existing records indicate that slave labor was not assigned to any of the automobile companies until August 1944 and "most documentation from the period indicates there were 50 or fewer Buchenwald concentration camp inmates at Ford-Werke at any given time from August 1944 to February 1945."[16]

"The distribution of dividends declared from 1938 through 1943 were blocked by the (German) government and no further dividends were declared until 1950."[17] The dividends from 1938 to 1943 were devalued in 1951 by 90 percent and Ford Motor Company used the resulting $60,000 credit to help repurchase outstanding stock.

Ford wrote off their investment in Ford-Werke of $8,034,049 and following the end of World War II submitted claims, under the 1948 War Claims Act, for losses in Europe for over $7,000,000. While only about 6 percent, or $42,000, of the claim was actually awarded it is not clear from the records how much, if any, of the award was actually paid.[18] In 1954 Ford, based on its recovery of the German property in 1948, restored its investment to the company books and valued it at $557,000.

14

The Veteran's Story

The public's first exposure to Ford and military veterans was in June 1916 following Poncho Villa's across the border raid that January, on the town of Columbus, New Mexico, which resulted in the mobilization of the U.S. National Guard for duty along the U.S.-Mexico border. That June the *Chicago Tribune* published an editorial summarizing their survey of large employers as to whether or not they would aid their employees financially as a result of being called up for National Guard duty. Frank Klingensmith, Ford Motor Company's treasurer, erroneously said no, leading to the headline, "Ford is an Anarchist." The editorial stated if Henry Ford continued to deny aid "he will reveal himself not merely as an ignorant idealist, but as an anarchist enemy of the nation." Actually Ford gave each of the 89 Ford employees who went to the border a numbered badge stamped M.N.G. (Michigan National Guard) entitling him to a job when he came back. In addition the Ford Sociological Department took care of needy families of absent soldiers.[1]

Ford demanded a retraction and when the demand was dismissed by the publisher, Robert R. McCormick, Henry Ford brought suit for $1,000,000. This led to one of the most widely publicized and followed trials in the country, lasting until August 1919. The jury found the *Tribune* guilty of libel and Henry Ford was awarded six cents. The jury did not think Henry Ford was an anarchist, but neither did it think he had suffered financially from the *Tribune*'s article. The press that vilified him during the trial claimed Ford had lost more than he had gained by the suit, but the common man, relating to Ford's lack of sophistication as exposed in the trial, felt differently. David Lewis in his *The Public Image of Henry Ford* claimed the trial helped in molding the image of Henry Ford (for better or worst) for the next twenty five years. In 1941 Colonel Robert McCormick, the owner of the Chicago Tribune sent Henry Ford a note apologizing for his attack.[2]

After the end of World War I Ford, who was a pioneer in hiring the handicapped, agreed to take 1,000 handicapped veterans as fast as they became available, but little else has been found on overall policies regarding returning veterans of this war. However, in 1928 Ford opened Camp Legion in Dearborn, Michigan, and Camp Willow Run in Ypsilanti, Michigan, providing farming opportunities during the summer for disadvantaged boys, most of whom were sons of disabled or deceased veterans. During the Depression year of 1933, Ford offered 5,000 jobs to members of the Wayne County (Michigan) Council of the American Legion.

In 1943 Ford sponsored the American Legion Junior Baseball League, awarding plaques to winning teams and $50 war bonds to each of their members. Ford and Lincoln-Mercury dealers joined in sponsoring their hometown teams. In 1947 Ford hired Babe Ruth as a consultant who, after a cancer operation, logged more than 40,000 miles appearing at league baseball diamonds across the country. That year Ford and its dealers cosponsored nearly 50 percent of the American Legion's Junior Baseball League's 8000 clubs. Ford's sponsorship continued for many decades.

Camp Willow Run was closed in late 1940 and Camp Legion was turned into a year-round project in January 1944 and used almost exclusively for sons of members of the American Legion.[3] This lasted only until April 1944 when it was converted into an occupational rehabilitation center for handicapped veterans under the auspices of the Henry Ford Trade School.[4] It was located on 300 acres along Southfield Road near Michigan Avenue, in Dearborn, Michigan, and was complete with barracks, dining hall, library, machine shop, chapel and farmlands. It taught veterans farming and mechanical skills and provided them room and board as well as paying them $3.00 a week. This was the first privately financed facility of its kind. All men, when considered rehabilitated, were offered jobs at Ford Motor Company but were under no obligations to accept such jobs. In September Henry Ford was awarded The American Legion's Distinguished Service Medal for assistance to disabled servicemen in establishing the Camp Legion School of Vocational Guidance. Two informational pamphlets were issued: *Welcome*, which included a self-addressed postcard for an application to Camp Legion, and *Sure There's a Job for You*, which was a 10 × 12 foldout picturing the facilities. The small village industry plant at Cherry Hill, Michigan, also provided work for disabled veterans for a short time in 1944 and 1945.

In April 1944 Ford pledged he would give job preference to ex–Ford employee servicemen in all his plants. Said Ford, "Other people have made a lot of money out of this war and the servicemen have made nothing, They deserve the first call." In July 1945 Ford announced that they would provide special equipment and free installation for amputee veterans' cars. One of the pamphlets issued for the amputee was *Take the Wheel Again* which illustrated use of the equipment designed for those men who had lost their hands. Ford declared, "No man who has lost a limb in the armed service is going to have to pay anything extra to drive a Ford car."[5] Ford was the only company to do this and continued to do so until the government provided a specially equipped car for every amputee veteran in August 1946. In addition Ford recommended to its dealers that they set aside 25 percent of their new cars for sale to ex-servicemen. Some did — some didn't.

In May 1945 Ford ran an ad entitled "All Honor to those who wear this button," which referred to a lapel pin featuring a small eagle within a wreath, nicknamed the ruptured duck. Authorized in 1939 with the start of the draft it indicated that the wearer had been honorably discharged from military service. It also signified that young men who appeared to be of draft age, and sometimes subjected to obnoxious remarks, had served their time and were not draft dodgers. Ford's ad was an effort to gain public recognition of this emblem and that wearer had been returned to civilian life after faithfully serving his country.

A 38 page *Guide Book for the World War II Veteran* was issued in May 1945 covering the returning ex–Ford serviceman's status as well as the opportunities open to all veterans as well as the availability of government assistance for education and home and business loans. In addition, due to all the Ford men who manned the 28 Ford ships sold or leased to the government during the war, the Merchant Marine Law was fully explained.

Starting with the April 1945 issue of *Ford Times,* a series of six articles entitled *The Veteran Comes Home* ran through August:

- No 1. April 1945 covered the introduction of the returning serviceman in the Ford labor pool. Special emphasis was placed on assessing the qualifications and ability of the disabled men to insure they could find a job that fits the veterans' limitations. "No job is ever created for the man."
- No 2. May 1945 described the hiring routine of a combat disabled veteran and how they first determined the job he would be recommended for.
- No 3. June 1945 covered the conference of groups of 20 men with Ford personnel giving them the opportunity to ask any and all questions and a briefing on the ten departments most would be assigned to.
- No 4. July 1945 explained the history of the Apprentice School, detailed the requirements for admission and the process for applying.
- No 5. August 1945 went into great detail, with examples, of classifying the disabled veteran and to insure the medical department was alerted to any impending change in classification.
- No 6. September 1945 covered the training available at Ford and Lincoln Mercury dealerships for the returning veterans. Two pamphlets were issued: *Mechanical Training Course for Veterans with Ford Dealers* and *An Opportunity for World War Veterans.*

In the spring of 1945 *Time* cited Ford as one of the five business organizations which had done the most to assist veterans in obtaining employment.

In their efforts to reduce Ford's enormous post-war losses, Camp Legion was among a number of Ford facilities closed between 1946 and 1950.

Ford of Britain provided their men joining the armed forces a pay supplement to bring their military pay up to their Ford wages for a period of three months. In addition, a trust fund was set up to provide for employees in military service or civil defense or their dependents who were in special need of help. It was funded by Ford's paying into it an amount equal to a certain percent of each employee's wages. Grants were made according to individual circumstances.[6]

15

Summary

In brief, the direct contributions of the United States to the Allied effort in World War I consisted mostly of manpower and motor vehicles, as very little other U.S. produced war materials reached the war zone before the armistice in November 1918. Both, however, proved to be vital with Ford providing most of the vehicles in the American effort. World War II turned out to be an entirely different situation and, while these stories detail only Ford Motor Company's contribution in both wars, they are also representative of the efforts put forth by all Ford vendors as well as the other American automotive manufacturers during the war.

There were major differences, however, in the approach the United States and Henry Ford took to the different wars. In World War I, while President Woodrow Wilson had pledged to keep America out of the war he was being urged by many to become involved. At the same time Henry Ford did everything he could to keep America from getting involved and, while he was not alone in his attitude or efforts, he was the most well known and one of the most vocal. The result was that neither the United States nor Henry Ford were significantly prepared for the defense of the United States prior to the actual declaration of war in 1917. In the dark days preceding World War II, President Roosevelt was, like President Wilson, urged by many including, once again Henry Ford, to keep America from becoming entangled in another European war. But, Roosevelt, in spite of this pressure, had the nation, including Henry Ford in spite of his objections, producing war materials for our defense and for our allies (via the Lend-Lease Program) before the attack on Pearl Harbor.

In both wars, Henry Ford earned a reputation as a pacifist. He thought war was a waste of men and productive capacity and urged on and abetted by greedy munitions manufacturers. Self-defense was another story. A somewhat ambiguous letter written by Henry Ford in 1915 aboard the SS *Oscar II* on his peace mission read, "We declare our opposition to any increase by the United States of her military and naval forces. This is not at all to demand immediate disarmament in our own country." He seemed to want it both ways.[1] However, when all the dust settled and it was apparent that war was unavoidable, all the resources at his command were turned to producing war materials with little concern for profits. In retrospect, considering the war materials produced by the Ford Motor Company in both wars, he was anti-war — not a pacifist. A slight distinction, maybe, but anti-war seems to fit Henry Ford better than does pacifist.

A cartoon published a month after the armistice captures the public perception of Henry Ford's war effort during World War I (*London Illustrated News*, December 11, 1918).

In both wars, Ford's most visible programs, the Eagle Boat and the Liberator bomber, received a great deal of criticism, mostly from people who had no idea of the staggering problems that were encountered and overcome. Production that lagged the public's exaggerated expectations led critics, at the time and even in recent years, to charge that Ford's troubles stemmed from not hiring experienced nautical and aviation construction workers to aid in building products they were unfamiliar with. In fact Ford did hire a number of nautical advisors in World War I to resolve specific problems and the AMC report verifies that Ford had also hired aeronautical experts to help in specialized areas. While this criticism that both projects would have run smoother with experienced workers seems a valid point, it is questionable that specialized tradesmen, if available, could have helped. First, Ford was asked to build the Eagle Boats and Liberator bombers because other sources were swamped with war production orders and few trained workers in those fields were available. In fact, in World War I, Ford had to pledge not to seek experienced workers from other shipyards. Second, Ford was building both the Eagle Boat and the Liberator bomber using vastly different methods of production compared to prevailing industry standards. This was no more apparent than in World War II when Ford was asked to build items designed by others, particularly the Pratt & Whitney aircraft engine, Consolidated bomber and the Waco glider. While Ford understood that none of the three companies were producing in volume they did expect to obtain plans that would allow Ford to proceed to lay out their assembly process. In all three cases plans were so inaccurate and incomplete that thousands of hours were spent by Ford engineers and draftsmen literally creating complete and accurate plans before any production planning could take place. Ford's assembly line methods did not lend themselves to the experience of the nautical or aviation tradesman skilled in these industries. Many, if not most, workers in these industries were accustomed to hand fitting parts and making adjustments when necessary to make things fit—a method completely at odds with mass production. A comment in a January 1944 Ford publicity release about Willow Run, that also applied to other Ford war production, summed it up:

> The early critics claimed that our tooling cost several times that of a comparable plant using old-line aircraft production methods. That was true. But we produce bombers worth the total cost of our tooling every few days now at Willow Run.

Attitude

Two unwritten principles served to guide Ford production methods. They were both tied to cost and quality concerns and were ones their managers had been imbued with since the start of the company. They proved to be of major importance in Ford's wartime contributions. The first principle held that accepted ways were always to be challenged as any process could be analyzed and improved. The other principle, based on their manufacturing experience of building over thirty million vehicles since 1903, was that mass production could be obtained only by precision manufacturing of interchangeable parts. Ford production men felt they could do any job better, faster and cheaper and in fact did improve production methods and save the government money, in both wars, on nearly every defense project they undertook.

Process

In order to install a mass production system for any product Ford would first spend untold hours breaking every job down to its most elemental basis. Once that was determined they would then spend thousands of engineering hours and untold hundreds of thousands, indeed millions, of dollars to develop procedures, methods and machines to implement the most efficient production system that, through dies, blanking machines and punches, would produce thousands of a required part to the same dimension time after time. Then each unskilled worker would be taught one or two simple assembly jobs. Machines would be used wherever possible to insure precision and to guide the worker in the final assembly process. This system of production, for the volumes involved, always ended up reducing costs while producing quality wares. The only cost reduction exception in World War II was in Ford's production of jeeps where contracts were doled out over a period of years to six different assembly plants. No single contract was large enough for Ford to invest in the tools and machinery necessary to maximize production.

Also to be noted, even with all the production sourced to Ford's branch plants and village industries, the amount of sourcing to outside vendors, encouraged and sometimes directed by the government, varied greatly. Examples of outsourcing ranged from the jeep where 43 percent of material cost was provided by outside companies, to the glider at 12 percent, the Liberator bomber with less than 10 percent and the Pratt & Whitney engine and gun director which were almost wholly handled in-house. But in all cases, in-house or vendor, quality was continuously verified. Ford's control systems had been developed over years of experience in producing vehicles and the lessons learned were applied to vendors to insure every item was produced to the same standards Ford imposed on their own facilities. In many cases Ford designs or re-designs were accepted by the government as quality standards for all producers, as in the case of gliders where a Ford built glider was sent to all other builders as a standard. This continued emphasis, combined with Ford's vast purchasing power and experience, insured quality while containing costs.

The perennial question is how many more B-24 bombers could have been produced if Ford had followed the aviation industry in the use of the soft Kirksite dies. Years later Charles Lindbergh wrote that he "would have been in favor of using soft metal dies," but ended his letter with "everything considered, it seems to me that the extraordinary thing is the speed, rather than the slowness, with which it [bomber production] was done."[2] Nevins and Hill commented that using Consolidated's actual production in 1942 of 1,140 planes, with experienced workers as the benchmark, Ford, which could not have produced any planes prior to July 1942, could have produced only about 500 planes under the best of circumstances. However, they point out, Ford did not have the trained workforce that Consolidated had and, in any event, coupled with the difficulty in attracting even untrained workers 100 planes seems about as much as could have been expected, versus the 56 that Ford actually built in 1942.[3] The downside to producing these 100 planes was that the system would not have been in place to produce the thousands of planes that were actually produced in the following years.

Facilities

One of the major factors that allowed Ford to develop and produce many of the wartime products in quantity, quality and a timely manner was the availability of 23,341,000 square feet of facilities spread across the United States at the beginning of the defense effort. The Rouge, alone, offered 10,000,000 square feet of factory floor space, 23 miles of roadway, one and one-third miles of docks, 100 miles of conveyor systems and a complete inter-plant railroad system of 125 miles with its own locomotive repair shops. Within the Rouge were coke ovens, blast furnaces, open hearth furnace, a rolling mill with a capacity of 3,000 tons of steel daily, a modern glass plant, the world's largest production foundry, an incomparable tool and die shop, cement plant, tire factory, assembly line and more. Then there were the Highland Park and Lincoln factories, huge in their own right, and the many branch and village facilities. In many cases Ford was able to overcome the critical lack of suitable steel and vendor capacity for new tooling by producing their own steel and designing and producing their own unique and replacement tool requirements. In another sense this was also true of workers. When lack of facilities and workers started choking production at both the airplane engine plant and Willow Run, the pressure was relieved by farming out many of the jobs to the branches and village industries where space and experienced workers were available.

In addition, as Ford was a privately owned company with access to enormous financial resources, they were able to make decisions quickly and provide funding immediately, where other manufacturers had to wait for committee approval and government funds to move forward. Ford, in the case of the aircraft engine plant, provided the initial funds that allowed for the immediate start of construction, although later, expenditures without prior government approval were forbidden. In many cases Ford quickly converted many of their existing facilities and only seven new facilities were required. The largest of the new facilities was Willow Run and the rest were located within the Rouge: airplane engine plant, airplane engine test cell facility, aluminum foundry and casting plant, magnesium foundry and an airplane engine foundry. With years of experience in plant construction, Ford was able to insure rapid and economical construction with proven architectural and engineering firms by engaging the contractors and supervising the actual construction.[4]

Finally, Ford had the experienced manpower, both management and labor, to quickly start urgent programs. The Ford management team had, for years, planned and built major facilities and organized them for the most efficient utilization of production all over the world and were aided by a cadre of specialized groups: purchasing, engineering, construction, machine design, metallurgical and chemical control, tool and die, traffic, etc. Added to this were the experienced supervisors and skilled labor groups, representing virtually every trade. They were the men that facilitated the expansion to meet growing war needs. Ford's manpower in 1941 was 123,477 employees. By November 1943 the various war contracts had mushroomed the employee requirement to 203,398, finally tapering off to 149,856 in December 1944 as war contracts were curtailed or canceled.

Cooperation

Ford, as did other manufacturers, faced new challenges every day in manufacturing items completely foreign to their experience. Ford worked closely with the government in improving or significantly modifying the M4A3 tank and universal carrier, M-8 and M-20 armored vehicle and the jeep as well as developing breakthrough production methods in many of the other contracts. They solved untold numbers of problems and, with the understanding that this was everybody's war and a collective effort was critical, they joined the Automotive Council for War Production and the Central Aircraft Council formed of all aircraft manufacturers. They met at regular intervals to share ideas in an attempt to help each other improve the quantity and quality of their war products. The prevalent secrecy common to automotive companies in pre-war years dissolved. Trade secrets became common property for everyone's use. Nowhere was this more evident than Ford's willingness to share their patents free of royalties; these were not only the patents developed from war production, but also the many patents they had developed prior to the war.

Hand in hand with the liberal use of Ford patents was Ford's assistance to other manufacturers. With over 30 years of experience in mass production methods, Ford received hundreds of requests from other manufacturers and the government seeking assistance in the production of various war materials. In some cases it extended to helping others set up their operations to utilize Ford patents and in others, such as the production of 75mm projectiles, they not only developed the production method and supplied all the data to another supplier, but also provided engineering assistance to get the supplier started in production.

In another significant situation Grumman Aircraft Corporation was unable to obtain critical forgings, delaying delivery of planes to the U.S. Navy. Ford helped design castings to replace the forgings and made 1,500 sets to satisfy the immediate need. Ford then sent its own engineers to another foundry to install the Ford process to continue production of these vital castings for Grumman.

Still another example was the centrifugal casting of aircraft engine barrels developed by Ford. Ford was called on to teach other foundries how to cast the barrels, which resulted in much heavy forging machinery being made available for other critical war work. Throughout the war, Ford consistently made available its engineering and technical resources to the government and industry and in many cases, where they could not be of help, they directed requests to sources known to be capable of handling the desired work. The value of these services was estimated at over $18,000,000.

Profits

In World War I, Henry Ford disdained making a profit on the production of war materials, declaring, "Everything I've got is for the government and not a cent of profit." However it wasn't until March 1924 that the Treasury Department determined Ford Motor Company's tax obligation and even then the government reserved the right to make revisions. On Ford Motor Company's gross receipts of $108,851,330, Henry Ford's share of the profit amounted to $926,780 after taxes, or eight-tenths of 1 percent. However, in closing out war contracts with the government, Henry Ford had ordered his company to never dispute a federal estimate or charge unless it was palpably in error, an action that undoubtedly saved the government more money than his final profit.[5] By the time the total cost of his pledge was finally known, Henry Ford apparently chose to ignore it.

Unlike World War I, at the start of World War II, Henry Ford said he would forgo all profits if his competitors would also refrain, which they did not. *Time* magazine in 1942 quoted Henry Ford, "If we come out with as much as we went in, we'll be all right."[6] Late in 1944 when a *Fortune* magazine reporter asked him if he would return profits, as he said he was willing to do after World War I, Henry Ford replied no, that he felt it necessary to

WELL-EARNED HONORS
to Somerville Ford Workers!

● The Army-Navy "E" award banner is not lightly given. It is a citation that must be earned through sustained accomplishment.

The men and women of the Somerville plant of Ford Motor Company are being so honored because of the excellent job they have done in the volume production of one of the most vital vehicles of war—the Universal Carrier.

Perhaps better known as the Bren Gun Carrier, this famous track-laying, amphibious, heavily-armed car has helped the United Nations beat back our foes on many fronts.

More than 20,000 Universal Carriers have been built and delivered by the Somerville Ford plant . . . on time or ahead of time . . . and many very important improvements in both design and construction have been contributed by Ford.

We extend our admiration and our sincere compliments to every man and woman of the Somerville plant for their individual parts in the splendid work which has earned this coveted honor from our armed forces.

Universal Carriers are powered with Ford engines—earlier models with the 85-horsepower V-8, current American production with the 100-horsepower Mercury engine.

THE FORD MOTOR COMPANY
Dearborn, Michigan

Boston Newspapers

Ford plants received the Army Navy "E" award for production excellence 18 times. Only 5 percent of World War II manufacturers received the award (from the collection of The Henry Ford).

maintain the relative strength of his company.[7] With that in mind, Ford's profit margin was by far the smallest of the big three automobile manufacturers as well as the other producers of the B-24 bomber. The following are the only realistic comparisons found.

PERCENT OF OPERATING PROFITS TO SALES
ALL WAR PRODUCTION 1942–1945

	1942	1943	1944	1945
Ford	1.2	6.1	4.7	(0.2)
Chrysler	7.8	7.7	7.6	4.9
General Motors	11.8	11.3	10.8	4.9

B-24 PRODUCTION 1942–1945

	1942	1943	1944	1945
Ford	1.2	6.1	4.7	(4.2)
United Aircraft	11.0	7.4	6.1	5.1
Consolidated-Vultee	13.6	8.4	7.1	4.1

The reduction in bomber production starting in late 1944 resulted in the loss of economy of scale and had the biggest impact on Ford's results in both 1944 and 1945. The effect on profit was exacerbated when the government directed Ford to maintain a bomber production workforce capable of producing 405 bombers a month when, at the same time, they had reduced Ford's actual production schedule to less than 215 planes a month.

Ford received contracts for 23 war products ranging from Army squad tents to the giant B-24 Liberator bomber with a total value of $6,000,000,000. After war's end cancellations the total value of war products actually produced and accepted by the government was $3,961,605,000 ($46,752,441,000 in 2008 dollars).

Attesting to Ford's wartime contributions, eight plants received 18 of the coveted Army Navy "E" awards for excellence, an award that was given to less than 5 percent of all war production manufacturers.

Chester, New Jersey	5 awards
Richmond, California	3 awards
Iron Mountain, Michigan	3 awards
Ypsilanti, Michigan	3 awards
Aircraft Engine Division (Rouge)	1 award
Willow Run, Michigan	1 award
Somerville, Massachussetts	1 award
Twin Cities, Minnesota	1 award

While Ford was not the largest producer of war materials, they received the greatest publicity (both favorable and unfavorable early on), and their record was nothing less than outstanding.

Due to the source of most of the materials referred to in this book, the story is obviously biased towards Ford. However, it in no way diminishes their wartime production achievements — the numbers speak for themselves.

Appendix

World War I Production and Finance Summary[1]

Contract	# Units	$ Gross Receipts	$ Net Income
Liberty Engines	3,950	35,339,900	4,123,145[2]
Aero Cylinders	433,826	4,252,259	830,427
Caissons	9,837	7,667,187	509,634
Tractors (farm)		1,474,840	134,099[2]
Tractors (tanks)	18	155,454	8,268
Armor Plate		272,716	819
Listening Devices	100	204,826	18,852
Body Armor		247,002	19,476
Helmets	2,731,573	298,899	89,156
74mm Exp Shell		2,457	223
Gun Mounts		464	0
Ordnance Hand Books		2,855	257
Other		32,758	8,133
Cars and Parts (vehicles)	30,734	12,097,367	2,673,563
Eagle Patrol Boats	60	46,104,042	954,937
Branch Building Rental		698,297	135,379
Grand Total		108,851,330	9,454,046

[1]Accession 572 Box 26 and Accession 902 Box 12 dtd March 1922
[2]Profit required by U.S. Treasury regulations

World War II Production Summary

Major Products	Ford Code	Start	Finish	Quantity[1]	Fixed Price Cost Plus	Value	Quantity[2]	Quantity[3]
Pratt & Whitney Engine	GBG	Aug '41	May '45	57,851	CP/FP	$962,358,000	57,851	57,851
Amphibian jeep	GPA	Sep '42	May '43	12,782	FP	$38,986,000	7,603	12,778
Jeep[4]	GP	Feb '41	Jan '42	4,458	FP	(below)	0	0
Jeep (Willys engine)	GPW	Jan '42	Jul '45	277,896	FP	$366,407,000	277,896	277,896
Gun Director M-5	GAW	Oct '42	May '42	400	CP	$60,170,000	1,202	1,202
Gun Director M7	GAH	Aug '42	Nov '43	802	CP	(above)	(above)	(above)
Armored Car T-17	GQ	Oct '42	Mar '43	250	CP	$22,654,000	250	(below)
Armored Car M-8	GAK	Mar '43	Apr '45	8,410	CP	$128,922,000	12,314	12,564
Armored Car M-20	GBK	May '43	Jun '45	3,791	CP	(above)	(above)	(above)
Liberator B-24	GK	Sep '42	Jun '45	6,790	CP	$1,142,830,000	8,684	8,684
Liberator B-24 KD	—	Jul '42	Jul '44	1,894	CP	(above)	(above)	(above)
British Axel	GAE	Jun '43	Aug '44	19,520	CP	$6,641,000	35,309	17,639
British Engine	GAE	Jun '43	Aug '44	26,086	CP	(above)	(above)	17,670
Generator P-1	GAL	Dec '42	Dec '44	75,166	CP	$14,425,000	87,390	87,390
Generator R-1	GBN	Jan '45	Jul '45	11,224	CP	(above)	(above)	(above)
Glider CG-4A	GAG	Sep '42	Jul '45	4,314	CP	$70,365,000	4,290	4,203
Glider 14A	GBG	Jan '44	Dec '44	87	CP	(above)	(above)	(above)
Jettison Fuel Tank	GPG	Jan '45	Jul '45	17,008	CP	$6,921,000	17,007	17,008
Jet Pulse Engine	MX544	Dec '44	Aug '45	2,501	CP	$4,725,000	2,401	2,411
Tank M4-A3	GAD	Jun '42	Aug '43	1,683	CP	$405,631,000	2,718	1,690
Tank Destroyer M10-A1	GBA	Oct '42	Aug '43	1,035	CP	(above)	(above)	1,038
Tank Engine	GAA	May '42	Aug '45	20,999	CP	(above)	26,954	26,979
Tank Engine	GAF	Sep '43	Sep '45	3,688	CP	(above)	(above)	(above)

Item	Code	Start	End	Qty	Type	Amount	Recap[1]	Recap[3]
Tank Engine	GAN	Aug '43	Dec '45	366	CP	(above)	(above)	(above)
Tank Engine	GAY	Sep '43	Nov '43	26	CP	(above)	(above)	(above)
Tank Engine—Recon	—	Jan '43	Dec '44	1,648	not listed	not listed	not listed	not listed
Tank Gun Mounts	—	Feb '42	Aug '43	5,475	not listed	not listed	not listed	not listed
Turbo Supercharger	GE	Aug '42	Oct '44	52,276	CP	$64,416,000	52,281	52,281
Universal Carrier	GAU	Feb '43	May '45	13,893	CP	$101,946,000	13,893	13,893
Rate of Climb Indicators	GAV	May '43	Dec '43	5,475	CP	$1,549,000	5,360	5,360
Squad Tents	—	Jan '45	Sep '45	—	FP	$994,000	not listed	9,498
Bomb Service Truck	GTBC	May '44	Oct '45	7,053	FP	$12,546,000	7,053	7,053
Cargo Trucks	G8T	Sep '42	May '45	77,915	FP	$134,161	77,915	77,604
Cargo Trucks (Army/Navy)	GTB	Apr '42	Oct '44	8,218	not listed	not listed	not listed	not listed
Moto-Tug[5]	—	not listed			not listed	not listed		3,025
Cargo Trucks (Army/Navy)		Jul '41	Aug '42	42,676		Probably standard Ford vehicles		
Pickup trucks 1½ ton		Feb '42	Mar '42	12,420		Probably standard Ford vehicles		
Automobiles		Nov '41	Mar '42	10,476		Probably standard Ford vehicles		

Other

Item					Type	Amount		
Steel					FP	$43,882,000		
Coke, Charcoal, Oil, Tar & Ethel Acetate					FP	$12,298,000		
Marine Revenues					FP	$2,199,000		
Liumber					FP	$980,000		
TOTAL CONTRACTS						$3,961,605,000		

Not itemized above are 4,889 tons of magnesium and unknown quantity of armor plate.

[1] Recap—month by month war production record—Jan '41 through Aug '45
[2] Recap—Fixed and Cost Plus contract record—1941-1945
[3] Recap—flyer published September 1, 1945
[4] Jeep—other month by month recap shows GP 5,163
[5] Moto-Tug—assembly subcontracted to vendor—other records indicate 10,877 units.

Rouge Plant Map

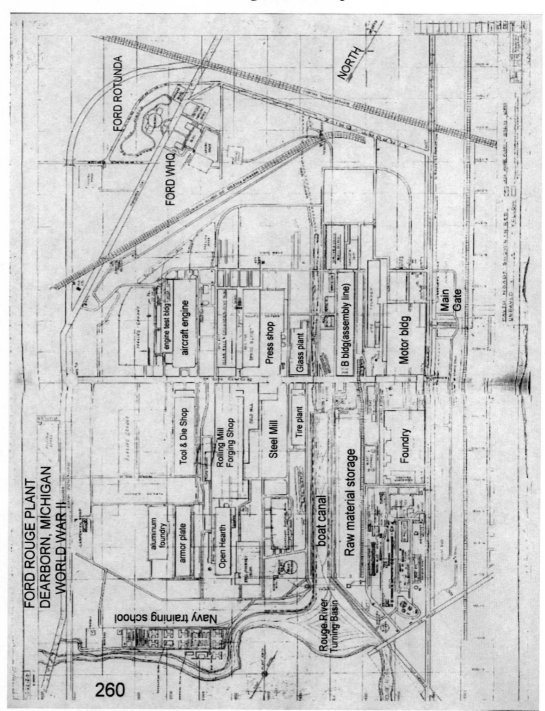

Monthly Unit Production of B-24 Bombers

Month	Sets of Spares	Knock-downs Douglas	Knock-downs Consolidated	Complete Ford
1942				
July		2		
August		0		
September		2		4
October	1	7		2
November	1	0		7
December	1	0		10
TOTAL	3	11		23
1943				
January	4	11	10	17
February	4	30	10	35
March	3	30	15	59
April	8	27	23	100
May	14	21	38	115
June	8	28	48	106
July	9	45	40	125
August	26	40	65	125
September	31	52	85	125
October	33	52	100	150
November	26	64	100	165
December	26	72	100	190
TOTAL	192	472	634	1,312
1944				
January	36	78	100	210
February	35	97	75	238
March	27	78	62	324
April	14	64	50	325
May	10	72	18	350
June	13	66	finish	383
July	7	17		415
August	9	finish		432
September	11			375
October	20			348
November	18			318
December	14			296
TOTAL	214	472	305	4014

Month	Sets of Spares	Knock-downs Douglas	Consolidated	Complete Ford
1945				
January	10			324
February	10			296
March	5			310
April	5			252
May	8			173
June	5			86
TOTAL	43			1441

Year	Spares	Knock-downs Douglas	Consolidated	Complete Ford	Total
1942	3	11		23	37
1943	192	472	634	1312	2610
1944	214	472	305	4014	5005
1945	43			1441	1484
TOTAL	452	955	939	6790	9136

World War I Songs and Poems About Henry Ford and His Cars

Mr. Ford You've Got the Right Idea

Words by Ray Sherwood
Music by J Fred'k Coots
Copyright 1916

The ship of peace has sailed away to seek a foreign shore
    and many people laugh and say it's queer
A million mothers kneel to pray. They've felt the sting of war
    they're praying for the ones they hold so dear
But when Columbus sailed they laughed and thought he was unsound
    they never thought he'd prove to them this good old world was round.

    Mister Ford you've got the right idea
        you're a champion of humanity
    There's millions of mothers who's hearts you'll fill with joy
        if Crown heads said "stop the war, we'll save your darling boy"
    And millions who scorn will soon turn to mourn
        they'll soon learn that you're sincere
    And they'll all cheer for the nation, that had taught them arbitration
        Mister Ford you've got the right idea.

They don't know what they're fighting for but still they fight away
    and no one knows when peace will ever reign
You'll pin a sign up on the door: "Let's arbitrate today."
    The mission that you're on is not in vain
And though you may not silence the guns, the spirit that you lend
    will be the stepping stone to bring this slaughter to an end.

Ford's One Man Chaser

Words by Harry S Coleman
Music by Alexandria Nomis
Copyright 1918

Henry Ford got a notion and he got it in his bean
    that he could lick the Kaiser and all his submarines.
So he made a "one man chaser" just as swift as it could be
    and they took the foreign waters like a swarm of bumble bees.
Then they searched those death tomb waters for the enemy to see
    and if periscopes reveal them, then the results like this will be
Just a grease spot on the water of the foreign bloody sea.

    Henry Ford's little chaser, churning in the sea
    Henry Ford's little chaser, protecting you and me
    Henry Ford's little chaser, the world soon will see
        cannot find an equal in the great deep sea
    Henry Ford's little chaser, bound to whip the Kaiser
        and all our enemy.

The Kaiser got a notion and he got it in his bean
    that he would take a trip to review his submarines.
So he took his swiftest chaser for those subs to go and see
    and while strolling though the water what a strange thing he did see
One of Henry's one man chasers was reflected to his lee
    then the Kaiser got excited 'till the hair stood on his head.
For he could not dodge this chaser Ford's revenger for the dead.

    The Kaiser's swiftest chaser, sailing though the sea
    The Kaiser's swiftest chaser, defying you and me
    The Kaiser's swiftest chaser, will soon be off the map
        he'll sink all those chasers in the great deep sea
    The Kaiser's swiftest chasers, cannot sail the waters
        to suit his jubilee.

Elizabeth Ford

Following is an excerpt from a Marine officer's letter.

And the Ford which Mrs. Pearce gave us will go down in Marine Corps history at any rate. Elizabeth Ford as the regiment knows her, has a unique career — she carried everything from sick men to hard tack — then she had two months in the trenches near Verdun and at the end seemed as though she would have to go to the scrap heap. In some way the men, who have an affection for her that you can hardly comprehend, patched her together and came up here and she rose to the heights of her service and her records. That night we took Bouresches with twenty odd men.... The road was under heavy shell and machine gun fire. For the next five days she made the trip night and day and for one period ran almost every hour for thirty-six hours. She not only carried ammunition out to the men who were less than 200 yards from the Boche, but rations and pyrotechnics; then to the battalion on the left of the road in the evil Belleau Woods, she carried the same, and water, which was scarce there. The last time I saw her she was resting against a store wall in the little square of Lucy-le-Bocage, a shell wrecked town, and she was the most battered object in the town.

Elizabeth Ford
By Wallace Irwin

We carried her over the sea, we did,
    And taught her hep, hep, hep —
A cute little jinny, all noisy and tinny,
    But full of American pep.
Recruited into the Corps she was —
    She came of her own accord.
We flew at her spanker the globe and the anchor
    And named her Elizabeth Ford

Cute little 'Lizabeth, dear little 'Lizabeth,
    Bonnie 'Lizabeth Ford!
She was short and squat, but her nose was set
    For the Hindenburg line — O Lord!
She hated a Hun like a son-of-a-gun,
    The Kaiser she plumb abhorred,
Did chunky Elizabeth, hunky Elizabeth,
    Spunky Elizabeth Ford.

We took her along on our hikes, we did,
    And a wonderful boat was she
She'd carry physicians, food or munitions,
    Generals, water or tea.
She could climb a bank like a first-rate tank
    And deliver the goods abroad —
When we touch our steel Kellies to "Semper Fidelis"
    Remember Elizabeth Ford.

Cute little 'Lizabeth, dear little 'Lizabeth,
    Bonnie 'Lizabeth Ford!
She took her rest in machine gun nests
    And on bullet swept roads she chored
Where the Devil Hounds were the first on the grounds
    Of a section of France restored —
Why, there was Elizabeth, chunky Elizabeth,
    Spunky Elizabeth Ford!

But 'twas on the day at those murder-woods
    Which the Yankees pronounce Belloo;
We were sent to knock silly the hope of Prince Willie
    And turn him around d. q.
We prayed for munitions and cleared out throats
    With a waterless click — good Lord! —
When out of a crater with bent radiator
    Climber faithful Elizabeth Ford.

Cute little 'Lizabeth, dear little 'Lizabeth,
    Bonnie 'Lizabeth Ford!
With a cylinder-skip she had made the trip,
    Water-and-cartridge-stored.

With her hood a wreck and a broken neck
  She cracked like a rotten board.
Hunky Elizabeth, chunky Elizabeth,
  Spunky Elizabeth Ford.

When they towed her out of town the next day
  Said Corporal Bill, "Look there!
I know of one hero who shouldn't draw zero
  When they're passin' the Croix de Guerre.
Who fed the guns that's startin' the Huns
  Plumb back to Canal du Nord?"
So his cross — and he'd won it! — he tied to the bonnet
  Of faithful Elizabeth Ford.

Cute little 'Lizabeth, dear little 'Lizabeth,
  Bonnie 'Lizabeth Ford!
Where shrapnel has mauled her we've never overhauled her,
  Her wheels and her gears restored.
Her record's clean, she's a true Marine
  And we're sending the Dutch War Lord
A note by Elizabeth, chunky Elizabeth, Spunky Elizabeth Ford!

Chapter Notes

Abbreviations

BFRC — Benson Ford Research Center of The Henry Ford
OR — oral reminiscences
AMC — refers to the study made by Industrial Plans Section, Logistics Planning Division Plan (T-5) Air Materiel Command, Army Air Force.

Preface

1. "The Guides Wore White," *Ford World*, November 26, 1965.
2. The Henry Ford, Dearborn, Michigan, is the new name of the Henry Ford Museum & Greenfield Village and is the repository of most Ford Motor Company records prior to 1963.
3. *Henry Ford's Airport and Other Aviation Ventures*, 1994; *The Aviation Legacy of Henry & Edsel Ford*, 2000; *Henry Ford's Aviation Ventures 1924–1936*, 1995, VHS & DVD.
4. Recap — month by month production — January 1941 through August 1945, Acc. 435, Box 39, Folder "Auditing Summary All Contracts."

Chapter 1

1. Lewis, *Public Image of Henry Ford*, page 91.
2. "Leland, Lincoln and the Liberty Engine," in *WHEELS*, Journal of the National Automotive History Collection, February 2005.
3. Nevins and Hill, *Ford: Expansion and Challenge 1915–1916*, page 55.
4. BFRC, accession 1, box 12. This accession contains a number of telegrams covering Ford's attempt to get a German plane with a Mercedes engine. In addition he talks about his intention to build 150,000 airplanes a year for use in France. Ridiculed at the time and an undoubted exaggeration, it was not completely unreasonable when you consider his plants were producing 3,500 cars a day, a much more sophisticated item than a stick and fabric airplane.
5. Henry Ford and Sons, owned by Henry and his son, Edsel Ford, and Henry's wife, Clara, was established to build farm tractors in 1915, as Ford Motor Company stockholders had complained that Henry Ford was diverting funds for the production of cars to his personal interest of building farm tractors.
6. "For Official Use Only: The Army Goes Car Shopping," *Automotive History Review*, Fall 2004. Most of the information on vehicles used in France came from this source.
7. *Ibid.*
8. Dickey, *The Liberty Engine 1918–1942*.
9. BFRC accession 507, box 26 *The Packard Liberty Motor*, January 1919. Dickey's *The Liberty Engine 1918–1942* describes a slightly different version of the development of the engine.
10. BFRC accession 285, box 32, 75 Liberty engines a day.
11. *America's Munitions*, pages 274, 275 production of forgings and bearings. In 1919 Benedict Crowell, assistant secretary of war and director of munitions, had published *America's Munitions 1917–1918*. It relates the status of all the U.S. Army weapons system at the start of the war and actions taken up to the Armistice in November 1918.
12. BFRC accession 1408 and 472, box, 26 cost of Liberty engine.
13. BFRC accession 1, box 172. The Navy had previously used the Ford-built Liberty engines for the first transatlantic flight in 1919. Not to be outdone the Army made a 9,000 mile round trip in four World War I type de Havilland airplanes in 1920. "Before the flight all the pilots asked for ships equipped with Ford Libertys. We never had a missing cylinder on the entire flight." *Ford News*, November 1, 1920.
14. Bill Stout, in his autobiography, *So Away I Went*, said he designed a small, single seat Cootie

airplane in 1919 to use the original Ford 2 cylinder Buzz Bomb engine but it would never develop more than half of its rated horsepower and as a result Stout's Cootie never flew.

15. Jack Beebe was a champion hydroplane racer and designer of the time, and the DePalma Manufacturing Co was founded by Ralph DePalma, a famous race driver of the period, to build racing cars and engines.

16. "Ford Builds First Robot Bomb Engine," *Ford Times*, January 1945. This relates the building of the two-cylinder engine, leaving the impression that it was the engine selected for the Bug. A *Detroit News* article of November 24, 1961, states the Ford engine was the one selected for the Bug. Documents in the United States Air Force Museum in Ohio refute these contentions and all existing photographs show the Bug with a four-cylinder engine.

17. Technically the Eagle Boats were ships. A boat is a vessel under 65 feet in length but in development, the Eagle was referred to as a boat and the name Eagle Boat stuck.

18. "The 100 Foot Submarine Chaser and the Eagle Boat," *Naval Institute Proceedings*, May 1919.

19. Bryan, *Henry's Lieutenants*, page 155. Knudsen went on to become President of General Motors in 1937 and in May 1940 was appointed Commissioner of Industrial Production in World War II by President Franklin Roosevelt.

20. BFRC accession 116, box 1 Kearny plant.

21. BFRC accession 116, box 1 Rouge buy back.

22. "The Eagle Boats of World War I," *Naval Institute Proceedings*, June 1973.

23. BFRC Vertical File. World War I — Eagle Boats.

24. "The Story of 199 Ships," *Ford News* August 1928. Following World War I, many of these wartime ships were offered for sale providing they be scrapped so as not to interfere with peacetime boat building. The story of Ford's purchase and disassembly of 199 of these ships in the Rouge was covered in 29 installments in the *Ford News* starting in August 1928.

25. "Ford Family Boats," *V8 Times*, November-December 2003.

26. BFRC accession 1409, caisson production.

27. BFRC accession 572, box 2, cost of tanks.

28. BFRC accession 572, box 26 armor plate.

29. *Ford News*, July1, 1921, helmet production.

30. BFRC accession 267, box 5, helmet cost.

31. BFRC accession 903, box 2, summary letter.

32. Painter, *Henry Ford Hospital: The First 75 Years*, page 43.

33. Burgess-Wise, *Ford at Dagenham*, pages 14, 15. A Ford of Britain Web site (accessed November 28, 2008) states that small tanks were built at the Trafford Park plant, the first Ford plant in Britain.

34. Wilkins and Hill, *American Business Abroad*, page 80.

35. Lewis, *Public Image of Henry Ford*, page 95.

36. BFRC accession 572, box 26, Couzens letter on profits.

37. Lewis, *Public Image of Henry Ford*, page 96.

38. All three of Edsel Ford's sons served in the U.S. military in World War II.

39. Nevins and Hill, *Ford: Expansion and Challenge 1915–1933*, page 57.

40. Sammie was the World War I equivalent of GI.

41. *The Ford Man*, September 3, 1918.

42. Wilkins and Hill, *American Business Abroad*, pages 78–79.

Chapter 2

A major source for Chapter 2 is BFRC, LaCroix Accession 435, Vol. 1, box 1.

1. *The Henry Ford Letters*, 1933, portfolio of letters published by Ford Motor Company.

2 Weigly, *History of the United States Army*, 1967, page 403.

3. O'Callaghan, *The Aviation Legacy of Henry & Edsel Ford*, pp. 114–115. Chapter 9 deals with the Ford-Lindbergh relationship.

4. "The Ford Defense Effort in America," *Time*, March 23, 1942.

5. *Life* magazine, August 1940.

6. AMC, page 23.

7 Ford Publicity Release number 21, dated February 18, 1943.

8. Bryan, *Friends, Families & Forays*, "Ford and the Disabled," page 326.

9. Twenty-five thousand of the Packard Motor Car Company's white workers struck in June 1943, protesting promotion for blacks.

10. "Working Side by Side," *Michigan History*, January-February 1993.

11. *Henry Ford and the Negro People*, 1941, a 22-page booklet published by the National Negro Congress which urged the Negroes to unionize, took great exception to the idea that Henry Ford was their friend.

12. AMC page 89, "The Army directed Ford to prepare for the inclusion of 25% women in the work force."

13. Ford Publicity Release number 36, dated August 26, 1943.

14. Cabadas, *River Rouge*, page 102.

15. Lewis, *The Public Image of Henry Ford*, page 363. Based on war contracts awarded through September 1944, the only figures available, General Motors was the largest producer with $13,800,000, followed by Curtiss Wright with $7,100,000 and Ford with $5,300,000.

16. "Production Expert Completes 35-Year Career at Ford's," *Rouge News*, May 12, 1950.

17. Bryan, *Henry's Lieutenants*, page 29

18. Stern, *Secret Missions of the Civil War*, page 149. Copperhead referred to a Northerner who favored the South and wore a copper pin made from the liberty head cutout from the old large one-cent coin minted until 1857.

19. Lindbergh was reinstated and promoted to the rank of Brigadier General by President Dwight Eisenhower in 1954.

20. Lindbergh's personnel records, Ford Motor Company Archives.

21. O'Callaghan, *The Aviation Legacy of Henry & Edsel Ford*, Chapter 9.

Chapter 3

A major source for Chapter 3 is BFRC, LaCroix Accession 435, Box 39 Vol. 2, page 3, and Box 2 Vol. 7.

1. "Birth of the B-24," *Ford Times*, June 1945. In late 1941, Fleet sold his interest in Consolidated to Vultee Aircraft and in March 1943 they officially merged becoming Consolidated Vultee Aircraft Corporation, commonly referred to as Convair.

2. AMC report, pages 2, 7, 8.

3. BFRC Acc. 796, Sorensen memo of trip dated January 18, 1941.

4. Sorensen, *My Forty Years With Ford*, page 280.

5. AMC, page 13.

6. Hollander and Marple, *Henry Ford: Inventor of the Supermarket*. Some of the food from Camp Willow Run was sold to the employees' commissary opened by Henry Ford in several locations in the Detroit area from 1919 to 1942.

7. By the end of 1944 working floor space dedicated to the B-24 would total 7,069,000 square feet — Willow Run, 4,734,617 square feet; Rouge Plant, 787,318 square feet; Highland Park, 1,116,176 square feet; Lincoln Plant, 382,257 square feet; and all others 47,632 square feet.

8. *Willow Run Plant Data No. 23* (employee newsletter), dated January 15, 1943.

9. AMC, page 30.

10. Oral reminiscences, William Pioch.

11. "Tooling Ford Bombers at Willow Run," *American Machinist*, December 10, 1942.

12. AMC, page 42.

13. Oral reminiscences, Logan Miller.

14. Nevins and Hill, *Ford: Decline and Rebirth*, page 225. "What may have been lost in 1942 was rapidly made up in ensuing months." It was estimated that by using the soft dies perhaps 100 planes could have been produced in late 1942 instead of the 56 actually built.

15. AMC, page 84.

16. Warren Kidder, in his minutely detailed history *Willow Run, Colossus of American Industry* (1995), the most thorough examination of Willow Run published, lists April 1944 production as 455 planes in 450 hours or one every 59 minutes.

17. Carr and Stermer, *Willow Run*, page 211. Union check-off records show 88,630 workers hired in the 31 months between December 1, 1941, and June 30, 1944, substantially higher than Ford's figures of 80,744 hired in 41 months.

18. AMC, page 91.

19. Lingerman, *Don't You Know There's a War On?*, Chapter 3.

20. Carr and Stermer, *Willow Run*, page 338. This book details the societal problems with in-migrants and natives in the area and covers extensively the housing scandal.

21. Kidder, *Willow Run*, page 182.

22. These prices and comparisons are from the 1947 report to the Price Adjustment Board, page 16. Various different prices for finished B-24s are published, but few indicated whether they included fees or government supplied equipment. B-24s coming off the line in 1945 contained $133,992 worth of government supplied equipment, e.g., radio equipment $45,000; Pratt & Whitney engines and propellers, $37,798; and turrets, $24,582.

23. AMC, page viii.

24. *Ibid.*, page 23.

25. "What's to Become of the Huge Willow Run Bomber Plant?" *Sunday Mirror*, May 5, 1945.

26. Kaiser-Frazer would cease automobile production and produce C-119 cargo planes for the Air Force during the Korean Conflict before finally selling the facility to General Motors in 1953. In 1946 the Edsel Ford Post of the American Legion in Willow Run secured B-24 number 139 from the government to be displayed at the post. Unfortunately too many of those associated with wartime Willow Run moved on and No. 139 slowly deteriorated until it was little more than a pile of junk. In 1950 it was sold for scrap.

Chapter 4

Major sources for Chapter 4 include BFRC, LaCroix Accession 435, Box 39 Vol. 3 & Box 2 Vol. 7 and Ford Builds for War — Gliding Wings, c. 1945, Ford Photographic Department.

1. While the German assault on Crete was successful, the causalities were so high among these elite troops that no further airborne attacks were made by the Germans.

2. Prior to World War II most car bodies were framed out in wood and then covered in sheet metal.

3. "Army Glider Construction," *American Aviation Historical Journal*, Winter 1989.

4. The Airframe Building was housed in the old Tri-Motor assembly building at Ford Airport.

5. Other Ford sources state the initial glider test took 45 minutes.

6. The Air Commando or 1st Air Commando Group, as it became, was established to provide aerial support to the British units combating the Japanese in Burma.

7. The crates for one glider required 11,000 feet of lumber, nearly enough to build a small, five-room cottage. Following the end of the war there were reports of new, uncrated surplus gliders being purchased for the wooden crate with the glider being discarded.

8. Various sources in Ford Motor Company records indicate slight differences in production. Serious students of United States glider production differ slightly even from the Ford numbers.

9. "Army Glider Construction," *American Aviation Historical Journal*, Winter 1989. By war's end only 5 percent of all wartime factories had been awarded the Army Navy "E."

Chapter 5

Data on the Pratt & Whitney Aircraft Engine are from BFRC, LaCroix Accession 435, Box 39 Vol. 2, page 20, and Box 1 Vol. 1. Data on the Pulse Jet Engine are from BFRC, LaCroix Accession 435, Box 2 Vol. 3, Page 74, and Box 2 Vol. 6.

1. Two other interpretations regarding Henry Ford's pacifism have been advanced. "On the Assembly Line," *Iron Age*, June 27, 1940, commented: "Ford [had previously stated] he would not build military engines except for defense. This is one of those not-quite-clear points: Ford appears to have been willing to help tool up one of the European nations [France] for a defense in a threatening war, but not [England] in an actual war program. This distinction is a fine one ... but is believed to have been an important one to Mr. Ford." In *My Forty Years With Ford*, page 275, Sorensen comments on "a tactless statement by Lord Beaverbrook that Ford had accepted an order for 6,000 Rolls Royce engines and implying that he was now supporting the British. Actually we had not accepted an order from Britain. Our dealings were entirely with American officials." Henry Ford knew that 60 percent of the engines would go to Britain, but Beaverbook's statement implied a different situation, the reasoning being similar to that in the *Iron Age* article in 1940.

2. BFRC, Vertical File, World War II — "The Greatest Wedding of American Industry," manuscript by Edmund Eveleth, Pratt & Whitney Executive.

3. "Sorenson of the Rouge," *Fortune*, April 1942. This highly complimentary article probably did not sit well with Henry Ford. Another comparison made showed that it would take 1,167,020 Ford V8 engines to equal the horsepower of the 57,851 Pratt & Whitney engines made by Ford.

4. BFRC, Accession 606, Sorensen correspondence re: Fordair S. A. of France.

5. BFRC, Vertical File, World War II — "The Greatest Wedding of American Industry."

6. *The Evolution of the Cruise Missile*, Page 64.

Chapter 6

1. Source for data on the aircraft ignition system: BFRC, LaCroix Accession 435, Box 39 Vol. 2, page 24, and Box 1 Vol. 4.

2. Source for data on the aircraft generator: BFRC, LaCroix Accession 435, Box 39 Vol. 3, page 71, and Box 1 Vol. 4.

3. Sources for data on the turbo supercharger: BFRC, LaCroix Accession 435, Box 39 Vol. 2, page 54, and Box 2 Vol. 5; "Genius of the Stratosphere," *The American Weekly*, December 30, 1945; "A Brief Story of the Ford Built Turbo supercharger," *Hangar Happenings* (Yankee Air Force), May 2001.

4. Source for data on the rate-of-climb indicator: BFRC, LaCroix Accession 435, Box 11.

5. Source for data on the altitude chamber: BFRC, LaCroix Accession 435, Box 2 Vol. 8.

6. Source for data on the quick change engine: BFRC, LaCroix Accession 435, Box 39 Vol. 2, page 25.

7. Source for data on the jettison fuel tank: BFRC, LaCroix Accession 435, Box 39 Vol. 3, page 74, and Box 2 Vol. 7.

Chapter 7

1. Source for data on the armor plate foundry: BFRC, LaCroix Accession 435, Box 39 Vol. 2, page 39, and Box 1 Vol. 2.

2. Source for data on the aluminum foundry: BFRC, LaCroix Accession 435, Box 39 Vol. 2, page 37, and Box 2 Vol. 6.

3. With the outbreak of war, steel became critical and the construction of this plant would be the first to substitute wood as much as possible. As a result 1,603,000 board-feet of wood substituted for 2,376 tons of steel.

4. Source for data on the magnesium smelter: BFRC, LaCroix Accession 435, Box 2 Vol. 8.

5. In June 1943 Ford received a contract for 300,000 pounds of magnesium for manufacturing incendiary bombs for Britain.

6. Source for data on the magnesium foundry: BFRC, LaCroix Accession 435, Box 2 Vol. 8.

Chapter 8

A general source for performance data for wheeled and tracked vehicles in Chapter 8 is TM 9-2800 War Department Technical Manual — Standard Military Vehicles, September 1, 1943.

1. Jeep (capital J) is a now a trademark of the Chrysler Corp.; jeep (small j) is a noun to describe a small four-wheel-drive vehicle. Source for data on jeeps: BFRC, LaCroix Accession 435, Box 39 Vol. 3, and Box 1 Vol. 1.

2. Both of the Ford Pygmy units survive. The Ford-body unit is in the Alabama's Veterans Museum, Athens, Alabama, and the Budd-body unit is owned by a collector in London.

3. "Progress in the Ford World," *Ford News*, January 1942.

4. There are no records of any of the government jeep contracts in the archives of the Ford Motor Company or the Benson Ford Research Center.

5. In a Ford public relations flyer issued at the end of the war jeep production is listed as 277,896. This, however, is the total of only the GPW units. For some reason the 4,458 early GP models produced are ignored. Some historians arrive at a different total number of jeeps produced.

6. *Here is Your War*, page 234.

7. "Ford to Build "MUTT," *Ford Times*, October 1959.

8. Source for data on the amphibian jeep: BFRC, LaCroix Accession 435, Box 1 Vol. 1.

9. Amphibious Scout Cars, February 1942, Ford Photographic Department (film).

10. Source for data on armored cars: BFRC, LaCroix Accession 435, Box 39 Vol. 2, and Box 1 Vol.2.

11. The Hercules engine was designated by Ordnance as it was used in other Army vehicles similar to the M-8 and simplified standardization for the Ordnance Department.

12. This is a case where Ford records differ. Other researchers offer different numbers.

13. Source for data on military trucks: BFRC, LaCroix Accession 435, Box 39 Vol. 3.

14. Source for data on the Moto-Tug: BFRC, LaCroix Accession 435, Box 36.

15. In 1948, Henry Ford II canceled the tractor agreement with Ferguson, leading to a nasty court fight. Ten years after the handshake it was difficult for the courts to determine who had agreed to what and in 1952 a consent decree was rendered requiring Ford to pay Ferguson $9,250,000, most of which went to his lawyers.

16. BFRC, Vertical File, World War II, Passenger Cars, "The Passenger Car Goes To War," draft.

17. Nevins & Hill, *Ford: Decline and Rebirth*, page 205.

Chapter 9

A general source for performance data on wheeled and tracked vehicles in Chapter 9 is TM 9-2800 War Department Technical Manual—Standard Military Vehicles, September 1, 1943.

1. Source for data on tanks and tank destroyers: BFRC, LaCroix Accession 435, Box 1 Vol. 2.

2. Lingemann, *Don't You Know There's a War On?* See Chapter 4 for a description of how priorities were set and materials allocated during World War II.

3. Source for data on the Ford tank engine: BFRC, LaCroix Accession 435, Box 39 Vol. 2, page 34.

4. Nevins & Hill, *Ford Decline and Rebirth*, page 194.

5. "U.S. Tanks Live Longer," *Ford Times*, February 1945.

6. Ford, *The Sherman Tank*, page 26.

7. Ironically, by September 1943, with heavier tanks needed, the government gave Ford a contract to develop a 700 HP, 12-cylinder engine patterned on the 8-cylinder tank engine which had been developed from the company's original 12-cylinder airplane engine. Thirty-six experimental 12-cylinder engines were built with the last one being delivered May 5, 1947.

8. Source for data on the Universal Carrier: BFRC, LaCroix Accession 435, Box 39 Vol. 2, page 44, and Box 1 Vol. 2.

Chapter 10

1. Source for data on the gun director: LaCroix Accession 435, Box 2, and Box 8 Vol. 8.

2. "Automotive Armament News," *Chicago Daily News*, December 19, 1942.

3. Source for data on the Ford Tire Plant: BFRC, LaCroix Accession 435, Box 1 Vol. 3.

4. Source for data on the ordnance depots: BFRC, LaCroix Accession 435, Box 39 Vol. 2, pages 64, 68.

5. I have been unable to find any reference to this award.

6. Source for data on squad tents: BFRC, LaCroix Accession 435, Box 39 Vol. 3, page 93.

7. Other Ford records indicate 9,498 squad tents were produced.

8. *The Ford Fleet* by Snider, Clair, and Davis is the only book on Ford marine history.

9. S/S designated steam-powered ships. M/S designated diesel-powered motor ships.

10. *Ford News*, 1928–1929 The story of the purchase of the 199 ships was related in 29 weekly chapters. Enough scrap metal was recovered to fill Ford's auto production needs for a year.

11. M/S *Green Island*, built to Ford's specifications, was the world's first all-welded ship. Stopped by a German U-boat, all hands were ordered into lifeboats. With all boats safely away the ship was torpedoed.

12. *Ford Times*, October 1945.

13. Source for data on Ford timber, mining and charcoal operations: BFRC, LaCroix Accession 435, Box 39 Vol. 3, page 122.

14. By-Products was a separate operation within Ford and included products produced through the operation of the coke ovens, blast furnaces, open hearth furnaces, steel mill, saw mills, etc. Products included ammonium sulfate, benzol, cement, charcoal, coal tar, lumber and other items totaling $9,000,000 in sales in 1939 alone. In addition to by-products, salvage reclamation was mandatory at Ford. The General Salvage Department at Highland Park had been established to recycle everything possible. For example, broken or worn drills would be made into small drills or ground into screwdrivers. Worn-out mop and broom handles would be turned into screwdriver and chisel handles. Worn-out screwdriver handles would be reworked for smaller tools, etc.

15. In 1932 Ford personnel at Iron Mountain developed the first briquette for home and commercial use. The briquettes, along with small grills, were sold though Ford dealers until the plant was sold in 1951 to the Kingsford Chemical Company which continues to merchandise the briquettes under the Kingsford name.

16. Source of data on inventions and patents: BFRC, LaCroix Accession 435, Box 39 Vol. 3, page 127.

Chapter 11

A major source for Chapter 10 is BFRC, LaCroix Accession 435, Box 39, Vol. 2, and Box 1 Vols. 3 and 4.

1. O'Callaghan, *The Aviation Legacy of Henry & Edsel Ford*, pages 158–161. The Ford Air Transportation Office was established in November 1941 to provide test pilots for Willow Run. Following the war it continued in operation to handle Ford's peacetime air transportation needs. Ford Airport was closed for good in 1947 when its offices and planes were relocated to the Wayne County Airport (now Detroit Metro) in Romulus, Michigan.

2. Lumber harvesting on Ford timberlands, originally done by Ford lumberjacks until the early 1930s, was contracted out to local logging firms which followed the Ford policy of selective harvesting.

3. Cherry Hill, Michigan, was in operation from 1944 to 1945. Immediately following the war, mechanical work was available here for rehabilitation, disabled veterans. While there are few records concerning Dexter and Hudson, Michigan, a Ford record dated January 1, 1945, lists all three of these sites as producing "commercial items."

Chapter 12

A major source for Chapter 12 is BFRC, LaCroix Accession 435, Box 1 Vol. 2.
1. Barbara Shafer, "They Kept 'Em Flying," *Michigan History*, March-April 2005.

Chapter 13

1. Saunders, *Ford at War*, page 9. Not stated was the fact that Hitler was threatening the invasion of Britain and all sorts of defensive schemes were being devised. Many of these schemes are described in the book *Operation Sea Lion*, which was the German code name for the invasion.
2. *United States News*, July 10, 1942. In the first half of 1942, 327 merchant ships had been sunk in the waters of the Western Hemisphere while the United States had built only 228 merchant ships. During this time, Ford-built World War I Eagle Boats were among the vessels striving to protect our coasts against the U-boat threat.
3. David Burgess-Wise, "Ford and the War in the Air," *Battle of Britain Anniversary Brochure*, undated.
4. Saunders relates in *Ford at War* that highly delicate jig borers made by the Swiss were shipped to Ford in England through German-occupied France and sympathetic Spain.
5. "Emergency Food Vans & Ford," *Ford Times* (British edition) July-August 1941; U.S. Publicity Release # 48, February 5, 1944.
6. Ford Military Vehicles (British Commonwealth) for Canada states 429,197 military vehicles including 33,988 Bren gun carriers.
7. *50 Years Forward with Ford*, 1953, Ford of Canada, 50th anniversary newsletter.
8. Saunders, *Ford at War*, page 36.
9. Letter to Air Materiel Command, June 7, 1947, page 27.

10. Nevins and Hill, *Ford: Decline and Rebirth*, pages 103, 104.
11. Ford Motor Company, *Research Finds About Ford-Werke Under the Nazi Regime*, 2001, page 29.
12. *Ibid.*, page 32.
13. Simon Reich was an author and professor at the University of Pittsburgh.
14. Ford Motor Company, *Research Finds About Ford-Werke Under the Nazi Regime*, page 53.
15. *Ibid.*, page 53.
16. *Ibid.*, page 69.
17. *Ibid.*, page 116.
18. *Ibid.*, pages 108, 109.

Chapter 14

1. Nevins and Hill, *Ford: Expansion and Challenge*, page 129.
2. Lewis, *The Public Image of Henry Ford*, page 104.
3. *Ford Times*, January 7, 1944.
4. *Ibid.*, April 14, 1944.
5. Lewis, *The Public Image of Henry Ford*, page 386.
6. Saunders, *Ford at War*, page 11.

Chapter 15

1. *Autograph Collector Magazine*, June-July 2007, quotes this letter, sold in 1999 by Christie's auction house.
2. BFRC accession 940, Box 27. Letter dated November 13, 1959, from Lindburgh to Ernest Hill, co-author of *Ford Expansion and Challenge: 1915–1933*.
3. Nevins and Hill, *Ford: Decline and Rebirth 1933–1962*, page 225.
4. At the end of World War II, the government sold the Willow Run plant to Kaiser Frazer and Ford purchased or demolished the other government-owned facilities located in the Rouge.
5. Nevins and Hill, *Ford: Expansion and Challenge*, page 84.
6. *Time* magazine, March 23, 1942, five-page article.
7. "The Ford Heritage," *Fortune* magazine, June 1944.

Bibliography

General

Ford Motor Company Archives
Benson Ford Research Center of The Henry Ford
(cited as BFRC)

Books

Althin, K. W. *C. E. Johansson, 1864–1943, The Master of Measurement*. Stockholm: Nordisk rotogravyr, 1948

Beasley, Norman. *Knudsen: A Biography*. New York: McGraw-Hill, 1947.

Bonin, Hubert, Yannick Lung, and Steven Tolliday, eds. *Ford: The European History, 1903–2003*. Vol. 2. Paris: Edition P.L.A.G.E., 2003.

Bryan, Ford. *The Eagle's Nest on the Rouge*, undated manuscript, BFRC Vertical File.

_____. *Friends, Families & Forays*. Detroit: Wayne State University Press, 2002.

_____. *Henry's Lieutenants*, Detroit: Wayne State University Press, 1993.

Bucci, Federico. *Albert Kahn: Architect of Ford*. New York: Princeton Architectural Press, 1991.

Burgess-Wise, David. *Ford at Dagenham: The Rise and Fall of Detroit in Europe*. Derby, England: Breedon Books, 2001.

Cabadas, Joseph P. *River Rouge: Ford's Industrial Colossus*. Minneapolis: MotorBooks/MPI, 2004.

Carr, Lowell, and James Sterner. *Willow Run: A Study of Industrialization and Cultural Inadequacy*. New York: Harper, 1952.

Crowell, Benedict. *America's Munitions 1917–1918*. Washington, DC: Government Printing Office, 1919.

Daniels, Josephus. *Our Navy at War*. Washington, DC: Pictorial Bureau, 1922.

Darwin, Norm. *The History of Ford in Australia*. Newstead, Victoria: Eddie Ford Publications, 1986.

Dickey, Philip. *The Liberty Engine 1918–1942*. Washington, DC: Smithsonian Institution, 1968.

Duffield, Edgar. *Ford Through European Eyeglasses: 1907–1947*. Chelmsford, England: Mercury Press, 1947.

Easdown, Geoff. *A History of the Ford Motor Company in Australia and New Zealand*. Sydney: Golden Press, 1987.

Ervin, Spencer. *Henry Ford vs. Truman H. Newberry: The Famous Senate Election Contest*. Manchester, NH: Ayer, 1935.

Fleming, Peter. *Operation Sea Lion*. New York: Simon & Schuster, 1957.

Ford, Roger. *The Sherman Tank*. Osceola, WI: MBI Publishing, 1999.

Frank, Reinhard. *German Trucks & Cars in World War II*. Vol. 8, *Ford at War*. Atglen, PA: Schiffer. 1993.

Geary, L. *Ford Military Vehicles*. Romford, Essex, UK: Ian Henry, 1983.

Hafeli, Ken. *Henry Ford's Timber Operations in the Upper Peninsula*. Undated manuscript. BFRC Access 1216.

Hershey, Burnet. *The Odyssey of Henry Ford and the Great Peace Ship*. New York: Taplinger, 1967.

Hollander, Stanley, and Gary Marple. *Henry Ford: Inventor of the Supermarket*. East Lansing, MI: Bureau of Business and Economic Research, Michigan State University, 1960.

Ketchum, Richard. *The Borrowed Years: 1938–1941*. New York: Random House, 1989.

Kidder, Warren. *Willow Run: Colossus of American Industry*. Lansing, MI: n.p., 1995.

Lewis, David. *The Public Image of Henry Ford: An American Folk Hero and His Company*. Detroit: Wayne State University Press, 1976.

195

Lingeman, Richard. *Don't You Know There's a War On?* New York: Putnam: 1988.

Lopez, Donald. *Into the Teeth of the Tiger.* Washington, DC: Smithsonian Institution Press, 1986.

Mooney, James L. *Dictionary of American Naval Fighting Ships.* Vol. 6. Washington, DC: Government Printing Office, 1976.

Nevins, Allan, and Frank Ernest Hill. *Ford: Decline and Rebirth 1933–1962.* New York: Charles Scribner's Sons, 1962.

_____ and _____. *Ford: Expansion and Challenge 1915–1933.* New York: Charles Scribner's Sons, 1957.

O'Callaghan, Timothy. *The Aviation Legacy of Henry & Edsel Ford.* Detroit: Proctor Publications, 2000.

Painter, Patricia Scollard. *Henry Ford Hospital: The First 75 Years.* Detroit: Henry Ford Health System, 1997.

The Passenger Car Goes to War. Undated manuscript, BFRC Vertical File.

Pyle, Ernie, and Kelly Orr. *Here Is Your War: The Story of G.I. Joe.* Lincoln: University of Nebraska Press, 1943.

Roberts, David. *In the Shadow of Detroit : Gordon M. McGregor, Ford of Canada, and Motoropolis.* Detroit: Wayne State University Press, 2006.

Saunders, Hilary St. George. *Ford at War.* London: Harrison and Sons, 1946.

Scott, Graham. *Essential Military Jeep.* Minneapolis: MotorBooks/MPI, 1996.

Segal, Howard. *Recasting the Machine Age: Henry Ford's Village Industries.* Amherst: University of Massachusetts Press, 2005.

Simmons, Brig. Gen. E.H., and Col. J.H. Alexander. *Through the Wheat.* Annapolis: Naval Institute Press, 2008.

Snider, Claire J., and Michael W.R. Davis. *The Ford Fleet (1923–1989).* Cleveland: Freshwater Press, 1994.

Sorensen, Charles, Samuel T. Williamson, and David L. Lewis. *My Forty Years with Ford.* Detroit: Wayne State University Press, 1956.

Stern, Philip Van Doren. *Secret Missions of the Civil War.* New York: Wings Books, 1990.

Tuckey, Bill. *True Blue: 75 Years of Ford in Australia.* Edgecliff, NSW: Focus, 2000.

Weigley, Russell. *History of the United States Army.* New York: Macmillan, 1967.

Werrell, Kenneth. *The Evolution of the Cruise Missile.* Montgomery, AL: Air University Press, Maxwell Air Force Base, 1985.

Wilkins, Mira, and Frank Hill. *American Business Abroad: Ford on Six Continents.* Cambridge: Harvard University Press, 1964.

Wilson, M. F. *The Story of Willow Run.* Ann Arbor: University of Michigan Press, 1958.

Periodicals

Aero Digest
Air & Space
American Aviation Historical Journal
American Machinist
Antique Automobiles
Automotive and Aviation Interests
Automotive History Review
Autograph Collector
Dictionary of American Naval Fighting Ships
Chicago Daily News
Friends Journal, Air Force Museum Foundation
Fordowner
Fortune
Hangar Happenings, Yankee Air Force Museum
Life
Michigan History
Michigan Historical Review
Motor News
Naval Institue Proceedings
Off-Road Adventures
The American Weekly
The Dearborn Historian
The Iron Age
The Way of the Zephyr
Sea Classics
Skyway
Time
V8 Times
Vintage Ford
Wheels, Journal of the National Automobile History Collection
Worlds Work

Ford Motor Company Publications

Amphibious Scout Cars (film)
Ford Times
Ford Man
Ford News
Ford World
In The Service of America (booklet)
In The Service of America (film)
Rouge News

Publicity Releases

Research Finds About Ford-Werke Under the Nazi Regime
The Willow Run Story (film)

Index